An Atlantic Crossing?

The Work of the International Examinations Inquiry, its Researchers, Methods and Influence

Comparative Histories of Education

Series Editors: MARTIN LAWN & ANTÓNIO NÓVOA

Created as part of national narratives of progress, and bounded by state borders and systems, histories of education now require an expansion into the horizontal plane, to develop an intellectual field focusing upon objects, ideas and relations, across borders and sites.

This series is intended to encourage the exploration of new questions and areas, through which comparative histories of education can be formed, recognising heterogeneity, flows of ideas and technologies, cross border designs, international networks and material collections. It also aims to encourage contributions from different disciplines, raise historical and comparative arguments for the study of educational issues, and encourage creative approaches that can contribute to a renewal of educational historiography.

Previous volume in this series

MATERIALITIES OF SCHOOLING
design, technology, objects, routines
Edited by MARTIN LAWN & IAN GROSVENOR
2005, paperback, 218 pages
ISBN 978-1-873927-30-4
www.symposium-books.co.uk/books/bookdetails.asp?bid=12

An Atlantic Crossing?

The Work of the International Examination Inquiry, its Researchers, Methods and Influence

Edited by
MARTIN LAWN

Comparative Histories of Education
Series Editors: Martin Lawn & António Nóvoa

SYMPOSIUM
BOOKS

Symposium Books
PO Box 204 Didcot Oxford OX11 9ZQ United Kingdom
the book publishing division of wwwords Ltd
www.symposium-books.co.uk

Published in the United Kingdom, 2008

ISBN 978-1-873927-26-7

Typeset by wwwords Ltd
Printed and bound in the United Kingdom by Cambridge University Press

Contents

INTRODUCTION

An Atlantic Crossing? The Work of the International Examinations Inquiry, its Researchers, Methods and Influence

MARTIN LAWN

The work of the International Examinations Inquiry (IEI) is almost forgotten now and yet it was an international and well-funded scientific project, operating over seven years, which attracted key world figures in educational research and undertook significant exchanges of data and experiment. Originally, it comprised the USA, Scotland, England, France, Germany and Switzerland, and then it grew to include Norway, Sweden and Finland. The core research group met three times: in Eastbourne in 1931 and Folkestone in 1936 (both in England) and Dinard, near St Malo (in France), in 1938. The key problem which united the researchers was the expansion of secondary education and the determination of the most effective way of examining pupils for entry into the secondary school. Each of the national case studies tried to produce information which could help, nationally or internationally, to support changes or improvements in examining – from intelligence tests to essay marking (Appendix 1). The value of the IEI is that it reveals the difficulties that historians of education have in chronicling the exchanges of scientific ideas and researchers who work across borders. In this project, psychologists and comparativists can be seen in the task of engaging with each other's work, and providing supportive and necessary conditions for these exchanges, and in turn effecting an international space, at the same time as they are producing a national one.

Historians of education, traditionally tied quite closely to the development of national systems of education, have had difficulty in advancing narratives which see the international as being present in the construction of the national system and its ideas and technologies, or that local agents of education are carriers of cross-border cosmopolitan or scientific ideas (see Hofstetter & Schneuwly, 2002, 2004). This is less so in peripheral or ex-colonial countries whose historians are more aware of the travel of technologies or systems of pedagogy, and of the power present in centre–peripheral relations, and its related categories of travel, of inquiry and education commerce. For example, within Scottish narratives of education, the Scottish Council for Educational Research (SCRE) was regarded as a peculiarly Scottish institution, closely linked in its foundation period (the 1920s and 1930s) with advances in Scottish education and the role played by the Educational Institute of Scotland, its major professional organisation (SCRE, 1947; Craigie, 1972). However, a close reading began to reveal the significance of the additional funding that the SCRE received in the 1930s, drawn from outside the country, which had created little attention in the accounts of its place in the national narratives of education. Crucial funding from the Carnegie Corporation in New York enabled the SCRE to become stabilised and to undertake ambitious and advanced scientific work in education (Lawn, 2004). The reference to Carnegie enabled further inquiry on the sociology of foundations and their power in social science (Fisher, 1980, 1983; Lagemann, 1989).The role of philanthropic foundations in educational research may be well known in US research but less known in societies without major foundations and yet within their sphere of US influence. Carnegie cropped up in the Commonwealth as an element in the establishment of national research centres in education (in New Zealand, South Africa and Australia), in England as the basis for the post-war National Foundation for Educational Research, and in publications and institutes across Europe as part of the International Examinations Inquiry.

The transcript volumes of the three IEI conferences were given to IEI members and are only available in places where project committee members gave their own copies to their university libraries. Contacts with European colleagues in the European Educational Research Association and in a meeting of the Nordic Conference on Educational Historical Research allowed some systematisation of inquiry into the IEI European projects and their personnel and products. In the last two years, in-depth research on this subject has taken place within a UK social science research project based at the University of Edinburgh which has allowed extensive documentary analysis in archives, including the Carnegie Corporation and Teachers College Archives in New York, the World Education Fellowship and Nunn and Clarke papers in the Institute of Education Archives in London, Scottish Council for Research in Education archives in Glasgow and a newly created Thomson Archive at the University of Edinburgh.[1]

This volume explores the work of the national IEI projects in relation to each other and to Carnegie in New York. European researchers are more and more able to engage in pan-European research projects of different kinds today, funded through the European Union and national agencies and foundations. But in the early twentieth century, cross-European projects were much more unusual. Scientific congresses, the growth of the New Education Fellowship Conferences and sponsored visits to other country's education systems were developing an elite of cosmopolitan educationalists, aware of other ideas and practices, and scientific results published elsewhere. The University of Jena, in Prussia, was one of the great pre First World War meeting places for advanced research meetings and courses in education; this was a result of a combination of the eminence of Professor Wilhelm Rein in Herbartian studies and the German establishment of doctoral studies. Several of the IEI members had met or travelled there. But the IEI is unusual because it was a funded, cross-border research project in education, focused upon a pressing policy issue, and involving top scholars from a range of countries (mainly European with a strong US contingent). It was more than a scientific congress, a pedagogical movement or a common research training experience. It was well funded by the Carnegie Corporation in New York and produced a series of significant publications on examinations and intelligence. Its status is uncommon. It is a funded scientific project, operating internationally, with a large core of members and a wider group of national participants; it draws together experts and policy activists from a range of places and places them in unusual proximity. In this way, it represents a new form of internationalisation. It defines a common problem, clarifies terms, engages in critical discussion, jointly produces and manages a series of linked projects and publishes its work internationally. It involves approximately one hundred leading researchers across Europe, at a time when there were not many of them. It appears to model or at least foreshadow a spate of post Second World War international studies and the establishing of common epistemic communities, in which loosely integrated professional, academic and policy actors form a network, and it establishes a model of work recommended for the post-war United Nations Educational, Scientific and Cultural Organisation (UNESCO). However, it is similar to certain kinds of scientific cum technological meetings in which the necessary standards for international trade or comparison are agreed; in this case, the policy area of school examinations becomes associated with the new science of intelligence with its related technology of testing. In effect, it tries to resolve new international standards on examining, testing and comparison, and associated factorial studies on intelligence and its advanced statistical arguments.

The International Examinations Inquiry takes place at a significant time in the emergence of international scientific work in educational research between the USA and Europe. It lies between a growing range of international conferences and congresses of the first part of the twentieth century and the post Second World War internationalisation of science, international organisations and knowledge transfers between the USA and Europe. So, it represents a midway stage between earlier individual contacts by well-travelled researchers, usually towards North America, and the development of joint research projects, sustained over time. First wave internationalisation, growing in the nineteenth century and throughout the early decades of the twentieth century, was based on study visits to determine how other countries, often commercial rivals, structured their educational systems – so from England, experts went to study school design in Germany, France and Holland and an official Department of Special Inquiries wrote papers on aspects of school design, curriculum or examinations in different countries. First wave internationalisation assembled exhibitions of materials and products suitable for schools, drawn nationally and internationally, which acted as models or templates for action; and in this period, created international Congresses, drawing together international expertise or confirming disciplinary or territorial boundaries, for example, the Empire Education Congresses (1911 and 1923) and International Moral Education Congresses. Congresses deliberately draw together experts from across continents for scientific intercourse but also to determine or rework a field of inquiry and its constituent elements – its concepts, practices and exchanges. Congresses may be intended as symbolic ruptures of a field, a deliberate attempt to reconstruct it by drawing it away from its earlier dominant sites and practices and from its senior host countries, and to create new hegemonic discourses within it. These meetings were described as aspiring to cooperate on the basis of participants' interests; they were viewed as producing a stage beyond simple national representation. In the 1920s, a recognition of the consequences of this process, a rapid form of cooperation produced by severe dislocation and restructured political conditions, created a discourse in which intellectual interchange was viewed as crucial and defined by its 'international mindedness'. Delegates and representatives were not to be seen as cooperating on the basis of national interests but disinterested internationalism and scientific interest. Shenton (1933) uses the term 'international' to apply to conferences in which nationals of various countries participated and reached agreement – either as individuals or representatives of their countries. These people were cosmopolitan because they came from all over the world, developed a common purpose, continuously cooperated, and aimed for mutual understanding.

An Intellectual Synthesis, an Administrative Solution and a Moral Reconciliation

When Monroe, the head of the International Institute at Teachers College, Columbia, described the initial conversation with Keppel, President of the Carnegie Corporation, New York, about international work, it was expressed in contemporary terms; doing something for education in Europe, something which would affect several countries. In this account, the independence of countries and the mutuality of their work was fundamental; it would be undertaken by 'representative educators' from each country, within independent committees and they would jointly construct their subjects of investigation (Appendix 2). The countries invited were chosen for their influential educational work. Other countries were considered at the outset (Belgium and Spain) but rejected for various reasons, and invitations were sent to interested representatives of other countries later (Netherlands and China). Later, Denmark and Holland, and the Dominions (of the British Empire) were to be approached but the War intervened.

The core participants met three times, between 1931 and 1938, in the Grand hotels of Eastbourne, Folkestone and Dinard (Appendix 2). The photograph of the last days of the network in Dinard shows many of them together, in the final hours of the meeting, with numerous research reports already published, aware of the impending European crisis, and thinking about the immediate future. They are all men. They are middle-aged or older, established in their fields, even emeritus. For many of them, this international project has been one of the most significant events in their work. They look assured that history and their peers will recognise them and will know what they achieved. Significantly, for a project on school examinations, and on the gateway between the primary and second stages of schooling, they are pictured as a school class. At one point, Desclos even refers to the group as a rather brilliant class. It is not clear why they attend the meetings or why individuals might stop, but only how they make statements or hold brief conversations when they do. For example, Spearman is a regular attender but hardly speaks and writes only a couple of pages in the reports. Boyd, the enthusiast for the project, appears only once. Others make dramatic exits: the sudden departure of the German researchers in 1933, the rather abrupt exit of Switzerland in 1935 (saying its project was done) and individuals (dying, resigning or ill). In their own countries, the Inquiry members are the early pioneers of educational research in its different forms – the study of intelligence testing, comparisons between national systems, promoters of the new child-based pedagogy – and they are all pioneers in the sense that they are working internationally. They are a heterogeneous group if classified by disciplinary interest; they include the founders and popularisers of the study of intelligence (Spearman, Thomson, Drever, Thorndike, Nunn, Ballard), the first generation of comparativists in education (Monroe, Kandel, Sadler and Ulich), and key members of a world progressive education movement (Zilliacus, Bovet, McClelland and Boyd). Sometimes they occupy more than one of these categories. They are not all professors: head teachers, statisticians and inspectors attend the meeting as well. Each country seems to have had its own way of organising and working: France provided some key intellectuals and administrators within a loosely distributed network of responsibility; England provided a mainly London-based education elite; Finland, its scholarly head teachers; and Switzerland, the organising capacity of the J.J. Rousseau Institute in Geneva. Scotland used the Scottish Council for Educational Research as its organising body; the distinctive element it contributed was a distributed network of professors, college lecturers and head teachers, and significant numbers of teachers and student teacher volunteers). A vivid eyewitness account of their interaction is given by Ballard describing their first meeting in 1931:

> In the spring of 1931 we held a three days' Conference at the Grand Hotel Eastbourne and were able to fraternize with Professor Paul Monroe, who had organized the conference; Professor Thorndike, of Columbia University, who looked like a very large and inspired schoolboy, and talked volubly and delightfully in a voice that was entirely his own and quite unforgettable; Professor Judd, of Chicago, who was reticent at first but blossomed out later as a concise and lucid speaker, and a splendid spinner of yarns; M. Desclos, of Paris, chairman of the French Committee and extraordinarily eloquent in our own language; Professor Pierre Bovet, of Geneva, bearded and benign; Professor Carl Becker, of Berlin, and Minister of Education under the Republic, whose untimely death a year or so later was universally deplored; and many other men of light and leading. I recall with special pleasure my talks with the late Professor Graham Wallas, who was a member of our Committee and had much to tell me about the old London School Board, and about the early days of the Fabian Society. ...
>
> The real purpose of this preliminary conference was to discuss the need for investigating the validity of the various systems of examination. When I remarked that in England examinations were under suspicion and in America under arrest, Professor Bovet added that in Switzerland they had been tried and convicted. (Ballard, 1937, pp. 206-207)

However, rules of operation did emerge from their meeting, and followed the lead of their two very experienced chairs, Monroe and Sadler, both of whom had spent most of their careers working in 'foreign' environments and reflecting upon their experiences. At the first gathering, Monroe opened by saying that the meeting had two main purposes – to 'exchange ideas and experiences on the subject' and to propose a project to the Carnegie Corporation, and he added that there would be no fixed programme, except in the first session. Sadler then opened his remarks by emphasising social justice, opportunity, individuals and sociality, before moving onto the specific issue of examinations. The meeting would discuss, clarify terms, and collect 'statements, criticisms and suggestions'. Statements were usually made in English but if in French or German, were then translated. Many of the participants appeared to be fluent in English, and this must have been a factor in their attendance. The decision to use English as the main language was never discussed openly; it could be expected that, at this time, German, and certainly French, would have been the main means of communication in education. But this was the beginning of an internationalism that reflected a new axis, America.

Paul Monroe.

Sadler and Hartog, from the United Kingdom, had worked closely together since Manchester University in the first decade of the century, and on a major commission in India in the 1920s. Sadler's ideas about chairing the IEI can be seen in a letter he wrote in 1930 about the work they were doing in India:

> If we fuse and find agreement, not only is the report in itself certain to be more useful to ... But it will mean that the factors in Bengal which are at cross-purposes are nevertheless not intractable and might be blended into a common purpose ... we are peace makers, and ours is at one and the same time the task of finding an intellectual synthesis, an administrative solution and a moral reconciliation. Of course our printed report in itself can do little more than give the keynote to future discussions and point the way to reform. But we are producing a new body of opinion, by communicating a new attitude of mind ... mere compromise would be worse than useless. The people (European and Indian) with whom we are dealing and for whom we are working are keen critics, suspicious, well informed, alert in their doubt about motives, ready to slander. Our only chance lay in intellectual thoroughness, in knowing more than they did, in getting such a grasp of the problem that our knowledge was deeper, wider, and more exact even than theirs. And then we had to kindle our knowledge, by sympathy, and by a wise and true belief in what can be done, and in what they can do. (Grier, 1952, p. 298; Sadler Letter Darjeeling, May 1930)

However, what might not have been discernible at the time is that the Inquiry had begun to devise a common means of conversation suitable for scientific purpose. They had adopted the diplomatic forms of political negotiation, guided by Sadler and Monroe, and created an informal but consistent form of diplomatic conversation, encouraging explanation and questioning for clarification, yet never inviting conflict or dispute. Indeed, as Withers (1999) notes:

> scientific knowledge and politeness, both as means and ends, were promoted through experimentation, the use of instruments and the rhetoric of polite conversation designed to instruct and to amuse and also to confirm politeness as part of a 'program of modernity'. (p. 36)

Of course what is not recorded can only be surmised, and there are silences in the transcripts which are difficult to judge. The early comparativists, Sadler and Kandel, were to be known for their respect for cultural uniqueness and identity threaded through national education systems and its discourses. Their expectation was of diversity of approach and difference of opinion in the meetings. Their method was comparison: their statements were wrapped around with careful cultural judgements, or tied to the specificities of cases, or deliberately ambiguous (problems were precarious or uncertain). On the other hand, intelligence-focused psychologists had a predisposition to a science in which generalisations across cultures were achievable. The language of this group of professors used new terms such as probability, reliability, diagnostic tests, standardisation, metaphors of medical diagnosis (the test as thermometer) and the fixity of ability. In the same way, they adopted as part of their conversation a reliance on the new tools of research; they co-opted statisticians, rare in number, to help explanations; they used survey research (still uncommon in education research in Europe) and they promoted intelligence testing, already in mass production in America. At the same time, the conversation was not just about the intricacies of evidence and scientific/practical perspectives upon it, it was a sort of a informal ceremony in which countries spoke through their representatives. They expected to be listened to, and they were careful in response. It was diplomatic as well as scientific. The Sadlerian formula, 'an intellectual synthesis, an administrative solution and a moral reconciliation', captures the ground upon which the IEI moved and the 'strategic diplomacy of its operations'. The formula combines the scientific, administrative and diplomatic elements through which Sadler (and Monroe) aimed to shape its deliberations.

Scientific discussion, exemplified in the work of the IEI, contained the languages and practices of the new research tools they used (statistics, surveys, tests, etc.), and it was an important technology in itself. It was to become the new common language of educational research, a kind of scientific Esperanto, circulated and constructed by the IEI across borders and through the permeable walls of their offices and projects. American psychologists, like Terman and Thorndike, used a new language of scientific objectivity, which they embedded with reassuringly solid metaphors drawn from engineering and medicine to legitimise their interpretations and proposals. And so did Thomson and Burt in the United Kingdom. Psychologists were engaging with current policy problems; in this case, selection for a mass secondary education, by emphasising their solid and practical capabilities in a metaphorical language of construction, allied to a new practice of quantitative, statistical research. It promised a usable truth through numerical analyses. Through the alchemy of their procedures, with a language of reliability and an emerging discourse of objective and universal standards, they were beginning to establish their authority over the older cultural connoisseurship and qualitative judgements of the earlier internationalists. In the IEI discussions, sensitivities about countries and their failures were compounded by expressions of certainty and of lack of awareness. Learning to discuss and to listen was a diplomatic necessity and a scientific obligation in the IEI meetings. The conversation as a whole was a scientific and careful discussion, discriminating about terms, cases, procedures and results. It displays the qualities Sadler opened with – there is exchange, clarification, discussion and negotiation. Desclos could describe the meetings as achieving rough but worthwhile results:

> we have become more modest, all of us, and much less dogmatic in consequence. We are more open-minded, it seems to me, this year than we were a few years ago, and moreover, we are much more nearly agreed as to the subjects of our research.

Carnegie, the funders of the project, had had to decide who should be invited, which countries should be represented and what expertise was needed. At the same time, they were offering a great opportunity to poorly financed researchers in Europe and a further chance to the New York International Institute to form another major global partnership.

> It was the realization of this situation which led Dr Paul Monroe, with his rich intimate and unparalleled familiarity with education, past and present, over the greater part of the globe, to recognize the seriousness of the problems involved and particularly through the impact of Western Civilization on the Orient and the Near East. It was through Dr Monroe's efforts that the Carnegie organizations, and particularly the Carnegie Corporation, interested in problems of an international character, chose as one of the first topics of their attention the subject of examinations. Under the sponsorship of the Carnegie Corporation, Dr Monroe, as Director of the International Institute of Teachers College, Columbia University, was appointed to organize and administer what came to be known as the International Examination Inquiry. (Kandel, 1936)

Monroe, thinking about whom to invite into the Inquiry, did not send out a call to key nations or well-known institutions, but to colleagues, and colleagues of friends. Monroe and Kandel, close colleagues at the International Institute in New York, must have pooled their wide experience and networks, and Monroe and Thorndike often had lunch together in their offices at Teachers College. Keppel lived near Thorndike and met him socially and his office was near the Teachers College site. Telephone calls and memos flew between them. Correspondence survives from Thorndike and Monroe to Keppel and meeting records between them about their planning and decisions. Professional and personal relations overlapped in this small internationalist community, working in the educational sciences. Either by training (especially in Germany and later in the USA), through scientific correspondence, conferences (especially the New Education Fellowship conferences in Europe) and associations or close cooperation, several members knew each other. They used place, reputation, publication and networks to assemble the project. How long this took is not clear. There is no formal pre-history of this Inquiry. But communications cannot have been easy. It was not just a question of whom to include but also the temporal questions of correspondence.

Isaac Kandel.

Their interaction was crucial to the success of the Inquiry. Although new as a project, some things were not left to chance. Professional friendships hinted at in other sources, and spatial and temporal overlapping in their histories, suggest that the members of this group had older connections, preceding their 1932 start. Two places are significant; the first is the University of Jena, in Prussia, especially between 1900 and 1915, and the second is Teachers College, Columbia University, New York, between 1918 and 1930. Jena was a significant place for Rusk, Kandel and Sadler. Teachers College was important for Sadler (who had given the Sachs Foundation lectures in 1930. Boyd had taught there in the early 1930s and Thomson had spent a year there as a visiting professor at the invitation of Edward Thorndike, in 1923/24. Hylla was an important student there in the 1920s. Also, the Inquiry overlapped in some of its membership with the organisation of progressive educationalists, the New Education Fellowship (NEF), formed in the 1920s. So, some members, attached to the Inquiry within national delegations and projects, knew each other through their internationalist identities in the NEF. Zilliacus, the key member of the Finnish project, described in the Inquiry as a Helsinki head teacher, had been educated at Bedales (a progressive school in Hampshire), in the USA and Germany, and became a leading member of the NEF. Through the NEF, he would have known Boyd (from Glasgow), possibly McClelland (from Dundee), Bovet (from Geneva) and Nunn and Sadler. In 1932, Zilliacus had published, on behalf of the NEF, the results of their inquiry into examinations (which had been pushed by Boyd). The NEF members would have known Becker and Ulich, leaders of the NEF in Germany, who either died or fled in 1933.

Frederick Keppel.

The kinds of letter sent out by Monroe and Keppel to many different putative IEI members are not known, and nor are records of their reception. When opening the first meeting at Folkestone, Monroe described the participants as contacted by Carnegie indirectly:

> they have chosen to make their contact with you gentleman of
> European educational institutions through the organization of

> which I have the honour to be Director, namely, the International Institute of Teachers College, Columbia University. (Monroe, 1931)

Each network partner viewed itself firmly from within its own state narrative, recorded its participation (if at all) as a minor aspect of its solid native history and in general, did not document the contributions to its own advancement made by these discussions and research work from elsewhere.

Edward L. Thorndike.

Although it might not be very clear how it started, without the financial support of the Carnegie Foundations the Inquiry would not have happened at all. Without its financing, the emergence of an international research project, producing intensive local research projects and linking them together by discussion and analysis, would probably not have taken place until the 1950s or 1960s. Carnegie New York was crucial in the development of this early internationalisation of research and the beginnings of closely focused national research activity across Europe and beyond. The funding of the Inquiry, paying for international travel, many research workers, publications and translations, was considerable. Carnegie was committed to establishing and developing it over seven years. The three major meetings, at Eastbourne in 1931, Folkestone in 1936, and Dinard in 1938, would involve core members from each national project, but those projects could involve up to ten researchers each. The SCRE, for example, received £10,000, a third of its overall financing in the 1930s (this sum is equivalent today to half a million pounds).

The significant funding of their work by Carnegie has the nature of a pure and altruistic act and ulterior motives do not feature in accounts of this funding. An American historian of education, Lagemann, in her history of Carnegie, is fairly open handed but raises difficult questions which should be applied to the Inquiry or its effects. What was Carnegie trying to do and were the Inquiry members aware of its purposes? In the USA, it had a history of supporting research institutes and expert scientists. Carnegie appeared to work with the grain of the experts' own view of themselves. A consistent idea, that of the independence of experts from government, available to deliver fair and objective knowledge, but free of governmental control, seems to have been the Carnegie approach in this period. Its money was used to further this strategy; as Lagemann argues, they had an

> ideal of an 'associative state', in which leadership and wide dissemination of information would enable all people without coercion to do their part in promoting prosperity and stability [and they believed that] scientific expertise and public education could advance the international interests of the United States, even against totalitarian societies, whilst safeguarding the nation's traditions of liberty and individualism. (Lagemann, 1989, p. 30)

Their grants were a positive choice – they supported, promoted and even intervened; these were not random acts or sometimes even benevolent acts. One of Carnegie's areas of interest was the protection of Anglo-Saxon 'race' privileges, and in their national and international grant giving, they supported experts who appeared to operate disinterestedly in their inquiries into difference. When Monroe summarised the work of the Inquiry in 1939, he affirmed that the Inquiry into effective examining in secondary education was really an Inquiry into social leadership:

> largely because secondary education, in whatever country it may be considered, has for its purpose the selection of the leaders who are to dominate or to direct the social, political and cultural movements in the future. As we discussed further we agreed that the major problem was the function of the secondary school in selecting these leaders.

While 'race' might not have been in the forefront of their experts' interests, nationally-based eugenic categories of intelligence and their nurturing through social policy were. Certainly, Carnegie had to find their experts for the Inquiry and shape them into this innovative institutional relation. The speediness of innovative foundations did not mix easily with the conservatism of universities, at this period. At the International Institute at Teachers College, Columbia University, the Rockefeller [2] and Carnegie Foundations had founded an active centre of internationalisation. When Monroe spoke, in the IEI meetings, he was offering a problem which suited Carnegie thinking; it was social, it was about elites, it involved technical and expert solutions and it needed scientific partners. Monroe must have offered a problem in line with their thinking, as a person who worked so closely with them already.

Henry Suzzallo.

Nationalising or Internationalising (Americanising) Educational Research

A focus on scientific networking within the study of the IEI reveals two interesting aspects; the cosmopolitanism of an elite group of educational researchers, with reputations crossing borders and often travelling and studying in other countries, and the 'internationalisation' of research theories and methodologies. In both cases, by the 1920s, the USA was becoming dominant, and its presence replaced the important sites and texts of Germany. Within the internal correspondence between the key New York actors (Monroe, Keppel and Thorndike), there is a clear sense of mission to modernise examining practices in other countries (in the new American way) and to 'offer' a distinctive and valuable research practice which could be used by European countries. For these three actors, there was an alliance of interests although their perspectives and responsibilities differed. The Carnegie Corporation, under Keppel, was widening its field of action in education in the 1920s, into cross-border actions in Europe, the British empire and even China. In this ambitious set of actions, it relied on experts. In this case, Monroe was an expert on other systems of education, particularly in the Orient, and was partly based in Istanbul; Thorndike was the major expert on testing and statistically supported experimentation, and had produced a series of publications about testing and examination in American schools. This alliance of interest, with its strategy and funding, worked with the grain of the IEI participant interests. They appeared to feel that the IEI was a useful opportunity for the modernisation of policy and scientific practice in research inside their own countries. If there was unease, it must have been expressed indirectly.

Education studies, and research, has been assumed to be local and national in its identity, closely aligned with the development of national education systems, and recorded, especially in the histories of education, within strong temporal and political boundaries. While production and commerce may assume trade across borders and between places, public service, and education within it, appears to be in place already. The educational sciences concentrated on problems of national interest and were nationally determined. They existed within wider networks of social relations and political power, and were shaped by the local environments in which its practitioners worked. The way that education, or more likely, schooling, was studied reflected its practical and policy problems, from shortages to capacity, and from books to creativity. Translation and mediation were the best that could be assumed in its relation with the wider world, and for this purpose, comparative education, a small sub-specialism, developed to inquire across borders. An important exception to this rule of local embeddedness in studies and research, according to Malmquist, was 'modern empirical-experimental research in education [where] there has been quite a stream of influence across the Atlantic, from the USA to different European countries' (1975, p. 55).

Yet interpretations drawn from a sociology of science perspective are more likely to recognise the way in which policy makers use and transport ideas and solutions across boundaries, especially when faced with social crises. In the case of the IEI, its dynamic was derived from the expansion of secondary education in Western societies, at a time when it was still an elite system, and from the shortage of new techniques in researching education systems. This dynamic was intertwined, and indissoluble; it was not coincidental or loosely coupled. The coming crisis in elite education caused the shift in ideas and research practices which the IEI represented and acted as a conduit for. Giddens argues that the governing of society by experts and the development of a field of applied educational research were linked projects that have to be seen relationally. Social science became institutionalised:

> The decisive advances in social science, as a whole, and in each of the separate social sciences, derives much more from the attempts of thinkers to come to grips with crisis situations in society at large and in the arena of the state ... New ideas are appropriated by policy makers and put in the service of attempts at social control or transformation: at the time, crisis situations serve to energise social reflection. (Giddens, in Wagner et al, 1990, p. xiv)

This perspective can illuminate the work of the IEI, an example of an attempt to transfer experimental knowledge (processes and techniques) across the Atlantic and consolidate it in Europe, to solve the pressing problem of assessment for secondary school expansion. The IEI constituted a meeting place for scholars, scientists and senior practitioners from several countries, and within countries, and the production of a series of national research projects and reports. Without financial underpinning, it would not have been easy for national members to meet each other, and difficult indeed for them all to meet at international meetings. Nor, without a Western crisis in school growth and selection would there have been an IEI at all; ideas of school selection, of closely focused educational processes, and of expert solutions were all present in the conversations and products of the project, as it faced what was seen as a pressing policy need for Western societies, how to move from an elite to a mass secondary system.

Americanising or Internationalising Educational Research

The IEI had spatial and scientific networks within it, which were placed in close relation to each other for the first time. Each national research team was constituted with a mix of crucial interests or specialisms. The nature of crucial representation varied across the sites but there was a mixture of specialism, practical and policy interest, and a sense of the best people to represent the country abroad. There appears to be three overlapping sets of academic specialists within the IEI; they are comparative educationalists, 'progressive' (New Education Fellowship) educators, and educational scientists (psychologists). These are not distinct intellectual categories or practices, and individuals may have more than one main identity, but they represent different approaches to educational work and across the range of their heterogeneous presence within IEI, quite diverse views and practices can be observed.

Illustrating Malmquist's point about streams of influence around experimental research in education, the IEI Conference transcriptions offer new insights into the way the three major experts in intelligence theory, measurement and analysis (Thorndike, Thomson and Spearman) use their knowledge and expertise to solve a crucial problem in the expansion of their education systems. Thorndike quietly fulfils his role as a facilitator, yet with the enormous authority of his own expertise and his role in influencing the construction of the Inquiry. Thomson works across the role of expert and policy actor. He comes across as almost apologetic about his huge involvement in intelligence testing for school selection. Whereas Thomson is practical, Spearman is theoretical and focused on basic science, emphatically reminding the audience of his ideas. Thomson is polite almost to diffidence, whereas Spearman is blunt, occasionally verging on the argumentative and rude. As a scientific conversation, it leaves Thomson and Thorndike engaging with their knowledgeable but inexpert audience, in a way that Spearman is completely unable to do. The IEI transcripts contain a three-way conversation among Spearman, Thomson and Thorndike that constitutes a 'psychometric masterclass' (Deary et al, 2008).

Recent disciplinary and national histories of social science have tended to view this period as raising significant questions about the 'Americanisation' of national intellectual traditions; indeed, in Pieter van Strien's phrase, to see this process as a form of 'scientific colonisation', an 'intellectual domination of an existing culture by a foreign, more powerful culture' (Strien, 1997, p. 349). This hegemony is achieved by voluntary submission, a recognition of cultural dominance, in which key members of the colonised culture travel towards it, learn its language and represent its ideas on return. In his study of social psychology in post-war Netherlands, Strien describes a meeting between the missionary zeal and 'feeling of superiority' among the Americans, bolstered by the Marshall Plan, and the willingness of Dutch scholars to 'subjugate' themselves. Obscuring their philosophical and sociological disciplinary base, and turning toward American empiricism, they began to segment and disrupt their own national disciplinary histories. Strien states that

> European social psychologists renounced the indigenous contributions of their contributions of their European predecessors, gave up the multi-disciplinary stance that was typical of pre-war European social psychology, and began to conceive their field as a sub discipline of psychology with a distinct experimental emphasis. (p. 359)

The conversation between the three leading experts (above) was driven by their scientific authority, listened into by interested parties in their field, and sometimes used in the development of national testing practices or in defining the field of research. It can be argued, though, that the 'American' drive helped to determine the scope and subjects of educational research in the following years. It was the one best solution on offer to the problems of secondary school selection. Its effects lasted until the 1960s in the United Kingdom. It was a universalising methodology, working across countries of widely different social and behavioural sciences, which came to dominate over locally embedded interests and traditions of inquiry. But this was an unequal process across the IEI countries and could not be treated as uniform subjugation without an added range of caveats.

However, it can be argued that it was the comparativists in education (Monroe, Sadler, Hartog and Kandel), the cosmopolitan leaders of the IEI, who eventually lost out in this process. Their sub-discipline and their own holistic perspectives on national systems of education was overtaken by the creation of measurement standards, usable in comparing schools, regions and even countries eventually.

Geographies of science (Crawford et al, 1993; Livingstone, 2003) recognise the cross-cultural links in science and the ways in which the communication of research was organised across distance and place. It was often unequal in production or capacity but it was capable, through its agreed operational standards, to move fluidly and fast. This process was aided by the development of trust in the IEI meetings, as well as by the data, reports and discussion in their meetings. The meetings in the Grand hotels at Eastbourne, Folkestone and Dinard were essential places of work, as well as a confirmation of the quality and esteem associated with their work. The Grand hotels were used as knowledge-producing sites and were just as specialist as laboratories, observatories and libraries. They were crucial to the diplomatic and polite exchanges which took place and the elimination of competitive, nationalistic relations. Difficult evidence-based conversations, revealing awkward data about national systems (and pride and identity) were managed carefully in a trust-based dialogue.

In scientific, as opposed to educational, histories, the emphasis is on internationalisation as a constant feature in the construction of the subject. So, the establishment of the national is understood to be in a context of the international and constituted within a professional scientific community (journals, associations, etc.) simultaneously. As each new nation state emerged (say from the 1850s on):

> a host of political, economic, social and cultural activities were brought under its sway and made national in scope and orientation. At the same time, advances in transport and communication technology made the citizens of nation-states much more aware of developments in other nations than before. The expansion of interests was apparent in the internationalization which occurred across a range of domains, among them industry, commerce, finance, politics, and demography. (Crawford et al, 1993, p. 12)

The key problems for international science were to do with establishing standardised methods of observation, units of measurement, taxonomies and equipment (Crawford et al, 1993, p. 14); international communications (rule-bound exchanges and associations); and universally accepted technical standards to manage the operation of new and shared technologies. Sometimes, single countries found that they were unable to create a critical mass of scientists to create a community, and unable to achieve the institutional, communications and knowledge requirements of a full-fledged community. Specialist associations helped by establishing and standardising the units and discourse of exchange. This was the role of the IEI. It was a community of educationalists and a scientific community of experts. Scientists acted within the borders of the nation to support national achievements and strategies *and* also internationally, to strengthen reputation, method, scientific equipment, and to test and exchange research results (Crawford et al, 1993, p. 28). This could mean that they often forged more meaningful and stable intellectual relations with colleagues in their field abroad than at home. These international relations helped to embed and validate new research perspectives, which in many cases in the IEI, then produced or reinforced national research institutes.

Conclusions

The Inquiry, set up by Carnegie and the International Institute in the 1930s, is intriguing because of its lack of visibility. In a sense, it disappeared on completing its work in 1939. Yet it was heavily funded, involved leading experts in the world on new directions in education, produced major research reports on examinations, and it reappeared as the underpinnings of later post-war secondary school reforms on access to secondary education across Europe.

Briefly put, this company of experts seem to be visible in their knowledge communities and their countries but invisible in their internationalism. Many of the leading actors in the IEI are very well known in their national narratives of education history but the flow of expertise in individuals or institutional links seems to move off the page of educational histories. These experts, when travelling, become missing persons. Even when not meeting, but working locally for the IEI, writing a report or corresponding with other members, there is little record of their networking and its effects. Where is the history of this flow of ideas and policy solutions delivered by the IEI except in local and national grounded cases which tended to ignore the international reference? The Inquiry left behind many significant research reports, embedded in national research histories, often as foundation documents in the mid-century reform of education (Sweden, England, Scotland, Germany and Finland). If they had a policy effect, they did so not at the time of their production in the late 1930s, but in post-war reconstruction. Several societies, especially Germany and Sweden, used their work to enable a system of examining to include tests and to manage the extension and differentiation processes of the new secondary education. In an article in 1944, on the need for a post-war International Education Organisation, prefiguring UNESCO, Kandel suggested that the Inquiry could be a model for the future; it promoted cooperation and cooperated on problems. Later, he became a major advisor to UNESCO in its first years.

Was Kandel prescient or unforgiving when he suggested, in 1955, from deep within his own argument about the value of comparative education, and reflecting upon the IEI, that

> It was only when representative speakers began to explain and define the objectives of education in the light of their respective cultural backgrounds that the differences began to be apparent. For each definition was redolent of the culture pattern and tradition which gave the national system of education its meaning. The existence of variety within a common framework of unity was recognised and, instead of a common attack on the examinations problem by an international group, it was decided to have the problem investigated in each country by a national committee.
>
> It cannot be denied that the progress of education can be advanced by the lessons derived from the new science of

> education through psychology and objective tests and measurements. But, as in the total area of man's quest for knowledge and understanding, there is great danger in ignoring the fact that science can furnish only partial answers to this quest. A philosophy of education may use the results that come from the application of scientific techniques, but the scientific study of education is not itself philosophical.

For him, education inquiry was a moral journey into self-reflection, about national sensitivities and aims, about difference and diversity, and about uniqueness. The idea of a common solution to international educational problems and new 'scientific study' had to be rejected (Kandel, 1955, p. 13). Is this what he was quietly thinking when others were discussing innovative methods of researching education and testing pupils? At the time of its writing, Kandel's words seem to be searching for an audience who still understands the moral purpose of education in international contexts, at a time when the idea of a moral purpose, the sense of culture and context, and cosmopolitan deliberation were drowning in the new scientific landscape of psychology and education. It is ironic as he was the main reason why the experts were able to work so effectively with each other in their powerful network. He was part of the enabling forces which constructed, funded and shaped the network in which they lost symbolic power to the quantitative comparativists. An early comment of Rusk, at the Eastbourne meeting, must have passed like a shadow over Kandel (and Sadler) and yet, from the perspective of the early 2000s, seems prescient.

> For some time past, there has been a discussion in America as to what was meant by comparative education. In the past it meant that a man went round among various countries and gave his opinion. Now that has been discredited so that our investigation and the adaptation of these tests might be made the beginning of a new comparative education on scientific lines. I should therefore merely like to intimate that we here might perhaps form the basis of a new science of comparative education. (Rusk, in Monroe, 1931, p. 262)

The Inquiry's work could be viewed within a legacy of products (research reports, conference meetings, manuals), in specialist training programmes and the highly trained experts, with shared socialisations; and in embryonic associations and continuing networks. They had begun to make a new space for educational research, no longer entirely national, more cosmopolitan, and within cross-border networks. They had built a pilot international institution, a disembedded laboratory, involving advanced and emerging research sites.

A sociology of science perspective would be disposed to see significant effects created by the IEI. It enabled high-level conversations about the technicalities of intelligence and its tests, the use of statistics in educational research and the complexities of comparison and intervention to move swiftly across borders. Research and policy publications, especially from the USA and the United Kingdom, were available at this time and served as a point of contact but the IEI enabled the range and magnitude of new ideas to be translated into consistent research programmes in separate countries, supported by world authorities in psychology, national systems of education and international comparison. Individual members of the core IEI group or even the national research teams would have had some knowledge of the subject of study, the perspective used and the methods of research. The opportunity to engage in solid and extensive research over time would have deepened this expertise, shaped strong local teams in national contexts and created key scientific reference points.

This appears to be the case in Germany where Hylla returns to the newly created DiPF (Deutsches Institut für Internationale Pädagogische Forschung) in Frankfurt in the early 1950s and translates American key test terms into a German glossary, and in Sweden where the post-war education reforms were influenced by the work of Hanninger, Grimlund and Wellander, all members of the Swedish research project. It was not the case in Switzerland where the original research team did not achieve its goals and Bovet produced an alternative project; nor does it appear so in France. The groundwork of the English team may have produced the significant texts of inquiry needed to create a climate of change and consolidate the stratification processes of their education system. The success of the Scottish work is more likely to be recognised in its fusing together of expert and professorial networks across the country and developing common research training programmes, as well as its confirmation that its population could be surveyed and tested with its consent and for its own good.

Did the three supportive elements of the IEI's scientific work studied here – its significant funding, its networks of trust and its communicative procedures (intellectual synthesis and moral reconciliation, in Sadler's words) – help to produce an internationalisation of research methodologies in education? It appears that in some ways it did, especially in the Nordic countries and in the United Kingdom. At least, it can be argued that if such a trend toward empirical-experimental research is discernible in this period and post war, then the IEI was a medium for its movement in Europe. Its means was the shared problem of examination for secondary education, a policy problem which the collaborating countries had in common.

Social science methods and ideas, even when bound by context and national purposes, can travel and policy crises serve to facilitate the appropriation of these ideas. In this case, an 'Americanisation' of educational research was useful to many of the participants although other factors (not least of which was the major disruption of the 1939-45 war) reveal the role of politics, internal disorganisation and strong national traditions as inhibiting the homogenisation of the field in Europe at this time. Dean Judd's comment, when writing to Keppel after the Eastbourne meeting, that the inquiry would introduce the 'science of education to countries in much need of it' seems apposite and maybe discerned as a Carnegie goal, just as much as modernising European examination practices.

In the way the IEI worked together, it appeared to influence the foundation of UNESCO, and in their national arenas (Kandel, 1955), it was useful in the establishment or development of national research institutes. Yet it is clear that its expectations about its work and the future were not realised. In this case, it appears that the stability of the network, and its mutual trust, was not the main problem it faced. It was the huge dislocation of the war in Europe. Even when facing war in 1938, the group at Dinard ended with an optimistic proposal:

> that an international Committee for the Study of Examinations should be instituted, to function as a co-ordinating committee representative of the various national delegations present at the Conference, and to include Denmark, Holland, Belgium, the Dominions and India. Prof J Drever, Convenor of the Scottish Committee has been appointed Convenor of the International Committee, and Prof GH Thomson has agreed to act as Secretary. (SCRE, 1938-1939, pp. 11-12. Monroe, 1939)

Perhaps its ambitions were realised but not in the ways expected.

Notes

[1] Created as part of a research project, *A Scottish School of Educational Research, 1925-1950* (ESRC Award RES-000-23-1246) (Deary, Lawn & Bartholomew).

[2] Rockefeller had similar operating goals to Carnegie, creating model institutional centres of research and fellowship programmes and promoting practical and scientific solutions to social problems. See Fisher (1980, 1983) and Bulmer (1998).

References

Ballard, P.B. (1937) *Things I Cannot Forget*. London: University of London Press.

Bulmer, M. (1998) The Problem of Exporting Social Survey Research, *American Behavioral Scientist*, 42(2), 153-168.

Craigie, J. (Ed.) (1972) *The Scottish Council for Research in Education, 1928-1972.* Edinburgh: Scottish Council for Research in Education.

Crawford, E., Shinn, T. & Sörlin, S. (1993) *Denationalizing Science: the contexts of international science.* Dordrecht: Kluwer.

Deary, I., Lawn, M. & Bartholomew, D.A. (2008) Conversation between Charles Spearman, Godfrey Thomson, and Edward L. Thorndike: the International Examinations Inquiry meetings 1931-1938. Unpublished Paper.

Fisher, D. (1980) American Philanthropy and the Social Sciences in Britain, 1919-1939, *Sociological Review,* 28(2), 277-315.

Fisher, D. (1983) The Role of Philanthropic Foundations in the Reproduction and Production of Hegemony: Rockefeller Foundations and the social sciences, *Sociology*, 17, 206-233.

Grier, L. (1952) *Achievement in Education: the work of Michael Ernest Sadler 1885-1935.* London: Constable.

Hofstetter, R. & Schneuwly, B. (Eds) (2002) Special Issue: 'The Emergence and Development of Educational Research in Europe', *European Educational Research Journal,* 1(1). http://www.wwwords.eu/eerj/content/pdfs/1/issue1_1.asp

Hofstetter, R. & Schneuwly, B. (Eds) (2004) Educational Sciences in Dynamic and Hybrid Institutionalization, *Paedagogica Historica*, 40(5-6), 569-589.

Kandel, I. (1936) The International Exams Inquiry, *The Educational Record*, 17 (Supplement No 9, January), 50-70.

Kandel, I. (1944) *Intellectual Cooperation: national and international.* Columbia University: Bureau of Publications (produced for the National Committee of the United States on International Intellectual Cooperation).

Kandel, I. (1955) *The New Era in Education: a comparative study.* Boston: Houghton Mifflin.

Lagemann, E.C. (1989) *The Politics of Knowledge: the Carnegie Corporation, philanthropy, and public policy.* Middletown, CT: Wesleyan University Press.

Lawn, M. (2004) The Institute as Network: the Scottish Council for Research in Education as a local and international phenomenon in the 1930s, *Paedagogica Historica,* 40(5-6), 719-732.

Livingstone, D. (2003) *Putting Science in Its Place: geographies of scientific knowledge.* Chicago: Chicago University Press.

Malmquist, E. (1975) *Educational Research in Europe Today and Tomorrow.* Amsterdam: Gleerup (European Cultural Foundation).

Monroe, P. (Ed.) (1931) *Conference on Examinations.* New York: Teachers College, Columbia University.

Monroe, P. (Ed.) (1936) *Conference on Examinations under the Auspices of The Carnegie Corporation, The Carnegie Foundation, The International Institute of Teachers College, Columbia University, at the Hotel Metropole, Folkestone, England, June 8-10, 1935.* New York: Teachers College, Columbia University.

Monroe, P. (Ed.) (1939) *Conference on Examinations under the Auspices of the Carnegie Corporation.* New York: Teachers College, Columbia University.

Scottish Council for Research in Education (1947) *The Scottish Council for Research in Education: its aims and activities.* London: University of London Press.

Scottish Council for Research in Education. *Annual Report 1938-39.*

Shenton, H. (1933) *Cosmopolitan Conversation: the language problems of international conferences.* New York: Columbia University Press.

Van Strien, P. (1997) The American 'Colonization' of Northwest European Social Psychology after World WAR II, *Journal of the History of the Behavioral Sciences,* 33(4), 349-363.

Wagner, P., Wittrock, B. & Whitley, R. (1990) *Discourses on Society: the shaping of the social science disciplines.* Dordrecht: Kluwer.

Withers, C.W.J. (1999) Towards a History of Geography in the Public Sphere, *History of Science*, 37 (Part 1, No. 115), 45-78.

APPENDIX 1.
Illustrative Project Bibliography

Hartog, P. & Rhodes, E (1936) *The Marks of Examiners*, p. 344. London: Macmillan.

The School and Examination System of Finland with Some Investigations into the Secondary School/by the Finland Examinations Enquiry (1939) Helsinki-Helsingfors: International Institute Examinations Enquiry.

Atlas de l'Enseignement en France (1936) Paris: Maisons du Livre.

Scottish Council for Research in Education (SCRE) (1933) *The Intelligence of Scottish Children: a national survey of an age-group* (also SCRE Publication No. 5). London: University of London Press.

Orrgard, Stellan. (1937) *High School Entrance-Tests and the Work of the Primary-School: a Swedish nationwide investigation in 1936.* Stockholm: P.A. Norstedt & Söners.

Pierre Bovet (1935) *Les Examens de Recrues dans l'Armée Suisse. 1854-1913. Enquête internationale sur les examens*, p. 208. Neuchâtel-Paris: Delachaux & Niestlé.

Some Aspects of Educational Sociology: a statistical analysis of selective experiences of the Studienstiftung des Deutschen Volkes (R. Ulich & E. Wohlfahrt, 1933, *Zur Bildungssoziologie des Academischen Nachwuchses in Deutschland*). Dresden.

APPENDIX 2.
IIE Membership of the National Projects

England

Cecil DeLisle Burns, Lecturer in Citizenship, University of Glasgow

Cyril Burt, Professor of Education, University of London; Psychologist, London County Council

Sir Percy Nunn, Principal, London Day Training College; Professor of Education, University of London

Sir Philip Hartog, (formerly) Vice Chancellor, University of Dacca; Chair, Auxiliary Committee on Education, Indian Statutory Committee

Lord Eustace Percy, Member of Parliament; (formerly) President, Board of Education

Sir Michael Sadler, Master, University College, Oxford

C.E. Spearman, Professor of Psychology, University of London

(In a second list, Percy is not included and Dr P.B. Ballard, Inspector, London County Council is added)

(Graham Wallas, Late Professor of Political Science, University of London, is added, replaced by Godfrey Thomson, from the Scottish Committee) (added in 1935)

E.C. Rhodes, Reader in Statistics, London School of Economics

C.W. Valentine, University of Birmingham (added in 1937)

F. Clarke, Institute of Education, London

France

Barrier, Inspecteur d'Academie; Adjoint au Directeur de l'Enseignement Primaire au Ministère de l'Instruction Publique

C. Bouglé, Sous Directeur, L'Ecole Normale Superiore

M. Cope, Présidente du Syndicat National des Professeurs des Lyceés de Garçons et l'Enseignement Secondaire Feminin

A. Desclos, Sous Directeur, Office National des Universitiés et Ecoles Francaises, Paris

Ch. Maurain, Doyen de la Faculté des Sciences, l'Université de Paris

Henri Laugier, Professeur de la Faculté des Sciences de l'Université de Paris; Professeur, Conservatoire National des Arts et Metiers; Directeur de l'Institut d'Orientation Professionale

G. Gastinel, Late Inspecteur General de l'Instruction Publique

Germany

Carl Becker, Minister a.D für Kunst, Wissenschaft und Volksbildung in Preussen; Professor an der Universitat, Berlin

Erich Hylla, Oberregierungsrat in Ministerium für Kunst, Wissenschaft und Volksbildung in Preussen; Professor an der Pädagogischen Akademie, Halle

Dr Robert Ulich, Ministerialrat im Ministerium für Volksbildung in Sachsen

(In a second list, Dr Otto Bobertag, University of Berlin is added)

Scotland

Thomas Henderson, Hon. Secretary, SCRE; Secretary, Educational Institute of Scotland (in a second list, Henderson is excluded)

W.A.F. Hepburn, Director of Education, Ayrshire

J.C. Smith, Senior Chief Inspector of Schools, Scottish Education Department

Godfrey Thomson, Bell Professor of Education, University of Edinburgh

Robert R. Rusk, Director, Scottish Council for Research in Education, Edinburgh; Lecturer in Education, Glasgow Training College

James Drever, Professor of Psychology, University of Edinburgh

William Boyd, Lecturer in Education, University of Glasgow

David Kennedy-Fraser, Psychologist, Glasgow Education Committee

William McClelland, Bell Professor of Education, University of St Andrews

John Mackie, Headmaster, Leith Academy

Norman T. Walker, Lecturer in Education, University of Aberdeen

Switzerland

Pierre Bovet, Professeur, l'Université de Genève; Directeur, l'Institut Universitaire des Sciences de l'Education, Genève

Jean Piaget, Directeur, Bureau International d'Education Genève; Professeur de Psychologie, l'Université de Genève

Brenner, Directeur, Lehrerseminar, Basle

Edouard Claparede, Professor of Psychology, Geneva; Director, Institute J.J. Rousseau

Robert Dottrens, Directeur d'Ecoles, Troinex, Geneva

Charles Junod

Albert Malche, Conseiller d'Etats; Professor, Geneva

W. Schohaus, Schweizerische Erziehungs Rundschau, Kreuzlingen, Thurgovie

Ida Somazzi, Seminar, Berne

Hans Stettbacher, Lehramtkurse, Universitat, Zurich

Teodoro Valentini, Professor, Scuola Normale, Locarno, Tessin

United States

C.H. Judd, Dean, School of Education, University of Chicago

Frederick Keppel, President, Carnegie Corporation, New York

Paul Monroe, Director, International Institute, Teachers College, Columbia University

Henry Suzzallo, President, Carnegie Foundation, New York

Edward L. Thorndike, Professor of Education, Teachers College, Columbia University

Isaac Kandel, Professor of Education, Teachers College, Columbia University

Walter Jessup, President, Carnegie Foundation, New York

W.S. Learned, Carnegie Corporation, Staff

Ben D. Wood, Administrative Staff, Columbia University

Finland

Laurin Zilliacus, Recktor, Tolo Svenska Samskola, Helsingfors

Carin Rosenius, Tolo Svenska Samskola, Helsingfors

Bertil Hedstrom, Lektor, Headmaster, Helsingfors

A.A. Koskenjaakko, Headmaster, Helsingfors

Norway

Johan Hertzberg, Headmaster, Stabekk State School, near Oslo

Sem Saeland, Professor of Physics, University of Oslo

Einar Hoigard, Lecturer in Education, University of Oslo
Kay Piene, Lecturer in Mathematics, Vestheim School, Oslo

Sweden

Nils Hanninger, Member, Board of Education, Stockholm
Hugo Grimlund, Headmaster, Vasa Secondary School, Stockholm
Tor Jerneman, Secretary, State Social Board, Statistics Expert
Brior Jonzon PhD, Chief Inspector of Elementary Education in Stockholm
Gustaf Lagercrantz, Bank Director
Nils Lundqvist PhD, Headmaster
Anna C Petterson, Headmaster
Karl Steenberg, Headmaster
Erik Wellander PhD, University Professor
Gustaf Mattsson, Headmaster

Plate 1. Eastbourne, May 23-25, 1931. Back row, left to right: 1 Suzzalo; 2 Connely; 3 Ulich; 4 Hylla; 5 Bobertag; 6 Spearman; 7 Rusk; 8 Thorndike; 9 Hartog; 10 Hepburn; 11 Cope; 12 Thomson; 13 Barrier; 14 Ballard; 15 Keppel; 16 Bouglé; 17 DeLisle Burns; 18 Judd; 19 Arsendeau. Front row, left to right: 1 Wallas; 2 Sadler; 3 Bovet; 4 Desclos; 5 Monroe; 6 Smith; 7 Becker; 8 unknown; 9 Nunn.

Connely. Koskenjaakko. Learned. Kennedy-Fraser. Rusk. Ballard. Keppel. Wood.
Arsendeau. Mackie. Gastinel. Godfrey Thomson. Jessup. Desclos.
Henderson. Hänninger.

Plate 2. Dinard, September 16-19, 1938.

Piene. Drever. Hamley. Jernemann. McClelland. Walker. Grimlund. Hedström. Krans. Höigård. Dawson.

Monroe. Hartog. Kandel Bouglé Spearman.

Zilliacus. Barrier. Smith. Kohnstamm Thorndike.

Blowing up the Citadel of Examinations: the English Committee and the Carnegie Corporation

MARTIN LAWN

SUMMARY The English Committee of the International Examinations Inquiry comprised some of the most well-known educationists and psychologists of education in England. It was London based and driven by Sir Philip Hartog, a close ally of the Chair, Sir Michael Sadler. It published a range of books including a bibliography and essays on the subject of examinations, and a close study entitled *The Marks of Examiners*, a controversial book. In the late 1930s, it was allowed to develop, with Carnegie funding, into a project for a national research institute, and its close ally, Sir Fred Clarke, worked with Hartog in the war years to this purpose.

> I am perfectly certain that in England you can only enter into the citadel of examinations as they are now, blow up what is bad and reconstruct what is good, you can only enter a citadel with a battering ram of facts, and it is as such a battering ram that I regard the preliminary enquiry which we have sketched out.
> (Hartog, in Monroe, 1931, p. 91)

> The object of the investigation is of a purely scientific character.
> (Hartog–Nunn Memorandum, 1 April 1932)

The first statement from Sir Philip Hartog, speaking about a subject that he had made his own for several decades in England, suggests an earnestness of purpose and radical intention which the International Examinations Inquiry (IEI) was an opportunity to further. Hartog is the key to the work of the examination researchers in England, drawn together by the IEI funding, as he had written about the problem of examinations twenty years before and he was a very close colleague of Sir Michael Sadler, the trusted leader of the English project.

Sir Philip Hartog.

One of the ironies of the English IEI Committee was that it had radical intentions, shared with Hartog, but it also constituted an elite itself. It was a modernising elite, and even had elements of a meritocratic approach to the problem of secondary examinations. Yet it represented Oxford colleges (Sadler), eminent professors of psychology (Spearman, Thomson and Burt), reforming school inspectors (Ballard), governmental advisers, and even an ex-Minister of Education (Lord Eustace Percy). Their interests ranged across the production of the new governing elite, through an expanded secondary education to interests in technical and statistical analyses of data. Together they constituted a well-balanced team. Well suited to the English ways of governing, through elite contacts, they were able to mediate between their radical intentions, scientific strength and conservative institutions.

The English Committee (EC) established itself fully soon after the first large conference of the IEI in Eastbourne, on 1 January, 1932. Over the next few years, the EC produced a range of useful and important research publications which had great effect at the time, judged by the comments in the press. Its members were judged to be both radical, in the sense that they researched the working of public examinations in England, and serious, as they represented some of the most well-known figures in education in England.[1] The EC expected its work to significantly change the examination system, not a surprising judgement given its membership and its research output. However, perhaps its greatest contribution was to enable a closer link to be made with the Carnegie Foundation in New York, which was part of a series of close links drawing English educational research into a British and a British empire context. Funding obtained through the IEI enabled England to establish its own post-war Education Research Foundation, tied closely to an emerging London Institute of Education. In both cases, the late introduction of Fred Clarke to the EC enabled this greater plan of modernising and enabling a 'British' approach to education research.

Moving away from the New Education Fellowship

From the outset, some members of the English Committee, in common with other national committees working in the IEI, had been involved with the New Education Fellowship (NEF). They were part of a European network of progressive educators of various kinds and they either knew about or were involved with an NEF study on examinations, begun in the late 1920s. *New Era*, the journal of the NEF, had had a series of articles on the problem of examinations, and in 1925 ran a series of papers on alternatives to examinations, and whether intelligence tests could replace them (vol. 6, no. 21). At the World Conference at Elsinore in 1929 reports on examinations were received from 22 countries: 'some of these reports were the results of intensive studies carried out over a considerable period; others were in the nature of less formal inquiries; still others were statements based primarily on experience and observation' (*New Era*, 1929, vol. 10, pp. 216-217, 'Examinations Enquiry Committee').

Michael Sadler, who was President of the English section of the NEF, spoke about the subject at its annual meeting in 1929 (reported in *New Era*, 1929, vol. 10, pp. 9-19, 'Examinations – an address by Sir Michael Sadler'). In a long paper, he argued that 'examinations are the English destiny' and that 'more and more, English boys and girls will have to pass examinations as part of the routine of their existence' (p. 12); exams cannot be dispensed with or abolished, although the fatalistic response of the English to it, he likened to the eighteenth-century view of the slave trade. However, he ended his argument by asking for some systematic research or scientific observation of the examination system in England and appealed for

> the Government or some affluent corporation determined to appoint ... a Commissioner to inquire into the working of our examination system, into the technique of question setting, into the methods of marking, and into the psychological effects of examinations on the candidates. The commissioner would need a staff of assistants and funds for the prosecution of extensive inquiries and test-experiments. (p. 19)

This idea was echoed at the Elsinore meeting and in *New Era*. The International Commission of the NEF published its report in 1935, *The*

Examination Tangle and the Way Out (Rawson, 1935), and throughout its pages members of the English Committee are referred to and quoted within it, for example, DeLisle Burns, Clarke, Sadler, Hartog, Valentine, Ballard and Burt. The final appendix is about Northumberland and its tests, the home base of Godfrey Thomson. The report recommends the use of record cards, the use of standardised tests in the classroom and reflects upon the unsuitability of examinations before the age of 16. This is worth mentioning because Beatrice Ensor, the secretary of the NEF, persistently approached Carnegie for funding for the NEF Commission and for involvement in the IEI in the 1930s, and was rebuffed. Carnegie officials tended to take the view that the work of the NEF on examinations was unscientific and premised on the idea that examinations should be abolished. Indeed, an early letter from Paul Monroe, the leader of the IEI project, to Percy Nunn in London seemed to be a reply to earlier requests for support and connections with NEF study: '[I think Sadler] makes the suggestion that if assistance for the examination inquiry should be given to the NEF the results would be most desirable and fruitful' (Nunn Papers, IE/TPN/8/11). Monroe then explains that the Rockefeller Foundation provides some funding for the NEF and its extensive programme (which precludes Carnegie from doing the same). Foundations try to avoid duplication. However, Monroe does recognise that the NEF examinations inquiry will be a technical inquiry and 'no doubt is the line of enquiry in which we may expect the most tangible and immediate results' (Nunn Papers, IE/TPN/8/1, 15 December 1930).

Sir Michael Sadler.

A strong internal correspondence takes place between Suzzallo (Carnegie Foundation, New York), Keppel (Carnegie Corporation, New York) and Monroe following letters from Ensor in which she stated that a promise of funding had been made to the NEF to support their examinations inquiry, that a number of NEF associates were to be invited to the Eastbourne conference and that acknowledgements should be made in the conference volume to the work of the NEF inquiry. Denying all promise of assistance, although they were actually not unwilling, Suzzallo and Keppel asked Monroe to manage the problem. Suzzallo wrote to Keppel that 'She is the most persistent woman on earth and she will, if we let her, make us feel that we have committed some sort of crime for which she thinks we will have to make amends' (18 September 1930, Memo, Carnegie Corporation Archives, Examination Study File 1930-33).

Two years later this is still going on. Monroe, reviewing the position, wrote to Suzzallo that he had left questions of cooperation to the English Committee although he argued that they could not be partners anyway:

> Her group is interested in destroying or removing examinations entirely. ... Consequently, it is quite impossible to get the authorities that are responsible for the administration of examinations to cooperate in the investigation of this subject and the investigation cannot be properly made without the cooperation of the authorities entrusted with the examinations themselves. (Monroe to Suzzallo, 7 November 1932, Carnegie Corporation Archives, Examination Study File 1930-33)

He expected the demands of the NEF to become 'increasingly exacting' if they engaged with them. Suzzallo agreed and intended to close the matter; he wrote to Keppel that Ensor was 'so persistent and clever in handling people ... I don't want any connection with her except to give her a gracious smile' (Suzzallo to Keppel, 23 November 1932, Memo, Carnegie Corporation Archives, Examination Study File 1930-33). The work of the NEF results in informal professional links within the IEI, and in the EC, but absolutely no formal linkages at all; almost the reverse. However, the correspondence says a lot about the Carnegie intentions and the line that the English Committee had to walk as insiders and reformers.

Developing a Project

A conference was organised at the Grand Hotel, Eastbourne, on the south coast of England, for 23-25 May 1931. Monroe had offered some money to Nunn which was to be used in its preparation. Nunn had been Principal of the London Day Training College since 1922 and in 1932 had supervised its metamorphosis into the Institute of Education, University of London, as its first Director. He was advised by Monroe that this meeting would have to create:

> the scheme of objectives for the study; and second, the question of technique, procedure and personnel; and third, to decide upon the [continuing] worthwhileness and desirability of such a Conference – the ultimate question. (Nunn Papers, IE/TPN/8/1, Letter, Monroe to Nunn, 15 December 1930)

Soon after, the IEI office sent to the English group copies of the US College Examinations Board work and its investigation into the use of testing in examinations and into mathematics and foreign languages; this could be seen as a model for its future work.

Sir Percy Nunn.

Hartog said, in Eastbourne, there needed to be 'A systematic investigation carried out with the help of the new statistical methods on actual scripts, written in answer to questions set by various examining bodies' (cited in Monroe, 1931, p. 32). England urgently needed to study the fundamental problems and techniques of examinations and this would have to take precedence over the sociological aspects of their organisation, authority and effects (Hartog, in Monroe, 1931, pp. 30-36).

The Eastbourne conference allowed the American group to comment upon the presentation of the need for an inquiry by the English team. An internal memorandum from Suzzallo to Keppel, within the Carnegie organisation, on 18 October 1931, described them negatively: 'They are not alert either to the scientific evidence in education, or to the rapid changes occurring abroad' (Carnegie Corporation Archives, Examination Study File 1930-33).

Judd, from the Chicago University School of Education, an observer at Eastbourne, wrote a short comment while on the *Europa* sailing back across the Atlantic and followed this up by a longer report later. Writing to Keppel, who is the president of the Carnegie foundation and at the centre of its planning, on 1 July 1931, Judd said that

> the English seemed to me to be floundering more than any of the rest. The particular group which was at the conference seemed to me without plan or program either in its social or educational outlooks. They seemed to me, with the exception of [DeLisle] Burns, to be many years behind the times. They are evidently in the first stages of scientific thinking. Their program of inquiry seemed to me purely sectional. (Carnegie Corporation Archives, Examination Study File 1930-33)

Judd is in favour of a longer view:

> Even the English study ... which seemed to me ... of little value would if carried on serve to introduce the science of education to countries in much need of it.

In his full report, Judd wrote that

> The English representatives behaved in a fashion which has come to be recognized the world over as typical of British candour. As distinguished from French and German delegations, the English group lacked solidarity and certainly lacked the quality of internal agreement. Only at one point did there seem to be a fair degree of agreement. All the English delegates seemed to hold that the typical examinations set by Oxford and Cambridge should be superseded by something less confident and less stereotyped. How to bring about the desired downfall of the ancient practices seemed to concern the English representatives more than did the determination of what was to be adopted after Oxford and Cambridge had been vanquished ...
>
> When it was pointed out that comparisons of markers' judgements and exposures of disagreements were published years ago in England and the United States, it was answered that Oxford and Cambridge examiners cannot be reached by any outside evidence. They must be convicted of personal sin: no amount of unrighteousness outside their own precincts will attract their attention. The English representatives were very earnest in their desire to break through the steel encasement, as one of them called the crust of conservatism, which now surrounds their ancient and leading foundations.
>
> One of the most vivid impressive descriptions of modern democracy was uttered by a member of the English delegation when he frankly stated that he for one did not believe in an elite.

> He pointed out that the day of selection and domination of society by a small ruling class has passed. He called for an entirely new concept of education and of democratic privilege. He pointed out that the present prime minister of England and the minister of finance have none of the university training which has been traditionally regarded as necessary for leaders in English public life. (Carnegie Corporation Archives, Examination Study File 1930-33, Judd Report, pp. 9-10)

Monroe tried to reassure Keppel (Monroe to Keppel, 8 July 1931, Carnegie Corporation Archives, Examination Study File 1930-33) that this view of the English group at Eastbourne represented an opportunity for collaboration and should not be seen as a weakness in the IEI endeavour:

> it is quite true, as Judd points out, that the point of view of these people is quite naïve and backward from the point of view of highly developed, sophisticated or scientific American approach to the methods of education, but after all, the main advantage of an international approach to a common program is that each national group should approach it from the basis of its own experience ... (Carnegie Corporation Archives, Examination Study File 1930-33)

A year later, and after the Eastbourne meeting had taken place, the IEI in New York was still waiting expectantly for the EC to be established in London. Monroe asked, with reference to the agreed monies from Carnegie:

> Should the money be paid to Sadler direct? or is there an official committee with a treasurer to whom this should be sent?
>
> I am sending you in a few days a copy of the Eastbourne proceedings which has been very slow in coming out. I shall be glad to know how many copies you would like for your group. The publications of the various groups might well follow the format of this publication and in general the color of the binding so that we may have something approximating uniform sizes. (Carnegie Corporation Archives, Examination Study File 1930-33, Letter from Monroe to Sadler, 15 December 1931)

Early the following year, the EC was established and its ideas formulated. In a confidential report to Monroe, the new EC was named as Sir Michael Sadler (chair), Sir Philip Hartog (Project Director), Sir Percy Nunn, Sir Cyril Burt, Graham Wallas, P.B. Ballard, C. DeLisle Burns and Charles Spearman. Monroe had suggested to the English Committee to invite Spearman and Lord Eustace Percy. At its first meeting Isaac Kandel came over from New York to attend it. Godfrey Thomson joined them when Walls died in its first year, following internal discussions about other possible candidates, including Maynard Keynes and Helen Wodehouse. E.C. Rhodes was employed as its statistician. It shared an office in The Temple with the Gilchrist Educational Trust.

Sir Philip Hartog, a close friend of Sadler since Manchester University and a close ally in their Commission on Universities in India, and mentioned elliptically in Sadler's? NEF address at Elsinore proposing an Examinations Commission, as the right person to lead it, was unanimously elected Director of the EC. Ballard described him as:

> the life and soul of the Committee. It was he who arranged for us our parts in the international conferences both at home and abroad, and it was he who edited the six volumes of reports ... he was also the main contributor to those volumes ... Without him, we should have achieved very little; with him as our Director our English contribution to the work of the IEI is something of which we have no reason to be ashamed. (M. Hartog, 1949, p. 132)

Dr P.B. Ballard.

Hartog was already an expert on examinations, publishing a book about them in 1918, and he soon took the lead in the EC; although part time, he worked almost full time in the office of the EC for the next seven years. His skills in mediation and diplomacy were utilised fully in those years, gaining access to examination board scripts and defending the research results in press Ballard described his work (and that of the Committee in effect) in this way:

> He had naturally a scientific mind and looked upon accuracy of measurement as an essential part of the scientific method but

> when he put the marking of essays to a scientific test it broke down hopelessly. The examiner had no unit of measurement and the mark he gave was simply a guess; perhaps a good guess, but still a guess. (M. Hartog, 1949, p. 137)

C.E. Spearman.

The EC decided to concentrate on two areas – fundamental problems and techniques of examinations and the sociological aspects of organisation and authority (the latter would allow comparison with other IEI countries). It intended to work with the Oxford and Cambridge Schools Examination Board, and their Local Examinations Delegacy, the London University Matriculation and Schools Examination Board, and the Northern Universities Examination Board. The general question which would shape their work was:

> Do the methods of examinations yield results which are reasonably consistent when different examiners mark the same scripts independently and when one examiner re-marks the same scripts after an interval of time? (Nunn Papers, IE/TPN/8/1)

And it was their intention that

> the range of the inquiry will be wide; the conclusions, it is hoped, decisive; but the findings will not have reference to the work of any one examining authority. (Nunn Papers, IE/TPN/8/1)

The sensitivity of the issue can be gauged from the agreement drafted between Hartog, Nunn and the London Board on 1 April, 1932. It emphasises the point that the investigation was into 'the general methods of examination used in England' (and by implication, not just on the London Board), it had a 'purely scientific character', the EC did not hold the view that examinations should be 'abolished' and that 'very little investigation of a purely scientific character has been carried out in this country' since the 1880s in Oxford. The EC wanted to use actual scripts in their study:

> they have no desire to be informed of the actual marks primarily allotted by the University to each script, nor could their investigations be regarded as forming ground for any special criticisms of the methods of the authority for which the scripts were written. (Nunn Papers, IE/TPN/8/1, p. 3)

Finally, they tried to convince the London Board that the international study was very important and that London had to have a key role as an important centre of organised examinations in England. They even offered to show them the results of their investigation before publication.

The EC planned a bibliography on examinations (compiled by Mary Champneys, Girton College and published as *An English Bibliography of Examinations* [1900-1932] in 1934) and a volume of essays; this would include an introduction by Sadler and other essays by DeLisle Burns, Ballard, Hartog and Burt. Negotiations continued in a slow and delicate manner with the examining bodies, from elementary to university, to secure scripts and cooperation, and it was noted that some examiners regard the study with 'apprehension'. The early publications were a recognition that they needed to start their work but were unable to begin large-scale investigations.

Monroe (writing to Keppel on 13 May 1932) reviewed the IEI centres:

> In England ... they have the benefit of the accommodations, the services of the secretaries, and the libraries of the Trusts, it is a very advantageous arrangement. Sir Philip Hartog gives at least half his time to it; Sir Michael Sadler is Chairman of the local group and takes charge of the negotiations with the university authorities. ... [Durham and London are fine] but have been temporarily checked by the negative attitudes of the first examination boards in Oxford and Cambridge. (Carnegie Corporation Archives, Examination Study File 1930-33, Report B901-11/19/31)

Early the following year, Rhodes, the statistician, had managed to set up and analyse a project on the examining of the School Certificate in English, through the Durham University Examination Board, whereby seven examiners worked on the papers from 48 candidates. The results were discrepant and it was assumed that they had different standards and objects in their minds: 'the discrepancies of marking of highly capable, conscientious and experienced examiners are such as to show that there is a very great element of chance in the present examination system' (Report of the International Institute Examinations Enquiry for England by The Director. Carnegie Corporation Archives, CCNY Series IIIA 141.3, June 1933, Report on Grant: B-901 11-19-31 D72,000).

This paper, 'Discrepancies between Examiners', involved a 'new statistical technique' which Burt described as being 'of great importance' in the IEI Minutes. It served to strengthen their purpose, as Hartog wrote that it should create:

> an interest in examining bodies which will ensure that the investigations which have been begun will be carried on by many other persons outside, in years to come, with a view to real and great improvement in the education system, in so far as it is affected by examinations (p. 11)

At an interim meeting of the IEI European leaders in 1933 in London, Hartog reported that the EC had prepared a volume of essays mostly by members of the Committee, a comprehensive bibliography of examinations dealing with publications in Great Britain and Ireland (from 1900 onwards), a list of examinations conducted by about 220 local education authorities in England, Wales, Scotland and Northern Ireland, a list of other examining bodies (about 200 exclusive of universities), and a note of examinations conducted under the sanctions of Acts of Parliament (that is, special examinations giving the licence to exercise the professions of solicitor or doctor, for example). The EC had begun investigations into the School Certificate Examination in English, History, and Latin; the College Entrance Scholarship Essay Exam; the College Entrance Mathematical Exam; and the place of the viva voce examination designed to test general ability and personality on the lines of the Civil Service Examination.

> The Director pointed out that the discrepancies in the marking of highly capable, conscientious and experienced examiners dealing with actual examination scripts were such as to show that there was a very great element of chance in the present examination system. They suggested that the differences between the different examiners were too great to be attributed to errors of carelessness or chance but they must be due to real differences in the judgement of values. He said that his Committee hoped to be able to push their analysis further on this point so that some much more substantial agreement in regard to the aims of particular examinations might be reached than was the case at present: and that they hoped that the investigations begun by them would be extended by other persons outside for many years to come, with a view to great improvements in the educational system ... (International Conference on Examinations: Interim Meeting.

> London, June 23 and 24, 1933. In Carnegie Corporation Archives, CCNY Series IIIA 141.3)

It is this area which was to constitute the second stage of the IEI EC work, and became the basis for their application for the next stage grant from Carnegie. For the generally supportive Monroe, this was a healthy sign that the EC had overtaken its shaky start and its odd circumstances; it was the only group in the IEI, at this stage, whose work did not take place under the auspices of an existing national organisation. Their methods of work were approaching the American style and focus of educational science research. They planned work on:

> the English essay in examinations and on the methods of improving the technique of the present examinations ... They think this a point of critical and fundamental importance ... [the Committee will receive] the sympathy and assistance of English teachers and Education Authorities and the cooperation of a number of voluntary workers .... The cadre of the present organization must continue.
>
> [The point of the work would be to] carry forward during the most critical stage the movement for a reform in the English examination system which the support of the International Institute and the Carnegie Corporation has made it possible to inaugurate. (Carnegie Corporation Archives, Examination Study File 1934-36, Monroe to Keppel – Report, 25 September 1935)

Monroe travelled the world but he would always try to visit London, and he appeared to be growing closer to the efforts of the EC. An additional publication on which Hartog had been working, *A Conspectus of Examinations*, was financed by Carnegie on Monroe's recommendation:

> this is a complete list and no other publication of its kind exists. It represents a vast amount of work by Sir Philip Hartog. No funds exist for publication and no item for publication was included in the last grant. In my judgement the volume it well worthy of publication. (Carnegie Corporation Archives, Examination Study File 1934-36, Report of the International Institute Examination Inquiry, p. 2)

In his annual report to Keppel at Carnegie in September 1936, he stated that

> The English volume 'The Marks of Examiners', though issued late in 1935, reached this country for distribution this spring. Their previous publication, the brochure 'Examination of Examinations' was a brief summary of the fuller work 'The Marks of Examiners', consequently the latter received very much less attention in the English press. The volume 'Examination of Examinations' called forth more than four hundred and fifty newspaper and magazine

> reviews and articles on the subject of examinations. While a number of reviews were called forth by the 'Marks of Examiners', it being a very technical publication, naturally did not receive as much attention. However, the closing statement in the London Times, under the date of July 4, 1936, will give some idea of the importance of the influence which this volume exerts; 'the book may come to be regarded as the herald of a great reform in our educational system. (Carnegie Corporation Archives, Examination Study File 1935-36, Monroe to Keppel, 10 September 1936)

So, for Monroe, England was on track, it was producing a work of reform, and it was supported by American influence, know-how and finance. Indeed, when the *Examination of Examinations* short report was published, the International Institute was to see the media response to it as a great success and a sign of reform pressure. A colleague, Nathaniel Peffer from Columbia, said that it had 'stirred up a hornets' nest' and that 'the review in nature is favourable on the whole and takes the position that at any rate it is good for the subject to have been ventilated, since it raises questions that ought to be faced' (Carnegie Corporation Archives, Examination Study File 1935-36).

Isaac Kandel gave a considered and detailed view of what happened in a report for Carnegie:

> [it] attracted immediate and widespread interest throughout the country. There is no better evidence of the public and social importance of the problem of examinations than the fact that about 130 newspapers in the country paid some attention to the report. The press itself accepted the results of the investigation at face value without any attempt to be critical but all drawing the main inference that examinations as at present conducted are unfair to the candidates. (Carnegie Corporation Archives, Examination Study File, 1935, 10 February 1936)

He reported headlines which included 'Uncertainty of Examinations', 'Chance in Examinations', 'Weathercock Minds' and 'Examination Luck'. Kandel produced a large number of extracts from the press – talk of erratic decisions, chance verdicts, lack of confidence (and pupil careers), 'what should be done' (*Manchester Guardian*), and 'vested interests of a commercial kind have been allowed to grow up around our secondary school examinations' (*Schoolmaster*) – and added that 'a few marks one way or the other may determine whether a poor boy or girl shall go to a secondary school or matriculation certificate which is now frequently demanded by employers' (Kandel, I., 10 February 1936, 'The English Examinations Report and the Public', in Carnegie Corporation Archives, Examination Study File 1934-36).

For Kandel, the response confirmed the conservative nature of the English educational establishment. Cyril Norwood, chairman of Investigators of School Certificate Examinations, and one of the most influential educationalists in this decade, despite frequently criticising the hampering influence of examinations, still maintained that 'broadly speaking, I should say that the system of examination marking is as accurate as human care can make it. There is not, in any case at present any practicable alternative' (Kandel, I., 10 February 1936, 'The English Examinations Report and the Public', in Carnegie Corporation Archives, Examination Study File 1934-36). Kandel remarked that the complacent attitudes of the educators and examiners is surprising because of all the criticisms of the narrow base of examinations since 1920, and attempts by local education authorities to improve selection methods (including through the use of testing). He argued that previous work on examination reliability did not disturb examiners like the IEI reports because of all the publicity given to them: 'there is ample evidence in their refusal to cooperate in the investigation that they are not anxious to have the situation disturbed ... The problem ... is far more far reaching than a matter of examination techniques; it inevitably becomes a problem of the distribution of education' (Carnegie Corporation Archives, Examination Study File 1935, 10 February 1936).

He saw the situation of the EC as strategic, that they had to prove in the most 'accurate and convincing manner possible the unreliability of marking in the existing practice of examinations in order to shake the prevailing complacency and before further investigations looking to reform could be undertaken' and that

> the English Committee had devoted its investigations to testing concurrences of a number of independent examiners and of independent boards of examiners in marking the same set of papers; the purpose of the second study was to test the claim that individual idiosyncrasies of examiners are ironed out when the marking is done by a board. As compared with earlier experiments conducted in this country the papers used in the investigations were actual papers written in actual examinations. These papers covered a wide range of examinations, both qualifying and selective, and included papers written in the Eleven plus or special place examination, a college scholarship examination, university honours examinations in history .... Examiners were selected from actual examining panels, were paid, and were given all the time that they needed. Every known variation of the examining technique was used in order to insure accuracy – the same system of marking was employed as in the original examination; the same examiners marked the same papers twice at an interval of a year; two groups of examiners under the direction of chief examiners, trial markings were submitted to criticism; an English essay was marked once by general impression and then by details; and numerical and literal marks were given. (Carnegie Corporation Archives, Examination Study File 1935, 10 February 1936, p. 5)

It must have been illuminating for Kandel and Monroe to be faced with the intransigence of educators and examiners faced with this kind of evidence; it is unclear if it was so enlightening for the members of the EC. This only confirmed to Monroe the strength of the EC work: 'Monroe said that on the whole the English had done the best job' (Carnegie Corporation Archives, Examination Study File 1934-36, Monroe to Keppel – memo of meeting, 3 February 1938).

Philip Ballard's comment on the furore, and overall about the IEI English Committee, was:

> [The English] Committee has, I venture to think, already rendered solid service to the community. The reader will doubtless call to mind the storm raised in the Press by the publication in December 1935 of the booklet by Sir Philip Hartog and Dr Rhodes, An Examination of Examinations.
>
> I admit that as a committee we are not popular – not at any rate among the defenders of the status quo. Our constitution has been called into question. We have been described as self appointed. That can be flatly denied. I readily concede that we do not serve under the auspices of the Board of Education, or of the British Universities, or of any public authority in this kingdom. But we did not elect ourselves: the original committee were chosen by the International Institute of Columbia University, New York, and chosen to take part in an international inquiry into the examination system in many lands. In other countries there are other Committees, all working in cooperation with us, and all financed from the same source – the Carnegie Corporation and the International Institute. (M. Hartog, 1949, p. 205)

About this time, Keppel had been having discussions with Fred Clarke, an Englishman who had been a professor in Southampton and Cape Town, and was currently at McGill University in Canada but had been trying for a while to return to England. Keppel treated Clarke as a useful source of information, even as a counsellor, about education in the British empire, and had been trying to help his return by establishing an empire-based advanced course at the Institute of Education under his direction. Keppel sent Sadler, a friend of Clarke, a note in December 1934, after talking to Clarke in New York:

> ... I have been wondering whether it would not be a good idea when he gets to England to bring him in touch with the Examinations Study in some informal way ... Clarke's mind throws light on everything it touches [and] the administrative future of the Examinations Study is not too clear .... There might be great advantage in having some man in the University of London who is familiar with the work of the Study as a whole. (Nunn Papers, IE/TPN/8/3, 31 December 1934)

He then wrote to Monroe:

> Professor Fred Clarke is moving from McGill to the Institute of Education in the University of London ... I thought it might be a good plan for him to be given a chance to familiarize himself with the Examinations Study. I think you know him. If you do, you know him to be a first rate fellow who pushes himself forward and who will know how to spread the gospel throughout the Empire. (Nunn Papers, IE/TPN/8/3, 31 December 1934)

Partly through their planning for a new educational science base in London, and their thinking about the new Institute of Education there, it had been agreed that the EC would get a substantial sum as part of the last tranche of the Carnegie grant. Hartog asked for $7,500-10,000 for three years in December 1937. This money would aid the establishment of a research organisation in England, a task which had become close to Carnegie's heart. However, the final IEI budget requests for future work caused some difficulties for Monroe, which he explained to Keppel. Apparently, the Scots and the French were spurred on in their demands by 'our rather generous treatment of the English situation, but they are quite different situations for the French have no probability of the founding of an independent research institute, while the Scottish already have this with an established means of support' (Carnegie Corporation Archives, Examination Study File 1934-36, Monroe to Keppel letter, 5 November 1938).

Within Carnegie, Hartog's proposal for continuing help was seen as 'legitimate, desirable and important' as long as the funding was matched from other sources. The Carnegie Treasurer said that the Corporation had:

> certainly got its money's worth out of the English committee thus far; I think its results are the best of all the project, except perhaps the Scottish group [and continued] I believe that the prestige of the Corporation and the Carnegie name would be much advanced in England by a 'constructive' result, which Sir Philip practically promises ... . Could the Corporation spare $15,000 over two years [$7500 a year] to get this project along to a point where it could be cut loose without forfeiting the promised results entirely? For my part, I should dislike to see any other name than Carnegie associated with this English enterprise through the committee's soliciting and getting funds from other sources. (Carnegie Corporation Archives, Examination Study File 1937-1945, HJS to Jessup letter, 16 February 1938)

As the French Committee received $4000 and the Norwegian Committee $3000 following these exchanges, the scale of the plan for England can be seen clearly. Following the state of war in England (declared on 3 September 1939), Keppel suggested to Monroe that 'we had better regard the money for the completion of the English study as in "escrow"' (Keppel to Monroe memo, 11 November 1939, Carnegie Corporation Archives, Examination Study File 1934-36); that is, the monies were to be held in trust by its agents, pending the fulfilment of the condition for which it was to be used. Hartog spent a great part of 1939 searching for matching funding from sources in England. He wrote to Sadler, through his secretary, in that year saying that

> He has had interviews with Dr Hall Smith, the Secretary of the Thomas Wall Trust, Sir Frank Watney, Clerk of the Mercers Company, and the Master and Clerk of the Merchant Taylors' Company. He is meeting Mrs EM Lowe, chairman Elect of the London County Council and Mr Robertson, Chairman of the Education Committee. On Thursday, he has interviews with Major Haden Guest, Secretary of the Leverhulme Trustees ... (M. Hartog, 1949 p. 139)

Clarke took over from Hartog an energetic commitment to the idea of a permanent organisation for research; both Sadler and Hartog had discussed between themselves the problem of a single institution, the Institute of Education, having this fund but decided that it had to be, rather than to wait for a national one to be organised. In January 1943, the first meeting of the Advisory Council of the Institute of Education Educational Research Fund heard Hartog, a member, talk about Carnegie's support for the continuation of 'systematic educational research' in England and Wales through this Fund (Clarke Papers, Institute of Education Archives). Clarke sent a letter to Jessop in 1943, at which time he was the Director of the Institute of Education in London, explaining what was happening with the money. Initially, it was just held without any ongoing activity but a Foundation for Research had been organised. The Carnegie grant was a 'contribution to educational research fund of the University of London Institute of Education, to match funds secured from other sources' and 'to be paid as a like amount should be secured from local sources' (Clarke Papers).

Clarke's letter included the Foundation Scheme, its Advisory Council members, and copies of letters from the National Union of Teachers and the President of the Board of Education (Carnegie Corporation Archives, Examination Study File 1937, Clarke to Jessup letter, 16 August 1943). Clarke had solicited funds from the National Union of Teachers and the Leverhulme Foundation and intended to write to others. He felt that the pressure for education research was growing (through the 1944 Education White Paper and the Norwood report) and that the President of the Board of Education acknowledged that things had to change.

The Foundation document makes clear that

> By the terms of the understandings entered into between the institute and the representatives of the Carnegie Examinations Enquiry [English Committee], the Institute is already pledged to take full responsibility for the administration of funds raised ...

The Foundation Advisory Council included Hartog, Spearman, Burt, Ballard and Clarke, showing the close connection between the IEI English Committee (now defunct) and the creation of an education research foundation for England. In effect, the Foundation became the research arm and responsibility of the Institute of Education; and as the latter became established, it also organised the country. Institute of Education staff would offer 'detailed scrutiny of research projects, advice and guidance to research workers, the devising of methods of research and the detailed planning of researches' (Carnegie Corporation Archives, Examination Study File 1937-1945, p. 2).

A later report to Carnegie in May 1944 by Clarke explained the growth of the Advisory Council and what it was doing as:

> the Corporation is fully entitled to all the information we can provide, for it would seem that the light it produced has set going what promises to be a wide spreading and lasting illumination.

Another undated Foundation report (post 1944) to Carnegie said that

> With the publication of its inquiry into the *Marking of English Essays* the English Committee of the IEI completed the last of its projects. It was felt by many people interested in educational research that the work of the English Committee should be continued and if possible extended in scope. To this end the Carnegie Corporation generously offered the sum of $10,000 towards the cost of initiating educational research on a broad basis on condition that an equal sum were obtained from interested individuals and educational bodies in this country. (Carnegie Corporation Archives, Examination Study File 1937-1945, p. 1)

At its 1943 meeting, the Advisory Council heard a statement from Sir Philip Hartog on the work of the Inquiry; he presented a list of 19 subjects which had been proposed by the English Committee of the IEI as suggestions for future research. After reflection, the Advisory Council gave priority to 'an enquiry into present methods of selection for secondary education' (Memo, Clarke Papers, September 1944, p. 3), and on:

> Educational Guidance and it was agreed that a comprehensive research should be planned on the problem of differentiating and classifying children at the end of the Primary School stage with the object of finding reliable criteria for allocating children to several forms of post-primary [secondary] education. (Carnegie Corporation Archives, Examination Study File 1937-1945, p. 6)

The main features of this research included: 'a set of tests to replace the single "intelligence test" in common use; reliable tests of attainment in the primary school; tests of ability in maths, science etc; records for primary and secondary' (Carnegie Corporation Archives, Examination Study File 1937-1945, p. 6).

In Conclusion

The work of the EC was solid and useful and became the context for the post-war development of the English education system. Its publications, produced mainly though Hartog, ranged across the field of examinations, indeed even established the field. It cannot be claimed that its influence extended as far as it was originally hoped, that is to a reform of the English examination system, or even as Kandel argued, a discussion about the distribution of education. Instead the significance of the work of the EC might lie in the direction suggested by Judd, the scientific revolution in education; that is, its way of researching and its promotion of testing, was to be its bequest to the future. It developed this through the Foundation for Research, later the National Foundation for Educational Research, and its early emphasis on differentiating and classifying children through testing and on the production of tests came to symbolise this new direction in educational research.

Note

[1] A sign of the expertise in the new area of testing within the EC is the fact that when the Consultative Committee reported in the early 1920s (*Psychological tests of educable capacity and their possible use in the public system of education –* The Hadow Report 1924), six of the EC members had been witnesses to it (P.B. Ballard, Cyril Burt, Percy Nunn, Charles E. Spearman, Godfrey H. Thomson and Graham Wallas).

Bibliography

Ballard, P.B. (1937) *Things I Cannot Forget*. London: University of London Press.

Carnegie Corporation Archives, Columbia Rare Book and Manuscript Library, New York – Examination Study Files 1930-33, 1934-36, 1937-45.

Champneys, Mary (1934) *An English Bibliography of Examinations (1900-1932)*. (Foreword – Sadler and Hartog). London: Macmillan and Co.

Clarke, Sir Fred, Papers, Institute of Education Archives, London.

Hartog, Mabel (1949) *Philip Hartog – a memoir*. London: Constable & Co.

Hartog, P.J.G. (1938) *A Conspectus of Examinations in Great Britain and Northern Ireland/by Sir Philip Hartog ... (with the assistance of Gladys Roberts)*. London: Macmillan & Co.

Hartog, P.J. (1938) *The Purposes of Examinations: a symposium, with an introductory survey*. London: Evans Brothers.

Hartog, P.J. & Rhodes, E.C. (1935) *An Examination of Examinations; being a summary of investigations on the comparison of marks allotted to examination scripts by independent examiners and boards of examiners, together with a section on a viva voce examination*. London: Macmillan & Co. (2nd edn, 4th Impression, 1936).

Hartog, P. & Rhodes, E. (1936) *The Marks of Examiners*. London: Macmillan & Co.

Hartog, P., Ballard, P.B., Gurrey, P., Hamley, H.R. & Ebblewhite Smith, C. (1942) *The Marking of English Essays*. London: Macmillan.

Hartog–Nunn Memo (1 April 1932) IE/TPN/8/1, IoE Archive, London (Percy Nunn papers).

Monroe, P. (Ed.) (1931) *Conference on Examinations: under the auspices of the Carnegie Corporation, the Carnegie Foundation and the International Institute of Teachers College, Columbia University/conference organized and proceedings*. New York: Teachers College, Columbia University.

Nunn Papers, Institute of Education Archives (IE/TPN), London.

Rawson, W. (Ed.) (1935) *The Examinations Tangle and the Way Out – report of the International Commission on Examinations of the New Education Fellowship*. London: NEF.

Sadler, M., Abbott, A., Ballard, P.B., Burt, C., DeLisle Burns, C., Hartog, P., Spearman, C. & Stirk, S. (1936) *Essays on Examinations*. London: Macmillan & Co.

Awkward Knowledge: the German delegation to the International Examinations Inquiry[1]

FLORIAN WALDOW

SUMMARY This chapter locates the position of the German delegation to the International Examinations Inquiry (IEI) both within German educational discourse at the time and within the context of the IEI. During its short period of activity, the German delegation produced some remarkable research that was quite unusual and ground-breaking in the German context, where empirical approaches to education and testing were rapidly being marginalised by a more philosophical orientation of education as an academic subject at the time. At the same time, the German delegation's position was of course formed by academic culture and educational discourse in Germany, especially by the idea of education as radically individualistic self-cultivation (*Bildung*). Conceiving of education as *Bildung*, however, potentially stood in conflict to applying psychometric testing methods. Thus, the German delegation's position was somewhat 'awkward' both in relation to the dominant pedagogical discourse in Germany at the time and to what might be termed the psychometric 'mainstream' at the Eastbourne conference.

Introduction

At the end of the first International Examinations Inquiry (IEI) conference at Eastbourne in May 1931, the German delegate Carl Heinrich Becker, former minister of education and cultural affairs in Prussia, expressed the hope that 'future centuries ... may date the history of education from the Eastbourne Conference' (Monroe, 1931, p. 256). As it turned out, nothing could have been further from the truth, at least from a German perspective. It is safe to say that the IEI has been completely forgotten in Germany. When a report produced in the context of the IEI finally came out in print in 2000, almost

70 years after it had been written, the editor did not even mention the IEI in his long introduction (Ulich & Wohlfahrt, [1933] 2000).

For sure, the fact that the National Socialist regime came to power in 1933 – i.e. shortly after the inception of the IEI – played an important role here. Not only were the international contacts of education as an academic discipline in Germany largely broken off, but the kind of research issues the IEI focused on were also marginalised and to a large degree suppressed by the Nazis. Exact, 'scientific' methods of assessment were seen by many as non-German (Laux, 1990, p. 89).[2] In the context of the organic people's community (*Volksgemeinschaft*), meritocratic selection and questions of equity in relation to the educational opportunities of pupils from different layers of society were no longer seen as important issues[3]. Germany withdrew from the IEI, and the two surviving members of the German delegation to the IEI were forced into inactivity or emigration (see below).

But already at the time when the first IEI conference took place, two years before the Nazis came to power, the type of research and issues discussed there were somewhat marginal and 'awkward' in the context of educational discourse and academic culture in Germany, and rapidly becoming more so. At the same time, the German delegation's position was formed by academic culture and educational discourse in Germany, making its position *within* the conference somewhat 'awkward' in turn, especially in relation to the prominent proponents of a psychometric approach who were present at Eastbourne.

Thus, in a sense the German delegation occupied an 'awkward' position within the context of the IEI, while at the same time the kind of research it produced only fitted somewhat 'awkwardly' into the current mainstream of pedagogical discourse in Germany, although for opposite reasons. This proposition constitutes the starting point of this chapter.

The chapter is structured in the following way: in the following section, I present the professional backgrounds and careers of the members of the German delegation to the Eastbourne conference of the IEI. In the next section I draw attention to some of the issues considered important by the German delegation that made their position 'awkward' at Eastbourne. The following section gives a brief overview over the research conducted within the framework of the IEI in Germany. Then, I locate the German delegation and its work within the context of education as an academic discipline and, more generally, academic culture in Germany, thereby in turn showing the delegation's 'awkwardness' in the German context. The final section contains a summary and some concluding thoughts.

The German Delegation at Eastbourne

Carl Heinrich Becker (1876-1933)

Before becoming an educational policy maker and administrator, Carl Heinrich Becker had had a distinguished career as a professor of oriental studies (Essner & Winkelhane, 1988). From about the First World War on, Becker became involved in educational policy making, and during the Weimar Republic he held high-ranking positions in educational administration, including two terms as Minister of Education and Cultural Affairs in Prussia (1921 and 1925-30). Becker possessed a wide net of contacts to politicians and scholars both inside and outside Germany and was among the German politicians who were most respected abroad. In an autobiographical sketch published in 1971, fellow-delegate Robert Ulich calls him 'the last educational statesman Germany could boast of' (Ulich, 1971, p. 428). Among the most important policy measures during his term of office was a major reform of the education of primary teachers.

Carl Heinrich Becker.

In 1930, Becker resigned from the ministry and resumed his academic career. Already in 1931/32, however, he was travelling in Eastern Asia on a mission from the League of Nations. Becker died in February 1933.

As education falls into the responsibility of the individual German states and as Prussia was by far the largest state at this time, C.H. Becker was, so to speak, the 'biggest fish' in German educational policy making and administration at the time of the IEI, a figure widely respected both in Germany and abroad.

Robert Ulich (1890-1977)

At the time of the first IEI conference, Robert Ulich was a high-ranking educational administrator in the Saxonian ministry of education (on Ulich's professional career, see Ulich's autobiographical sketch in Ulich, 1971; also Waterkamp, 1998). Among other responsibilities Ulich was in charge of the field of higher education in Saxony. Already before assuming this position, Ulich had been involved in educational policy making (mainly in the field of adult education) and popular education.

Ulich also possessed academic credentials: in parallel to his position as an administrator, he was Honorary Professor of 'Practical Pedagogy' at the Technical Institute of Dresden. Before becoming an administrator, Ulich had worked in the Leipzig Institut für Kultur- und Universalgeschichte, founded by the controversial social and cultural historian Karl Lamprecht. In 1930, through the help of Abraham Flexner and Isaac Kandel, Ulich had the chance to visit the USA for half a year; during this time, he lectured at Harvard and Teachers College, Columbia University.

Robert Ulich.

While at the Ministry (headed for most of the time of his office by Social Democrats), his progressive educational politics, e.g. in the field of primary teacher education, antagonised right-wing parties. Thus, when the Nazis seized power in 1933, Ulich lost both his position at the Ministry and his honorary professorship.

In 1934, Ulich went to the United States at the invitation of the Harvard Graduate School of Education.[4] In 1935, he was appointed to a professorship of education at Harvard, a position he continued to hold until his retirement.

Erich Hylla (1887-1976)

Originally educated as a primary teacher, Erich Hylla had a background as a school principal, school inspector and school administrator (on Hylla's professional career see Koinzer, 2006, and Führ, 1994). From 1922 he was part of a group of specialists at the Prussian Ministry of Education and Cultural Affairs, reporting directly to the minister.

In parallel to his work at the Ministry, Hylla was a prolific researcher, with a special interest in issues of testing and pupil selection, especially selection for the different types of secondary schools after the first four years of primary schooling (see, for example, Hylla, 1925).[5] Already while still a primary teacher, Hylla showed a keen interest in educational psychology and took part in workshops organised by the eminent educational psychologist William Stern for primary school teachers. It was at these workshops that Erich Hylla first met Otto Bobertag, with whom he later collaborated on several research projects and who also became a delegate to the IEI.

Erich Hylla.

In 1926/27, Hylla traveled widely in the USA, visiting schools and universities, among them Teachers College in New York. He wrote several articles and books about his travels (Hylla, 1928), trying to give the German public an insight into the American educational system and thereby also trying to further the cause of progressive school reform in Germany (Koinzer, 2006, pp. 136-137), and also translated Dewey's *Democracy and Education* (Dewey, 1930).

When the Nazis came to power in 1933, Hylla lost his position at the Ministry because he was considered 'nationally unreliable'. Throughout the Nazi era, Hylla was banned from doing qualified work within education in Germany; he was not even allowed to work as a primary teacher. In 1935/36 and 1938, he again spent some time in the USA, lecturing at Teachers College and Cornell. After the War, Hylla resumed his academic career, despite his impressive research record being hampered by the fact that he had entered the academic world through teacher education and thus did not possess a doctorate (Führ, 1994).[6] Issues of testing continued to be a major topic of interest for Hylla. Among his first publications after the War was an English–German glossary of testing terms (Hylla & Traxler, 1949). Ultimately, Hylla became head of the Hochschule für Internationale Pädagogische Forschung, later Deutsches Institut für Internationale Pädagogische Forschung, in Frankfurt am Main and continued to be an important figure within educational studies in Germany as one of the (at that time) few proponents of an empirical approach to education (Baumert et al, 1992, p. 6).

Otto Bobertag (1879-1934)

At the time of the first IEI conference, Otto Bobertag was one of the foremost educational psychologists and testing specialists in Germany.

Otto Bobertag.

In addition to his impressive research record, Bobertag also was a prolific translator, translating, for example, Edward Thorndike's *Educational*

Psychology (Thorndike, 1922) and Binet and Simon's intelligence tests and applying them to conditions in Germany (Bobertag, 1914). On several occasions, Bobertag collaborated with Erich Hylla (see, for example, Bobertag & Hylla, 1926).

Bobertag had worked with William Stern, one of the major pioneers of educational psychology and especially testing in Germany, at the University of Breslau before assuming a position at the Zentralinstitut für Erziehung und Unterricht in Berlin. The Zentralinstitut was a publicly funded non-university institution that was supposed to serve several functions, ranging from providing professional development for teachers and being a clearing-house for international educational contacts to research in educational psychology and testing (on the Zentralinstitut see Böhme, 1971). In 1934, Bobertag lost his position at the Zentralinstitut, which at that time was being remodelled along National Socialist lines. He died shortly after this from a heart attack.

Profile of the German Delegates: some shared characteristics

Some shared characteristics are worth noting about the German delegates: firstly, close personal contacts existed among them. Hylla worked closely with Becker at the Prussian Ministry of Education and Cultural Affairs. At the same time, Hylla collaborated with Bobertag at the Zentralinstitut. Becker also had close ties to the Zentralinstitut; from 1920 on he was deputy chairman of the 'Verein der Freunde des Zentralinstituts' and in 1930 he became a member of the institute's steering committee ('geschäftsführender Vorstand'; Pallat, 1933). Ulich knew Becker from other contexts in which they collaborated, e.g. from the German section of the New Education Fellowship, and considered the latter as his 'admired friend' (Ulich, 1971, p. 428).

Secondly, all of them were committed internationalists. Ulich and Hylla spent extended periods in the USA.[7] Hylla organised study tours through the USA for German teachers and administrators. Becker was a figure of international renown, possessing extensive contacts in other countries. Bobertag and Hylla were prolific translators. Ulich and Becker were actively engaged in the New Education Fellowship. Bobertag and Hylla worked at the Zentralinstitut für Erziehung und Unterricht, which had partly been founded to act as a clearing house for international contacts.

Thirdly, all of the German delegates were democrats, a minority position among German academics at that time (Ringer, 1990). Both Becker and Ulich served under social democratic governments, and both managed to infuriate right-wing parties with their work. The fact that Ulich, Hylla and Bobertag lost their professional positions after the Nazis came to power – Becker died a few days after the Nazis came to power in February 1933 – also testifies to their political orientation.

Fourthly, although all of the delegates possessed academic credentials, none of them was a full professor of education at a German university, a fact that is particularly significant in the context of this article. The delegates most heavily involved in research, Hylla and Bobertag, were active at a public non-university institution, the Zentralinstitut für Erziehung und Unterricht.

'Generalisation vs. Individualisation' and 'Efficiency and Culture': the German position at Eastbourne

In the following, I draw attention to two issues that were considered to be of paramount importance by the German delegation, while being in tension at least with the position of the psychometricians present at Eastbourne. According to the recorded conference minutes, only Ulich and Becker contributed to the discussion at Eastbourne to a significant extent.[8] There is a certain tension here, as Bobertag contributed most to the *published* research done within the context of the IEI in Germany; at the same time, he contributed least to discussions at Eastbourne.

The first issue I want to discuss here concerns the perceived tension between 'generalisation' and 'individualisation' of examinations. This tension was presented by Becker at the beginning of the conference as follows:

> The desire to objectify leads automatically to the generalizing, and hence to the mechanising, of the examination system ... For this reason many advocate a radical individualization of the examinations – the task should be set according to the disposition or inclination of the pupil; the testing should be done by the instructor himself. (Monroe, 1931, p. 15)

Becker suggests that this issue should be one of the central topics of investigation to be treated by the IEI. It should be noted that Becker does not present the extreme 'individualisation' position as his own, but at least he considers this tension to be a very real one and the problem caused by it as one of the major obstacles for constructing adequate examinations.

A second issue which the German delegation calls attention to is connected to the question of 'individualisation vs. generalisation' of examinations. It concerns what Robert Ulich calls integrating 'efficiency and culture in an examination' (Monroe, 1931, p. 119). The English term 'efficiency', which Ulich employs as a translation of the German '*Fachtüchtigkeit*', is somewhat misleading in this context. A more adequate (if more cumbersome) translation of '*fachtüchtig*' is 'possessing area-specific skills and being able to use them competently'. Put in very general terms, the tension between 'efficiency and culture' mentioned by Ulich amounts to the question of how to combine character formation on the one hand with the acquisition of work-specific skills on the other.

This issue was debated in many different contexts around the world at this time, not just within the IEI and not just with respect to the examination system (Ringer, 1992). What makes it distinctive here is Ulich's particular definition of general education as character formation and the importance he assigns to it. According to Ulich, the 'classical educational ideal of the concept of humanity' was shattered by the onset of modernity, i.e. the emergence of a world dominated by natural sciences and industrialism. Ulich argues for a resuscitation of education as personal self-cultivation, discarding certain elements that over time have cluttered the curriculum of general education (*Bildung*) – such as ancient languages – without being essential for achieving true *Bildung*. According to Ulich, the 'content of a culture obligatory for all must give place to an emphasis on *individual* development!' (Monroe, 1931, p. 117, emphasis added). This view of education has repercussions on how examinations should be conducted, on 'how to integrate efficiency and culture in an examination'. The examiner has 'to decide how far a student has merely acquired knowledge or has, with the acquisition of knowledge, at the same time enriched his personality' (p. 119). He has to have 'the gift of reaching conclusions about the character of a candidate through his manner and forms of expression as well as through his special knowledge' (p. 119). It is obvious that this cannot be reached by impersonal, 'objective' assessment; instead, empathy and intimate knowledge of the pupil are the most important traits the 'good' examiner has to possess.

For psychometricians like Thorndike or Spearman, Ulich's position and the 'individualisation' position to which Becker refers must have seemed like anathema (even though they did not react directly to Becker's and Ulich's contributions). The discussions throughout the conference were largely concerned with the question *how* to secure objective, valid and reliable measurements, including the question of how to standardise assessment among different examiners. In stark contrast to this, Ulich's position and the position referred to by Becker *negate* the very possibility of achieving this, at least through the methods advocated by the psychometricians. From this perspective, letting the instructor do the examining is not seen as a condition that potentially corrupts measurements, but on the contrary as a requirement for their validity. Apparently, though, discussions at Eastbourne did not fail to make an impact at least on Becker; towards the end of the conference, in his final summary of what in his opinion the IEI and especially the German group should do, he more or less *dropped* this issue (Monroe, 1931, pp. 256-259).

Research Produced by the German Delegation

In Germany, the research produced within the context of the IEI did not have a significant impact; in fact, it was hardly noticed at all. As was mentioned above, this was to a large part due to the fact that the Nazis came to power in 1933, effectively suppressing the kind of research that was done in the context of the IEI and driving the surviving German delegates into inactivity or exile. However, some of the research done in the context of the

IEI was very innovative in a German context, in some instances anticipating approaches that did not receive wider attention until several decades later.

The research produced by the German delegation can be divided into two main areas: *selection of university students for scholarships* and *selection of pupils at the primary–secondary school transition point.*

Selection of University Students for Scholarships

In collaboration with his Dresden colleague Erich Wohlfahrt, Robert Ulich produced a study on the 'educational sociology of academic recruitment in Germany' (Ulich & Wohlfahrt, [1933] 2000).[9] While an English 'abstract' of the report appeared after Ulich's emigration to the United States (see Monroe, 1939, p. 329), the original German version only appeared in print in 2000, almost 70 years after it was written. The empirical basis of the study consisted of data on students supported by the Studienstiftung des deutschen Volkes, a foundation that was supposed to provide scholarships for poor, but gifted students.[10] The main aim of Ulich's and Wohlfahrt's study was an 'analysis of different forms of selecting gifted students' (Ulich & Wohlfahrt, [1933] 2000, p. 31). A second aim was to investigate 'how certain forms of education and selection ... are connected to social, organisational and structural conditions of education' (p. 31) such as social background, type of secondary education, type of main subjects at university, etc.

The results of Ulich and Wohlfahrt's study come as no surprise to today's reader: among other things, the authors demonstrate that there is a nexus between students' social background, their choice of secondary school, their aspirations and their success within the educational system. Interestingly enough, they frame this result not in terms of a language stressing the importance of equal life chances for individuals, but in 'holistic' language that invokes the 'totality of the people':

> The process of [social] advancement, choice of profession and performance in working life in a people cannot simply be determined through adding individual performance in an atomistic way; rather, there are relations here between the individual personality and the powers flowing from the totality of a people. (p. 121)

The authors do not deduce from this, however, that children from humble backgrounds should be excluded from university. Rather, in concordance with the aims of the Studienstiftung, the authors argue for making an academic education available for gifted children from humble backgrounds; they see 'shared interests' among the 'traditional hereditary culture of a people, as far as it still is fresh and creative, and the will to advancement of truly gifted members of even the humblest strata of society'. Both are 'enemies of the mediocre masses seeking to gain entrance to the universities, founded on hollow swotting, a wrong assessment of working life and a spoiled sense of quality' (pp. 117-118). Thus, in Ulich's view, the future academic elite should consist of members of the traditional, cultured elite, supplemented by the minority of 'truly gifted' from the working class, while the middle-class 'swots' not interested in true *Bildung* should be kept out as far as possible.

These paragraphs reveal a position that is close to the stance Ulich assumed in discussions at Eastbourne. In Ulich's thinking, we thus have an interesting combination of demands for an improvement of the educational chances of the working class and meritocratic selection together with an anti-utilitarian, elitist conception of education as *Bildung* and certain echoes of society seen as an 'organic', 'non-atomistic' entity.[11]

Selection of Pupils at the Primary–Secondary School Transition Point

A second body of research is concerned with the selection of pupils at the transition from primary school to the different types of secondary school existing at that time in Germany (see footnote 3). Research in this area was conducted by Hylla and especially Bobertag; they were able to build on a considerable amount of previous work and data collected earlier.

In several articles, Bobertag points out the problematics of the situation concerning selection for the different types of secondary school (Bobertag, 1931, 1933). One argument that runs like a thread through all articles is that the system in place at the time of writing was far from selecting pupils on an objective basis. The main problem as identified by Bobertag and Hylla was that selection in most cases relied heavily on teachers' marks, and teachers were not good at assessing pupils' performance in an objective, valid and reliable way.

Bobertag and Hylla not only showed deficiencies in the current methods of selection, but also strived to actively improve them. A booklet entitled *Instruction Manual for Student Assessment in Primary School*, produced by Bobertag in conjunction with Hylla and a group of Berlin teachers, is of particular interest (Bobertag, 1932a). Its unassuming title is deceptive; what Bobertag and Hylla set out to do here is nothing less than provide Prussian primary school teachers with a test that was supposed to allow them to compare the results of their pupils or classes with the achievement of pupils in Prussia as a whole. A Scotsman or Swede might wonder what is so special about this, but in a German context, this project was ground-breaking. The test is designed for pupils in the fourth year of primary school, as selection for different secondary schools took place after this year (*'Übergangsauslese'*), making an objective measurement of pupils' achievement particularly important at this particular point in time. Although Bobertag and Hylla were not alone in trying to improve and make more objective the selection process at the end of class four of primary school (Ingenkamp, 1989), their test was the first school achievement test of its kind in Germany. The test did not receive much attention when it first came out, but it enjoyed a 'second life' after the end of the Nazi era. Hylla and the Berlin teacher and school psychologist K. Ingenkamp revised the test in 1947/48, and it was still in use in the early 1960s (Ingenkamp, 1962, p. 23; see also Ingenkamp, 1969).

The 'instruction manual' is written in a language that is supposed to be comprehensible even to teachers with no prior knowledge of experimental psychology or testing. It provides tests in six different subject areas: reading skills, vocabulary, applied calculating ('*Denkrechnen*'), language use, spelling and calculating with numbers ('*Zahlenrechnen*'; Bobertag, 1932a, pp. 5-6). The difficulty of the different test items was determined by Bobertag and his group using a large sample of Prussian pupils.[12] Teachers were provided with detailed instructions how to carry out the test. Then, teachers could determine their pupils' performance in relation to that of the sample with the help of detailed tables and instructions for correcting.

Bobertag also used the data on pupils' performance obtained in the course of the work to investigate how good teachers were at assessing the difficulty of a test item. For this, he asked a sample of teachers to assess the difficulty of the test items in the *Instruction Manual* and compared their answers to the measured difficulties. The results were very clear and demonstrated that teachers had enormous difficulties in assessing the difficulty of test items (reported in Bobertag, 1933). As a rule, teachers underestimated the test items' difficulty; also, there was an enormous variance in how difficult teachers assessed an item to be.

The German Delegation, Educational Discourse and Academic Culture in Germany

In order to make clear the context that shaped the position of the German delegates to the IEI, I will briefly sketch some important aspects of academic culture and more particularly educational discourse in Germany at the time. Applied to the position of the German delegation, this will hopefully shed some light on both why the German delegation differed in some important respects from the mainstream at the IEI and why its work was at the same time unusual in a German context.

'Bildung'

The first aspect I want to discuss here is the educational ideal of *Bildung*. Education as *Bildung* has been identified as *the* central concept around which German academic culture, including the higher tracks of secondary education, revolved at that time (Ringer, 1990; Drewek, 2002). *Bildung* centres on an unfolding of personality through self-cultivation, often by means of the interaction with venerated texts that were deemed especially appropriate for the purpose (Ringer, 1992).[13] *Bildung* is supposed to realise a potential that is 'already there' – in different forms and to a different degree – within individuals. *Bildung* thus is a notion with radically individualistic connotations; in this respect, it is the total opposite to a conception of education that assumes that people are socialised 'from outside'. At the same time, the emphasis on the self-cultivation of character also means that *Bildung* is opposed to the mere accumulation of facts and skills.

The radical individualism of *Bildung* was often complemented by a view of social relations that did not conceive of society as a sum of equal parts, but as an organic whole that can be described by what Fritz Ringer (1990, 1992) has called the 'symphonic analogy.' Society is here likened to an orchestra, in which all the parts are necessary for the success of the whole, but play very different individual roles.

'Geisteswissenschaftliche Pädagogik'

A second important aspect shaping educational discourse in Germany and thus also the position of the German delegates is constituted by the particular form in which education was institutionalised as an academic discipline in Germany in the first quarter of the twentieth century. Towards the end of the nineteenth century, i.e. before education was established as a separate academic discipline at German universities, experimental education and psychology had developed into a vigorous field of study, mainly accommodated within the field of philosophy (Ingenkamp, 1990). Peter Drewek has shown that in the time period 1910-20, the majority of university courses with educational content at German universities were experimentally oriented (Drewek, 1996). However, from the early twentieth century on, a counter-current gained in strength that conceived of the task of education as an academic discipline as a historical and especially philosophical reflection of education, based on a 'reiterated interpretation of its own history and the history of its presumed predecessors' (Schriewer, 2000, p. 78). This particular form of conceiving of the study of education was often termed '*geisteswissenschaftliche Pädagogik*', which may roughly be translated as 'education conceived of as a humanities subject'. *Geisteswissenschaftliche Pädagogik* was a conscious attempt to take a stand against early twentieth-century 'empirical education' (*empirische Pädagogik*) and educational psychology in its empirical form, which ultimately succeeded in shaping the way in which education as an academic discipline was institutionalised in Germany. From about the 1920s on, the school of *geisteswissenschaftliche Pädagogik* dominated educational studies in Germany, a situation that continued at least until the 1960s.[14]

Geisteswissenschaftliche Pädagogik was closely intertwined with a corresponding conception of psychology (Schubeius, 2002). This '*geisteswissenschaftliche Psychologie*' was consciously opposed to more 'scientific' and empirical approaches and aimed at a 'holistic view' [15] of its objects of study. Eduard Spranger, one of the most influential figures of education as an academic field in Germany and author of the pedagogical best-seller, *Psychologie des Jugendalters*, wrote in 1921:

> I see ... the rise of technical methods for assessing the intellectual capacities and regulating the choice of educational trajectories as symptomatic of the relationship between democracy and rationalism ... Here, individuality is seen as something that can be measured and expressed in numbers, not as a structuring principle of the soul ... Individuality can only be assessed through living intuition. (Spranger, 1921, p. 267)

Three years earlier, Spranger had written about tests for selection to secondary school that these 'serve to breed a type of intellectual upstart, as our most recent intelligence tests exclusively focus on soulless attributes of the soul' (quoted according to Drewek, 2002, p. 134).

The reasons for the institutionalisation of education as *geisteswissenschaftliche Pädagogik* have to be sought in particular social constellations and reactions to the dynamics of educational reform demands in the first quarter of the twentieth century (Drewek, 1996, 1998, 2002; Schriewer, 2000). A key issue here was legitimising the existing educational system and safeguarding it against change in an unwelcome direction (Schriewer, 2000, p. 75). *Geisteswissenschaftliche Pädagogik* blocked the questioning of existing educational structures through experimental pedagogy (Schriewer, 2000, p. 78), it kept primary school teachers' ambitions for social advancement through university education in check (Schubeius, 2002, p. 369), thereby also effectively keeping away a large group of students with predominantly lower-class background, and it assuaged philosophers' fear of being colonised and sucked up by the burgeoning field of psychology. The 'defensive institutionalisation' of education at universities (Drewek, 2002, p. 139) in the shape of *Geisteswissenschaftliche Pädagogik* thus served in essence socially conservative purposes. It was aided by the state administration through changes in the organisation of teacher education (Schriewer, 2000). A side effect of the emergence of *geisteswissenschaftliche Pädagogik* as dominant paradigm that is interesting in the context of this chapter is the fact that it led to an increasing isolation of German educational studies as concerns its international contacts (Drewek, 1998, p. 189). Some of the important representatives of *geisteswissenschaftliche Pädagogik* – e.g. Eduard Spranger, Werner Nohl and Erich Weniger – cooperated with Becker and Ulich in international contexts, such as the German section of the New Education Fellowship (Röhrs, 1997; see Watanabe, 2004; also Becker, 1932), but certainly, it is not a coincidence that none of them was present in the German delegation to the IEI.

The German Delegation and German Academic Culture

After this quick sketch of some central elements of educational discourse in Germany and German academic culture more generally, the position of the German delegation to the IEI hopefully has become more comprehensible.

As was discussed above, *Bildung* was the educational ideal of advanced secondary and higher education in Germany and a central concept around which much of German academic culture revolved. Education as *Bildung* is conceived of in such a radically individual and idiosyncratic way that it becomes almost impossible to assess one person's *Bildung* other than through the 'living intuition'. In a situation where apparently there is no yardstick for rational, generalised measurement, it indeed becomes difficult to argue for a 'generalisation' of examinations; hence the tension between a 'generalisation vs. individualisation' of examinations as introduced by Becker to the discussion.

At the same time, the radically individualistic character of *Bildung* has repercussions on how issues that today would be subsumed under the heading of 'equity' are framed. The question whether *Bildung* and its assessment are 'just' in a 'democratic' sense (i.e. in the sense of providing equal chances to all individuals) does not really enter into consideration, as *Bildung* is such an individual matter as to be in certain respects asocial or at least opposed to the liberal idea of society as sum of equal parts, favouring instead an 'organic' view of society where members' relations are structured according to the 'symphonic analogy'.

Concerning its relation to the distribution of power and social prestige, *Bildung* has a twofold nature: On the one hand, the concept of *Bildung* provided a powerful weapon against the traditional social order at the time of its origin in the late eighteenth century, in that it set an 'aristocracy of *Bildung*' – which was potentially open to people regardless of their social origin – against privilege by birth.[16] On the other hand, *Bildung* could be used as a means of social closure, turning it effectively into the prerogative of a particular social group. This happened increasingly from the second half of the nineteenth century onward (Ringer, 1992). In Ulich's views on who should be allowed to enter the academically educated elite, we find reflections of both aspects: on the one hand, Ulich demands the opportunity to achieve *Bildung* for the 'truly gifted' members of the lower classes; on the other hand, he wants to keep the 'swots' out, i.e. keep those from entering higher education who are not capable of or do not want to achieve true *Bildung*.

Bildung is essentially about self-cultivation and character formation. This is why Ulich stresses that examinations should not just measure 'efficiency', but also 'culture'. In order to do this, examinations have to be 'holistic', have to consider the whole personality according to contemporary German positions. This makes it necessary that the examiner has an intimate knowledge of the candidate and is able to more or less 'intuitively' grasp whether the candidate's character really has character developed (*'gebildet'*) in the proper way.[17]

While all of the delegates in some ways are products of academic culture in Germany, it already has become clear that the position of the German delegation is far from homogeneous. Robert Ulich's position surely is much closer to that of the *geisteswissenschaftliche Pädagogik* than, for example, Otto Bobertag's.[18] Hylla's position is probably somewhere between Ulich and Bobertag: While being full of admiration for some elements of the educational system in the USA and a proponent of empirical educational psychology, Hylla's position towards the American high school is very ambivalent and deeply coloured by its roots in educational discourses and academic culture in Germany (Koinzer, 2006).

Conclusion

The German delegates to the IEI were certainly 'modernists' in Fritz Ringer's sense, i.e. they were not members of the 'orthodox' anti-democratic, politically and intellectually conservative majority of German academics, but belonged to the minority of 'German mandarins' who sought to adapt existing culture and education to modern challenges (Ringer, 1990). The fact that they were prepared to discuss and seriously consider rational testing methods shows that they differed significantly from the mainstream current of contemporary educational thinking in Germany; thus the knowledge they produced was 'awkward' in relation to the German educational establishment and German academic culture.

At the same time, even if they were open to and willing to consider and accommodate outside influences, it becomes clear that the thinking of the German IEI delegates is a product of German academic culture and heavily influenced by the character of education as an academic discipline in Germany. This in turn makes much of what they say at Eastbourne and some of their research 'awkward' in relation to many other contributions to the IEI. As Fritz Ringer also points out, even the 'modernists' were products of their particular intellectual field. The modernists' position is characterised not by the wish to do away completely with German academic culture, but to transform and adapt it to modern times. Robert Ulich's autobiographical sketch, published 40 years after the Eastbourne conference, bears clear witness to that, providing a perfect illustration for the position of a 'modernist' in Ringer's sense: Ulich complains about the ways in which the initially valuable idea of classical humanist education has become distorted by practice and become an elitist vehicle of protecting the social advantages of the middle class and keeping out the working class. He argues for bringing out the truly important elements of education and giving even the workers access to them: 'true popularization is by no means a cheapening and dilution of knowledge, but rather an illumination of its essence by elimination of its technical accretions' (Ulich, 1971, p. 425).

This article opened with Carl Heinrich Becker's euphoric expectation that the first IEI conference may come to be seen as the point in time from which 'future centuries ... may date the history of education'. Writing one year after the Eastbourne conference, Otto Bobertag gives a more realistic assessment of the conditions under which the IEI was received (or rather ignored) in Germany:

> It is hardly possible to venture a guess whether it will be possible ... to construct and apply a method of objective student assessment. Currently, experiments and trials of these methods are totally absent from the German school system. Thus, it has to be assumed that the urge to make progress in this direction is largely lacking in German schools. It is unlikely that this will change in the near future. (Bobertag, 1932b, p. 377).

Bobertag's pessimism proved to be well founded. For many decades, the kind of empirical work Bobertag and Hylla stood for was marginal within educational studies in Germany, contributing to the fact that for a long time, student assessment in Germany was largely grounded in unreflected practice by practitioners (Terhart, 1999, p. 281). This is particularly remarkable in a tracked system like the German one, where the allocation of pupils to the different streams of the educational system is so important for pupils' future life chances.

Today, the German averseness to tests is rapidly disappearing. Educational testing has come back with a vengeance, a development that gained additional momentum through the so-called 'PISA-shock' (Gruber, 2006). Now, branches of educational studies other than '*empirische Bildungsforschung*', such as history of education or comparative education (apart from international student assessment) are frequently discredited and delegitimised both in public debate and within the educational research community (see, for example, Weiler, 2003; Kahl & Spiewak, 2005). But arguably, even in the vehemence with which the pendulum has swung in the direction of testing, there still is a faint echo of the conditions under which the German delegation to the IEI operated. In contrast to countries such as Sweden with a long history of testing in education (see Christian Lundahl's contribution to this volume), the German general public and policy makers and many German researchers simply have not had the chance to develop a critical, reflected stance towards the potential and the limits of testing.

Notes

[1] The research for this article was conducted within the research project 'International student assessments, national assessment culture and reform history' at Uppsala University.

[2] According to Erich Jaensch, educational psychologist and supporter of National Socialism, intelligence testing favoured Jews and was thus not

suitable as a means of selection (Laux, 1990, p. 128). Anti-Semitic undertones had been discernible in the discussion on experimental psychological methods for pupil selection for a long time already before the Nazis came to power (Ingenkamp, 1989, p. 177).

[3] However, this did not prevent German army psychologists from using the very same methods during the Second World War that were denounced publicly (Geuter, 1999).

[4] His stay was partly financed through the Carnegie Corporation, and in his autobiographical sketch, Ulich mentions explicitly that his contact with the Carnegie Corporation had been established through the IEI (Ulich, 1971, p. 432). Thus, one might conclude that the fact that he was able to emigrate and continue working as an academic in his field was facilitated by having participated in the IEI.

[5] This issue had become a contested topic through the introduction of a compulsory primary school for all pupils (including those intending to proceed to academic secondary school, the *Gymnasium*) through the *Reichsschulgesetz* in 1920 (Ingenkamp, 1990, pp. 174-181). Before this reform, pupils intending to attend the *Gymnasium* had in many cases been prepared in special preparatory schools, not the 'normal' *Volksschule* (primary school). A third type of secondary education, situated between the *Gymnasium* and the *Volksschule* in relation to curriculum and social prestige, was available at the *Realschule*.

[6] Even though J.C. Smith from the Scottish delegation addresses him as 'Dr Hylla' at Eastbourne; see Monroe, 1931, p. 132.

[7] Both Ulich's and Hylla's cases demonstrate once more the importance of Teachers College as a hub for scholarship within international and comparative education during these years; see Koinzer, 2006. In a questionnaire filled in by former students of the International Institute at Teachers College, Hylla describes his time there as 'a broadening of my outlook on life and a human enrichment, which no other single stage of my education or professional activities provided'. The archival materials from the archives of the Carnegie Corporation and Teachers College pertaining to the German delegates were generously made available to me by Prof. Martin Lawn.

[8] A German stenographer was not always present during discussions at Eastbourne. Therefore, some of the contributions of the German participants have not been recorded in the same detail as those from English and French speaking countries, which of course constitutes a certain obstacle for analysis.

[9] Ulich and Wohlfahrt were among the first to use the German term '*Bildungssoziologie*'. See the editor's introduction to Ulich & Wohlfahrt ([1933] 2000).

[10] The *Studienstiftung* still exists; however, the criteria according to which it awards its – very prestigious – scholarships have changed. Nowadays, scholarships are awarded on the grounds of academic and – to a lesser degree

– personal merit alone; a student's financial situation no longer plays a role (Kunze, 2001).

[11] Picking up terms first used by V.E.M. Kim, Dietmar Waterkamp characterises Ulich's vision of an 'educational utopia' as 'conservative, elitist and even aristocratic in outlook' (Waterkamp, 1998, p. 323).

[12] The sample consisted of a total of 37 classes with 1209 pupils, drawn from all parts of the metropolitan area of 'Greater Berlin' (*Groß-Berlin*). The authors concede that this limited the applicability of the test to classes and pupils from rural areas (see Bobertag, 1932a, p. 7).

[13] *Bildung* has certain parallels to and similarities with the French notion of *culture générale*, but there are also massive differences, one of the most significant probably being the radical individualism of *Bildung* compared to *culture générale* (Ringer, 1992).

[14] Bobertag complains in 1931 that 'in Germany, we do not have an empirical branch of educational studies – but instead we have all the more philosophy, theory of values and other educational ideologies' (Bobertag, 1931, p. 13).

[15] Fritz Ringer (1990) has shown how 'holistic' became a label that was used indiscriminately in all kinds of connections in German academic culture.

[16] In fact, this has been named as one of the reasons for the genesis of the concept of *Bildung* among the middle classes in the late eighteenth and early nineteenth centuries (Ringer, 1992).

[17] The parallels to the methods championed by contemporary historians belonging to the school of 'Historismus' and contemporary philologists are striking. See Ringer, 1992.

[18] Interestingly enough, when teaching at Harvard after his emigration, Ulich became a fully fledged '*geisteswissenschaftlicher Pädagoge*', thus making him 'awkward' again in relation to most of his US colleagues (Waterkamp, 1998).

References

Baumert, J., Eigler, G., Ingenkamp, K., et al (1992) Zum Status der empirisch-analytischen Pädagogik in der deutschen Erziehungswissenschaft, in K. Ingenkamp, R.S. Jäger, H. Petillon & B. Wolf (Eds) *Empirische Pädagogik 1970-1990: Eine Bestandsaufnahme der Forschung in der Bundesrepublik Deutschland*, vol. 1, 1-88. Weinheim: Deutscher Studien Verlag.

Becker, C.H. (1932) Der soziale Wandel und die Erziehung auf dem internationalen Pädagogenkongress in Nizza 1932, *Pädagogisches Zentralblatt*, 12(10), 482-489.

Bobertag, O. (1914) *Über Intelligenzprüfung nach der Methode von Binet und Simon*. Leipzig: Barth.

Bobertag, O. (1931) Variabilität und Konstanz von Begabung und Schulleistung, *Zeitschrift für pädagogische Psychologie und Jugendkunde*, 32(1), 12-27.

Bobertag, O. (Ed.) (1932a) *Anleitung zur Leistungsmessung in der Grundschule*. Berlin: Zentralinstitut für Erziehung und Unterricht.

Bobertag, O. (1932b) Ergebnisse einer Versetzungsstatistik in Preussen, *Pädagogisches Zentralblatt*, 12(7/8, 9), 359-377, 428-439.

Bobertag, O. (1933) Leistungsschätzung und Leistungsmessung in der Schule: Ein Beitrag zur Frage 'Was leistet unsere Volksschule', *Zeitschrift für pädagogische Psychologie und Jugendkunde*, 34(8), 377-393.

Bobertag, O. & Hylla, E. (1926) *Begabungsprüfung für den Übergang von der Grundschule zu weiterführenden Schulen.* Langensalza: Julius Beltz.

Böhme, G. (1971) *Das Zentralinstitut für Erziehung und Unterricht und seine Leiter: Zur Pädagogik zwischen Kaiserreich und Nationalsozialismus.* Neuburgweier: G. Schindele.

Dewey, J. (1930) *Demokratie und Erziehung: Eine Einleitung in die philosophische Pädagogik.* Breslau: Ferdinand Hirt.

Drewek, P. (1996) Die Herausbildung der 'geisteswissenschaftlichen' Pädagogik vor 1918 aus sozialgeschichtlicher Perspektive, *Zeitschrift für Pädagogik*, 34, 299-316.

Drewek, P. (1998) Educational Studies as an Academic Discipline in Germany at the Beginning of the 20th Century, in P. Drewek & C. Lüth (Eds) *History of Educational Studies* [Geschichte der Erziehungswissenschaft.], vol. 1, 175-194. Gent: C.S.H.P.

Drewek, P. (2002) Defensive Disziplinbildung: Die Akademisierung der deutschen Pädagogik im Kontext der Modernisierungsprobleme des Bildungssystems und der Erziehungswissenschaft am Beginn des 20. Jahrhunderts, in R. Hofstetter & B. Schneuwly (Eds) *Erziehungswissenschaft(en) 19.-20. Jahrhundert: Zwischen Profession und Disziplin*, 113-139. Frankfurt am Main: Peter Lang.

Essner, C. & Winkelhane, G. (1988) Carl Heinrich Becker (1876-1933), Orientalist und Kulturpolitiker, *Die Welt des Islams*, 28(1/4), 154-177.

Geuter, U. (1999) Psychologie im nationalsozialistischen Deutschland, in R. Knigge-Tesche (Ed.) *Berater der braunen Macht: Wissenschaft und Wissenschaftler im NS-Staat*, 94-110. Frankfurt am Main: Anabasis.

Führ, C. (1994) Institutsgründung als Lebensarbeit: Erich Hylla (9.5.1887-5.11.1976) und die Gründung der Hochschule für Internationale Pädagogische Forschung in Frankfurt a. M. als Beispiel deutscher Gelehrtenpolitik in der Nachkriegszeit, in *Bibliothek für Bildungsgeschichtliche Forschung des Deutschen Instituts für Internationale Pädagogische Forschung. Wiedereröffnung am 2. März 1994. Dokumentation*, 30-37. Berlin: Bibliothek für Bildungsgeschichtliche Forschung.

Gruber, K.-H. (2006) The German 'PISA-shock': some aspects of the extraordinary impact of the OECD's PISA study on the German education system, in H. Ertl (Ed.) *Cross-National Attraction in Education: accounts from England and Germany*, 195-208. Oxford: Symposium Books.

Hylla, E. (1925) *Der Übergang von der Grundschule zu weiterführenden Schulen.* Leipzig.

Hylla, E. (1928) *Die Schule der Demokratie: Ein Aufriss des Bildungswesens der Vereinigten Staaten.* Langensalza: Julius Beltz.

Hylla, E. & Traxler, A. (1949) *English–German Word List of Terms Used in Educational Measurement* [Deutsch–englische Fachwörterliste für das Gebiet der pädagogischen Messung]. Berlin: Pädagogischer Verlag.

Ingenkamp, K. (1962) *Die deutschen Schulleistungstests: Kritische Betrachtungen und Untersuchungen zur pädagogisch-psychologischen Grundlegung*. Weinheim: Julius Beltz.

Ingenkamp, K. (1969) The Administration of School Tests in Germany, in K. Ingenkamp (Ed.) *Developments in Educational Testing*, vol. 1. London: University of London Press.

Ingenkamp, K. (1989) Experimentelle Methoden in der Schülerauslese: Beispiele für den Einsatz experimenteller Methoden bei Begabten- und Übergangsauslesen vor 1930, *Zeitschrift für Pädagogik*, 35(2), 175-195.

Ingenkamp, K. (1990) *Pädagogische Diagnostik in Deutschland 1885-1932*. Weinheim: Deutscher Studien-Verlag.

Kahl, R. & Spiewak, M. (2005) Nur bedingt wissenschaftlich, *Die Zeit*, 10 March.

Koinzer, T. (2006) Das pädagogische Amerika in der Weimarer Republik: Rezeption und Externalisation der 'Schule der Demokratie', in F. Becker & E. Reinhardt-Becker (Eds) *Mythos USA: 'Amerikanisierung' in Deutschland seit 1900*, 135-150. Frankfurt am Main: Campus.

Kunze, R.-U. (2001) *Die Studienstiftung des deutschen Volkes seit 1925. Zur Geschichte der Hochbegabtenförderung in Deutschland*. Berlin: Akademie-Verlag.

Laux, H. (1990) *Pädagogische Diagnostik im Nationalsozialismus 1933-1945*. Weinheim: Deutscher Studien Verlag.

Monroe, P. (Ed.) (1931) *Conference on Examinations under the Auspices of the Carnegie Corporation, the Carnegie Foundation and the International Institute of Teachers College, Columbia University*. New York: Bureau of Publications, Teachers College, Columbia University.

Monroe, P. (Ed.) (1939) *Conference on Examinations under the Auspices of the Carnegie Corporation, the Carnegie Foundation and the International Institute of Teachers College, Columbia University*. New York: Bureau of Publications, Teachers College, Columbia University.

Pallat, L. (1933) C.H. Becker +, *Pädagogisches Zentralblatt*, 13(3), 113-117.

Ringer, F.K. (1990) *The Decline of the German Mandarins: the German academic community, 1890-1933*. 2nd edn. Hanover: University Press of New England.

Ringer, F.K. (1992) *Fields of Knowledge: French academic culture in comparative perspective, 1890-1920*. Cambridge: Cambridge University Press.

Röhrs, H. (1997) Gründung und Gestaltung der 'Deutschen Sektion' des 'Weltbunds für Erneuerung der Erziehung' (1921 bis 1931). Ein bildungspolitisch bedeutsames Kapitel der internationalen Reformpädagogik, in C. Kodron, B. von Kopp, U. Lauterbach, U. Schäfer & G. Schmid (Eds) *Vergleichende Erziehungswissenschaft: Festschrift für Wolfgang Mitter*, 688-706. Cologne: Böhlau.

Schriewer, J. (2000) Educational Studies in Europe, in E. Sherman Swing, J. Schriewer & F. Orivel (Eds) *Problems and Prospects in Education*, 72-95. Westport: Praeger.

Schubeius, M. (2002) Institutionalisierungsgeschichte der Psychologie und ihre Verbindung zur Pädagogik im Kontext von Schul- und Gesellschaftspolitik im Deutschen Kaiserreich und der Weimarer Republik, in R. Hofstetter &

B. Schneuwly (Eds) *Erziehungswissenschaft(en) 19.-20. Jahrhundert: Zwischen Profession und Disziplin*, 367-382. Frankfurt am Main: Peter Lang.

Spranger, E. (1921) Die drei Motive der Schulreform, *Monatsschrift für höhere Schulen*, 20, 260-274.

Terhart, E. (1999) Zensurengebung und innerschulisches Selektionsklima – die Rolle der Schulleitung, *Zeitschrift für Soziologie der Erziehung und Sozialisation*, 19(3), 277-292.

Thorndike, E.L. (1922) *Psychologie der Erziehung*. Jena: G. Fischer.

Ulich, R. (1971) An Autobiography, in R.J. Havighurst (Ed.) *Leaders in American Education: the seventieth yearbook of the National Society for the Study of Education*, Part 2, 414-444. Chicago: University of Chicago Press.

Ulich, R. & Wohlfahrt, E. ([1933] 2000) *Zur Bildungssoziologie des akademischen Nachwuchses in Deutschland: Zusammenhänge zwischen Herkunft, Schulvorbildung und Studium, nachgewiesen an den Mitgliedern der Studienstiftung des Deutschen Volkes 1925-1933; herausgegeben und mit einer Einführung versehen von Dietmar Waterkamp*. Münster: Waxmann.

Watanabe, T. (2004) Erich Weniger als Vorsitzender der deutschen Sektion des 'Weltbundes für Erneuerung der Erziehung', *Jahrbuch für historische Bildungsforschung*, 10, 217-233.

Waterkamp, D. (1998) Robert Ulich: ideal universalism. A German Emigrant's Contribution to Educational Studies in the USA, in P. Drewek & C. Lüth (Eds) *History of Educational Studies* [Geschichte der Erziehungswissenschaft], vol. 1, 311-332. Gent: C.S.H.P.

Weiler, H.N. (2003) Bildungsforschung und Bildungsreform – Von den Defiziten der deutschen Erziehungswissenschaft, in I. Gogolin & R. Tippelt (Eds) *Innovation durch Bildung: Beiträge zum 18. Kongress der Deutschen Gesellschaft für Erziehungswissenschaft*, 181-203. Opladen: Leske & Budrich.

Bovet's Dilemma – examinations or no examinations: the Swiss contribution to the Carnegie initiative

RITA HOFSTETTER & BERNARD SCHNEUWLY

SUMMARY At the Eastbourne conference on examinations organised by the Carnegie Foundation, Bovet asks a fundamental question: what are the effects of examinations on the school system and on teachers' work. This question is the expression of a dilemma he has: as an experimental pedagogue, he is in favour of scientific examinations; as a militant for New Education, he defends teachers' freedom, which can be hampered by examinations. In order to provide some answers to his questions, he analyses the origin and effects of large-scale examinations of army recruits in Switzerland (1854-1914) and the reasons for their suppression; among others, the action of the New Education influenced teacher trade union. The analysis of this Swiss historical experiment allows him to formulate his dilemma in a more sophisticated way, but it remains.

Pierre Bovet (1878-1965) was invited to Eastbourne, to the Conference on Examinations organised by the Carnegie Foundation in May 1931, as director of the Institut des sciences de l'éducation (ISE), then commonly known as the Rousseau Institute. He was both a representative of the New Education movement in Europe, indeed the world, and Professor of Experimental Pedagogy at the University of Geneva. We are familiar with the close relationship that existed between experimental pedagogy and New Education, each providing the other with a form of legitimisation (Hofstetter & Schneuwly, 2006). In the crucial question of examinations, what form did this relationship take? Did it complement or contradict the approaches and aims? Could it have served even to promote examinations? If so, of what nature and to what ends? These questions confronted Bovet with a dilemma, intensified during that conference where he most certainly met sympathisers of New Education, such as Prussian Minister of Education Becker, who visited him in Geneva, or Percy Nunn, but especially the greatest designers of scientific tests and examinations such as Cyril Burt, C.E. Spearman, Edward L. Thorndike and C.H. Judd.

Pierre Bovet.

The Rousseau Institute: between the credo for measurement and militancy for the '*école active*'

At that conference, the purpose of which was to review the question of examinations in different countries, Bovet represented Switzerland in the relatively minor role given to the country. But it was primarily as director, for two decades, of the Rousseau Institute, and as founder and first director of the International Bureau of Education (IBE), then under the direction of Jean Piaget (who had to decline the invitation) that Bovet spoke in Eastbourne. He was therefore witness to an innovative experience in Europe, since the Rousseau Institute was the first institute of educational sciences founded on the Continent in 1912, the international influence of which, as the instigator of a resolutely scientific approach to educational phenomena and as a leading light of New Education, was undeniable at the time. He bore witness in particular to the fact that the Rousseau Institute was behind the founding of the International Bureau of Education (IBE), which aimed to create a synergy among all those the world over working for education to contribute to international cooperation and, hence, to bring the peoples and countries of the world closer together. And it was thanks to a grant from an American foundation, the Laura Spelman Rockefeller Memorial Foundation – which operates in a similar way to the Carnegie – that the project was able to get off the ground in 1925. Supported by the Rousseau Institute, the IBE was at that time sustained by the Swiss Association for the League of Nations and by an initiative committee made up of some fifty famous names under the patronage of Albert Einstein and the director of the International Labour Office.

The problems on the conference agenda were the same ones that had, from the start, mobilised the main protagonists of the Rousseau Institute, its experimental psychology laboratory, its related services (including its experimental nursery school, *Maison des petits*, and its vocational guidance service), and even of the IBE, originator of a number of international surveys and conferences. The research work, publications, teachings and conference presentations of those representing these institutions at that time were designed essentially to help improve educational concepts, systems and practices. While becoming fervent propagandists of a new education more attentive to the specific needs of children and the laws of their development, in a romantic and naturalistic vision of education, they also intensified their experimental investigations, within schools and beyond, to enable them to forge tools to help make training systems and enterprises more efficient. In the wake of the pioneering work by their American colleagues, the Genevans put much effort into building and trialling an impressive array of tests and experiments.[1] Their attention was focused on analysing skills with a view to improving career guidance, optimising the rational organisation of work and, more broadly, studying the performances of individuals and institutions. Until the 1920s this notion, at the same time naturalistic and mechanistic, seems to have been received relatively harmoniously. But by the time the conference was held in Eastbourne, disharmony had turned to discord. The Institute was in crisis (especially financial). Eventually fully recognised by the official authorities anxious to keep it going, it became attached to the University (1929), which gave it a larger base but also redefined its orientations. The relief guard, in the person of Piaget to be precise, then took up the reins of the establishment, bringing the advantage of a more professional, especially psychological, approach to research. The Institute was urged to reduce its militancy (New Education) as well as its efforts in applied psychology, then at the centre of controversies not devoid of ideological and political biases. In May 1931, the Institute was still in the process of reorganisation to meet the challenge. The perfect conciliator, an expert in negotiation, Bovet, whose work in experimental pedagogy was then recognised, may have been confident that the Institute would expand. He did not know then that this would only be possible after an unprecedented crisis, which would relegate him to obscurity. And it is true that the very modest place he occupied at Eastbourne was perhaps an early sign of this reversal.

Bovet in Eastbourne: where the dilemma became clear in the light of international experience

Edited by Monroe, the book from the Conference on Examinations (1931) gives a precise idea of what went on during the three-day event comprising six meetings. It consists of shorthand records of the speeches given by the participants each day. Its concept is given straight away by Monroe in his introduction: 'I have provided no program except for the first session. Here I have asked one representative of each of the several national groups to present the problem as it lies in his respective country' (p. 4). Through lack of time, Bovet could not take part at the end of this first session, contrary to what was planned.

The three main presentations by Bovet were all devoted to the relationship between principles of New Education and 'examinations', the term in the conference title which describes the issue well by the very fact that it is all-encompassing, covering both traditional examinations and examination by more standardised means such as tests.[2] The speeches by Bovet reflect perfectly his dual identity as an ardent militant of New Education which led him to a certain scepticism about examinations, and as a defender of experimental pedagogy who had faith in the possibilities of measurement: an identity that put him in a distinctive position at this conference and that was to be reflected in the work he would do on examinations on his return to Geneva. We describe it as a dilemma which he does not make explicit as such, but which nevertheless emerges in his presentations, notably by the simple fact that he leaves questions open.

In his first speech, Bovet refers to two previous speakers who had examined the purposes of secondary education. Célestin Bouglé, a representative from France, deputy director of the Ecole normale supérieure in Paris, gave his view of secondary education by citing the old adage of Montaigne of 'la tête bien faite, plutôt que la tête bien pleine' (better a cultivated mind than a full head) and referring to the principle that follows from it of 'apprendre à apprendre' (learning how to learn), which brings into play, according to Bouglé, institutions of French secondary education such as the dissertation and interpretation of a text. Robert Ulich [3], councillor in the Ministry of Education of Saxony, for his part, alluded to the Prussian secondary school reforms introduced by Becker. They had enabled the realisation of what had been envisaged in Switzerland to change secondary education, but had not produced the desired result, i.e. a reform [4] aimed at 'making our young people aware of the *raisons d'être* of our people, of our democratic ideal, of this Swiss federalism, also, that seeks to recognise the rights of diverse general cultures' (Monroe, 1931, p. 63). Bovet states that Swiss secondary education did not meet either of the 'ideals' proposed: no dissertation and competition as in France aimed at developing the ideal of 'learning how to learn' and the 'cultivated mind', and no programme carried out as in Prussia enabling the development of solidarity and the democratic spirit. This led him to the question of how to 'show this inadequacy' in order to persuade the stakeholders, politicians, teachers, parents, to reform the failed system. Bovet exhorted the scientists in the auditorium, notably Thorndike, Burt and Spearman:

> You should give us examinations, tests, if you like – in short, the means to convince them that our schools do not teach our pupils to learn, the means to ascertain objectively around us this bankruptcy in our secondary education, with regard to both of the ideals represented tonight. (Monroe, 1931, p. 63)[5]

This emotive plea for the scientific means to assess the school system is articulated very clearly in his second speech, in which, moreover, he raised quite another problem altogether. We see in Switzerland [6] – and in numerous other countries – a dual movement in relation to examinations, especially among teachers:

- a real interest in (although there is also undeniable opposition to) tests, in objective measurements as proposed by Thorndike or Ballard;
- a great suspicion towards school examinations, which did not even exist any longer in some areas in primary school: 'In primary education, a characteristic movement has effectively abolished examinations completely and replaced them with teacher assessments; which is to say that, although we want to express ourselves in scientific terms, we have renounced experimentation for observation; but observation that continues throughout the year also involves experimentation' (Monroe, 1931, p. 98).

However, teachers made a clear distinction, continues Bovet: 'Teachers themselves use tests to measure scholastic achievement, but not to assess general culture, personality, the future possibilities of a child' (p. 98). From these observations, he poses a problem that had not yet been tackled by the conference: Bovet is interested not just in comparing the different examination procedures and their advantages and disadvantages, 'but also in comparing the results of examination on one hand, and those without examinations on the other' (p. 98); in other words, using comparative scientific studies to analyse the impact of eliminating examinations (he was known to favour the latter).

In his final speech on leaving Eastbourne, Bovet comes back to this problem, which was clearly close to his heart:

> I am especially concerned at the moment to find out what the position of the problem of examinations is and ought to be in the eyes of those among us who have stood now for many years for the abolition of school examinations. We have advocated that in the elementary schools, and we have advocated something like that in the secondary schools, where we have tried to replace their external and final *maturité* and *baccalauréat* by the following-up of students and pupils by the teachers themselves. The external examinations were to be entirely suppressed and replaced by this judgment given by the teachers themselves who see the students at work. We have not achieved that everywhere; we have achieved it

> in some elementary schools and we try to achieve it in secondary schools, and I think this would be a very interesting moment to see what the effects of this new trend of thought are. (Monroe, 1931, p. 253)

Bovet thought then that it was possible to provide the basis of a reply to this question within the three-year period proposed by the English delegates for starting experimental work in the various partner countries.

At Eastbourne, Bovet reveals a dual point of view, explicit in his second speech. Talking about a 'dual movement', he sees in fact a relationship between two trends that seem divergent: one opts for more examinations and tests, the objectivity of which must nevertheless be reinforced; the other for the abolition of examinations, which gives teachers more freedom. Of course, he shows that tests are only concerned with certain measurable areas, and that they are used by the teachers themselves without being imposed by the system. But his assertions fail to conceal a fundamental dilemma. This dilemma became even clearer in his two other speeches:

- in the first, he calls upon science to show the weakness of the system and to support the reforms in his eyes indispensable for secondary education; here we see at work a frequent alliance between reformist initiatives and scientific approaches;
- the second on the contrary, which opens up a completely different area of thought, on the fringe of the conference and making him look like an outsider, proposes to tackle experimentally the effect of the abolition pure and simple of school examinations.

He does mention school examinations; but the relationships between school tests and examinations were not explicitly discussed, and his quite radical positioning at the end of the conference suggests that the latter was what he was advocating in the first place. Did he not say that he was 'especially concerned' by this question? A dual dilemma therefore:

- for promoting the reforms – especially in secondary education – he calls for objective tests in experimental pedagogy, but these tests still had to be created and improved;
- his real preoccupation, in arguing for New Education, is ultimately elsewhere: to abolish examinations and measure, objectively, the effects of abolition, which he assumes to be positive for the work of teachers.

Bovet back in Geneva: a methodological dilemma – in which the experimentalist turns into a historian[7]

On his return to Geneva, Bovet immediately set to work to realise the research programme announced. He clearly did it alone; at no time does he mention possible collaborations with colleagues at international level in his 'international survey on examinations' – the subtitle of his work.[8] His aim: to confront directly the question of the effect of abolishing examinations.

The situation seemed particularly favourable in this regard in Switzerland, and especially in the canton of Vaud: a law was to be passed in 1930 that offered municipalities the option of abolishing annual examinations or keeping them. This was the perfect opportunity for a comparative study on the effects that abolishing examinations would have on the work of the teacher; purpose of such an investigation: to compare, from the viewpoint of the work of the teacher the municipalities that abolished examinations and those that kept them. Unfortunately, there remained alongside the municipality examination a cantonal examination, crucial for assessing scholastic performance and therefore decisive for teachers: Bovet's investigation becomes meaningless.

One issue remained: documenting the movement for the abolition of examinations that Bovet had postulated at Eastbourne. Two surveys show that the movement was very real in Switzerland:

- the first was initiated by the ISE [9] following a consultation of Swiss experts in Berne in March 1932, and carried out with assistance from the Pestalozzianum in Zurich; clearly, the results were so disparate that a systematic analysis was ruled out. However, the trend towards abolition pure and simple of examinations in some cantons and for them to become relatively unimportant in others was clearly perceptible;
- the second survey, parallel with the first and limited to French-speaking Switzerland, was carried out by the Teachers' Union: except in Geneva, examinations remained, but with control moving from teachers to inspectors and with less importance given to examinations.

What explanation was there for this trend towards the abolition and relegation in importance of examinations? To answer this question, Bovet here relinquishes the experimental process and the questionnaire method and adopts historical reasoning as a method of causal explanation. The argument that he developed initially is simple: methods for controlling work change with ideas and pedagogic institutions; the trend towards abolition, evident since the end of the First World War, was linked to the New Education movement. He sums up his historic survey in the following broad terms:

> The humanists of the 16th century wanted those in their schools to learn Latin and Greek; they knew the extent to which that was achieved [thanks to appropriate examinations]. The liberals of the 19th century wanted to spread elementary knowledge widely; they knew what proportion of their pupils learned to read, write and count. As for us, in the 20th century, whatever we are called, we shall be resolute in developing and cultivating the child, but we shall find ourselves quite average at knowing the extent to which we do what we aspire to and have a duty to do. (p. XV)

So the question that arose from this general historical exploration was the following: what is it that caused examinations to be introduced, then abolished? The approach for answering it was to be from historical evidence. However, a precise object was needed to conduct it: this would be the examinations for army recruits in Switzerland.

Examinations or None? A Question Put to the Test in Historical Experimentation

Examinations for army recruits in Switzerland were introduced relatively systematically from 1854, reports Bovet [10], then they saw a remarkable expansion until the turn of the century but were abandoned with the First World War. Despite several attempts to bring them back, they were not reintroduced immediately after the war.[11] This history enables us to review the factors that explain firstly the appearance then the success of these examinations on the national scene, and also their failure and disappearance. Here, history functions as a sort of real-life experiment enabling Bovet to isolate the factors behind a social phenomenon.

Why examinations for recruits? What are the conditions of their success? These are two significant prototypical questions.

Article 27 of the Constitution of 1874 made the Confederation responsible for ensuring that the education given by the cantons was sufficient. A federal measure accompanied it to enable the Confederation to assess the repercussions of the obligation of education provision and the impact of training systems under the cantonal states: examinations for recruits. 'The Confederation thus made use of the army to prepare for school unification ... to determine the value of the schools in such-and-such a canton, as the first report by the Bureau of Statistics explicitly states' (p. 6). This idea was rooted in practices that had already been under way in some cantons since 1854.

Bovet's analysis of the federal regulations governing the examinations for recruits shows that it was an extremely rigorous process.[12] The marks given for reading, composition, arithmetic and civics (geography, history and constitution of Switzerland) were defined in some detail. A 48-page brochure described how the examinations were to be set:

> Although the regulations deserve praise for the care with which they set out the meaning of the quantitative marks, the Guide is remarkable in the way it gives the questions set the character of a 'clinical examination'. (p. 42)

The experts, appointed from the teaching profession (primary inspectors and teachers), received ad hoc training and participated in the experts' annual conference. That conference played an important role in guaranteeing the universality and prestige of the examinations. For example, 27,000 pieces of written work were re-examined in order to detect cantonal experts who were too lenient. Marks were entered in the recruits' service records and therefore followed them throughout their lives. Sometimes the results were published, occasionally even including names, to ensure their impact. Effectively, it was a considerable challenge, as much for the recruits and teachers as for the cantonal authorities and the general public.

The results of these examinations were presented, interpreted and sent to the cantons by the Federal Bureau of Statistics, which further refined the data collected by introducing new categories such as illiterates, or by considering new factors such as the last school attended, occupation or the distance between school and home, for interpreting the data.

To make the data accessible to everyone, it was presented initially in the form of a general average for all branches, with cantons and even districts placed in order of rank. Quickly realising that this method of presentation combined too many dissimilar factors, the Bureau of Statistics opted for results in the form of a percentage (poor, average and good) for each branch, which was more meaningful and better able to describe the strengths and weaknesses of the system. But under external pressure, the Bureau was forced to revert to averages, as they were clearer to the public and easier to understand, even though they were thought, with good reason, to be misleading. 'So scientific principles and rational convictions are going to capitulate to the methods of shooting galas and gymnastics festivals: the report will give way again to the average mark' (p. 128).[13] By charts showing the long-term evolution of the marks, the Bureau showed that the proportion of poor results fell and the proportion of good results rose significantly. This led Bovet to deduce: 'In 1913, the exhilaration emanating from this second chart [of good results] rubs off in some measure on the first and red is also the colour of the small proportions of poor marks revealed by the report on the latest examinations' (p. 139); and the Bureau to question if this increase was not indeed a result of the very existence of the examinations for recruits: 'No one will deny the extraordinarily healthy influence that these examinations have had on the development of mass education in Switzerland' (p. 152). Almost all cantons reported the examination results to their citizens fully or in summary. Often there were arguments to improve the laws: 'Since 1875, there has hardly been a proposal of any importance made in the area of mass schooling in any canton that has not also been justified by a reference to the results of the recruits and to the warning signs, apposite or not, that they contain' (a report quoted by Bovet, p. 157).

But the very success of the examinations for recruits and the importance given to them sounded their death knell. Thereafter assessed mainly by the yardstick of these examinations, schools and those in charge of them, including teachers, based their methods and programmes on them. The cantons even used new institutions, the complementary schools, where young people could prepare and where the course contents were entirely determined by these examinations. Special courses were added specifically for the benefit of the recruits, orientated exclusively towards drill. From the start of the twentieth century, doubt began to creep in. Did examinations not limit the action of the school? Did they not define content too emphatically and too narrowly?

At the very time the great French educationalist Buisson took an interest in examinations and brought in a bill 'aimed at establishing an annual examination of primary education for conscripts, in imitation of what is done in Switzerland' (p. 180), examinations for recruits were stopped: 'War had come. Before gaining a foothold in France, the examination of recruits was dead in Switzerland' (p. 181).

For Bovet, the result of the historical experiment was clear and precise: during a short phase of history, corresponding to the introduction of a widespread state school system, in a federalist context moreover, examinations for recruits had been an essential tool for furthering the school: 'Introduced to record illiteracy and ignorance in order to help combat these evils, they achieved their aim; one can without naivety pay tribute to them for this fine result' (p. 199). But their very success corrupted them by imposing them as an exclusive method for controlling the work of teachers and orientating schools towards knowledge and techniques as a sole result of memorisation and drill, and thus limiting the freedom of teachers, primary teachers in particular. However, was it necessary to abandon examinations? Was that a way out of the dilemma? To answer that, Bovet analysed the repercussions of the history of examinations for recruits.

The Question Shifts and Remains Open: where everything ends in a kind of aporia

After the First World War, a long period began in which controversy surrounded the examinations for recruits. There were two clearly opposed factions. The cantons and their administrations were decidedly in favour of the examinations; they wanted to hold on to a means whereby they could control teachers. Teachers, however, vigorously opposed their reintroduction. Briod, a union representative of the primary teachers of French-speaking Switzerland, launched a fierce diatribe against the resumption of the examinations for recruits in the union's journal. Of course, they enabled progress to be made initially, but under their influence, primary education suffered a regrettable deformation. To break free from drill, examinations had to be abandoned and progress made in the school reform

> that tried to give schooling more joy and physical and moral wellbeing, by creating new sources of interest, by adapting the methods to child psychology, by cultivating the heart as well as intelligence, by bringing into school something of the life for which it must prepare the child. (Briod, 1920, quoted by Bovet, 1935, p. 157)

Thus it was in the name of the principles of New Education that the examinations were condemned. And it was not by chance that the 1920 congress of the Société pédagogique romande (SPR; the teacher trade union of French-speaking Switzerland), which steered it towards officially adopting these very principles, unanimously rejected examinations. As far as the teachers of German-speaking Switzerland were concerned, rejection was clear as well, under the principles of the *Arbeitsschule*.

The authorities nevertheless were keen to reintroduce examinations. The solution was found by following the paths proposed by two former staff members of the ISE. Duvillard (1922), a former teacher, pupil of Claparède, then head of the research bureau attached to the Department of Education of Geneva, proposed two different examinations [14]: the first was individual, on reading, writing and arithmetic, and used modern means in the form of tests; the other was communal and its object was civics. This idea was to be developed in several trials by Heinis, an occupational psychologist, also a student of Claparède then teaching at the Institute, who put the idea into practice by developing examination procedures influenced by applied psychology. But to no avail: after a long debate the reintroduction of examinations for recruits was rejected by the national parliament. The basic arguments were those of the teachers, taken up by a number of members of parliament. It was the opposition of teachers that killed it off, as was exposed by a fervent defender of the examinations in the National Council: 'they see in examinations of all types a sabot that blocks the exercise of freely individual teaching' (quoted by Bovet, 1935, p. 194).

For Bovet, the cause was understood: the examinations for recruits in their standard form were no longer justified; and it was in large part the New Education movement that had driven them out, through teachers who were devotees of school reform. But what was to be done then? With the disappearance of the examinations for recruits, Bovet's dilemma was not over by any means. And the abolition of examinations in primary school, which he noted with satisfaction, again under the influence of the same movement, leaves unresolved the other problem that he poses as experimental pedagogue: the necessary control of scholastic performance, which influences – and Bovet is aware of it – the work of the teacher and contents taught by methods giving precedence, come what may, to the mechanical dimension of teaching to the detriment of the freedom of the teacher and the needs of the children. How is this dilemma to be overcome? He treads cautiously and tries to find a solution to reconcile what is his fundamental dilemma: control of the school and freedom of teaching. The path he proposes is narrow and, above all, cannot yet be embarked on. It is more the sketch of a route, which seems to leave the problem unresolved.

The *école nouvelle* (p. XII), more clearly than the 'old', attempted to take on two quite distinct tasks: to cultivate and to instruct. These two tasks are particularly evident, he says, in two people representing the renewal in the United States: Dewey for whom the school must focus on the needs of the children, and Thorndike, who wishes to measure school performance objectively. The two can be combined, Bovet believes: Washburne did it in Winnetka, and in Europe it was Claparède who united the two trends. But how was that to be given concrete expression? The idea was simple: these two tasks cannot be assessed by the same tools. For knowledge and techniques, he advocated, tests were appropriate and were well tried and tested.

> For the other type of control, adapted to the other task of the school, culture, no suitable procedures have so far been found. Therefore it is impossible to relinquish them. We are too interested in finding out if the school and the teacher are carrying out their full task.... As long as man values culture as much as education and has not found a satisfactory way to control that particular part of the task of the school, examinations of whatever nature will be a danger. (p. 199)

Conclusion

Did Bovet resolve the dilemma that appears in his speeches at Eastbourne? It cannot be denied that he clarifies the problem he faced: how to reconcile a critique of examinations with a defence of tests. How does one defend simultaneously a liberating vision of the school and the profession of teacher exempt from the yoke of administration, and yet use tests to assess the school objectively, its performance, the achievement of the objectives set for it, including the one, supreme for Bovet, of the 'cultivated mind' and of 'learning how to learn'? And how does one obtain methodological means for analysing the effects of examinations scientifically? Bovet succeeds in answering the latter question by a historical methodology placing under the microscope the repercussions of the examinations for recruits: effects at first positive that generated momentum, but which contained perverse effects and limiting factors that would later predominate. The examination appears thus as an instrument dependent on well-defined pedagogic circumstances. It has no value in itself. To examine or not to examine? The answer depends on the context. The demonstration is convincing.

So what do we make of the new context in which Bovet operates? Bovet tries to overcome the dilemma he faced here by not letting go of anything, by trying to keep everything; one could even say in a way, by not taking a position. The distinction between the two tasks of the school allows him to do this. There is, on one hand, instruction based on repetition and drill, on the creation of habits. And here examinations to measure performance do exist according to him: the tools of applied psychology that have the advantage of not, as is too often the case, confusing the two tasks. On the other hand there is what he calls 'cultivating', which addresses not 'receptivity' but the 'activity' of the pupil: 'his interests always aroused, to which we appeal whenever we try to develop the child, to cultivate his mind and his heart' (p. XIV). No tool exists to assess the effects of action in this domain.

The price to be paid for resolving the dilemma is high: a bipartition of the school that still relies heavily on receptivity, memory, the creation of habit, which is hardly in keeping with the ideals of New Education. Indeed, this is the price to be paid for redeeming tests and their utility and functionality; for retaining the 'experimental pedagogy' dimension; for keeping to the tradition defined by Claparède and his 'Thorndike' side. The other price to be paid is the lack of articulation with the other task of the school and the appearance of a new dilemma: since tests cannot show us 'the extent to which we do what we aspire to and have a duty to do' (p. XV), we have no means to 'control that particular part of the task of the school'. It follows that

> examinations, in whatever form will be a danger. They will always risk giving substance to a false idea: or the idea that education is the only important thing as it is the only thing we try to measure; or the idea that education and culture are one and the same thing, as we measure them with the same instruments. (p. 199).

Finally would Bovet's dilemma still be ours? Does Hopmann (2007) not point out a similar question when he says about PISA:

> What will happen to the school subjects left out, to the special-needs that are marginalised, to school tasks which have nothing to do with higher-order academic achievement, to the school functions which move beyond a one-dimensional kind of knowledge distribution? (p. 400)

And does Bovet's instinctive mistrust of measurement by tests, and therefore of the standards for constructing them, not find an echo in the plea by Herzog (2008) against the idea that the product of the school could be assessed like that of a factory? Bovet vaguely anticipates these problems, but like a number of those of the period, he is convinced that the improvement of pedagogy comes at the same time through New Education, and its emancipatory potential, and through experimental pedagogy, whose scientific nature – proven by the rigour of its tests and measurements – will boost the performance of education systems. The solution he proposes for the dilemma was technically, psychologically and ideologically the only one possible for him and his epoch: doing both at the same time. And therefore perpetuated the dilemma experienced.

Notes

[1] A list of the tests and measurements is found in Hofstetter (in press), who also gives a detailed description of the militant commitment of the protagonists of the Institute and the crisis of the 1930s.

[2] He spoke moreover on a terminological question, proposing to substitute 'intuitive or qualitative method' and 'objective or quantitative method' with the terms '*Generalisierungsmethode*' and '*Individualisierungsmethode*' and, in the discussion on the civil service entrance examinations, mentioned the work done by his institute for the post office.

[3] The shorthand report of Ulich's speech does not mention this allusion to Becker; perhaps because, as Monroe states in his introduction, there was no German shorthand typist and the German speeches 'are usually given only in fragmentary form'.

[4] Bovet refers here to the propositions of Barth, widely discussed in the 1920s, but which did not come to anything; see Barth, (1919). Bovet states that the book: 'expressing the almost unanimous desire, even though badly realised, of all secondary education, aims to give the Swiss "maturité" a regime as far removed as possible from that of the French baccalauréat, or the German pre-war Abitur, with more emphasis on essays and practical work' (1935, p. VII).

[5] Apart from the points that he regarded as crucial – the very necessity for school examinations and knowledge of the effect of school – Bovet also takes up a methodological point emphasising what Switzerland could contribute: 'The very fact that we are a country so divided, with so many local and cantonal systems, and with those three influences of Germany, France, and Italy, together with that of our own school tradition, would perhaps make it possible to draw interesting comparisons between the practice and systems in different parts of the country' (Monroe, 1931, p. 252). And he states this idea by yet another dimension: 'This very fact of the smallness of our country, the possibility of looking into the details and in most cases even to personal factors and aspects of the situation, seem to me to make the results perhaps more difficult' (p. 253) He also offers collaboration in the collection of documents internationally by the IBE and in Switzerland by the ISE.

[6] In 1920, the Teachers' Union of French-speaking Switzerland passed a resolution adopting the principles of New Education and the active school, at the instigation notably of Duvillard (for its importance see farther on in the text). Bovet himself was on the committee of the union. Of course the movement got considerably weaker during the 1920s, but did survive when Bovet intervened.

[7] The remainder of the text is based essentially on Bovet (1935), publication of which was made possible by a grant from the Carnegie Foundation. In the introduction to his book of 209 pages, Bovet analyses first examinations generally and their suppression in Swiss schools. The core of the book is a history of examination of army recruits in Switzerland. After the presentation of their prehistory in the cantons and of the elaboration of their federal regulation, he treats different aspects of these examinations: the experts, their role, their education and their collaboration; the signification of the recruit examinations; the political discussions in the parliament on the meaning of these examinations; their analyses by the Federal Bureau of Statistics; the mode of presentations of the results for the public and the public interpretation of the results; and the probable influence of the recruit

examinations on schools and on the canton's educational policy. The last chapter presents the debate for and against recruit examinations after their suppression in 1914, and discusses the more general question of what kind of examinations for what kind of teaching and learning in school. A large appendix of sources concludes the book.

[8] It seems that this was also the case for the other surveys carried out on the initiative of the Carnegie Foundation: these were in fact national surveys, driven by an international programme.

[9] References to this questionnaire are made at different places in 1933: a short note by Stettberger in the journal of the Pestalozzianum; several mentions in the minutes of the teacher trade union and of the ISE. All these notes and mentions say that many teachers respond to it. But we could find no trace of the questionnaire itself, nor of a publication of the results and can only rely on the presentation by Bovet.

[10] Lustenberger (1997) even dates them to 1830; more recently Crotti & Kellerhals (2007) have described the political context of the examinations for recruits, in relation to the PISA surveys.

[11] Lustenberger (1997) shows that they were reintroduced after the Second World War, but in a very different form.

[12] Bovet enthusiastically comments: 'This care taken to specify the exact conditions in which each mark on the scale must be allocated seems quite remarkable. If we are not mistaken, it gives this document an important place in the history of this objective control of scholastic performance, of so much interest nowadays in the United States and elsewhere. Recent works on this subject date the conscious and methodical efforts for an objective assessment of scholastic knowledge to the Vaney grading scales in Binet's *Année psycholgoique* in 1905, or to a lecture by J.-M. Rice at the meeting of School Superintendents in Indianapolis in 1897, which led to the first works by Thorndike. When one looks at the "prehistory" of this movement, there is a report of a sampled scale of writing in use in Greenwich in 1864, quoting a page by Horace Mann. But these isolated facts, while interesting, cannot be compared in importance with our examinations, whose organisers sought for forty years, with the success that we shall see, to refine the technique and determine it precisely. At least fifteen years before Cattell began to popularise the idea of tests, performance tests were being used unwittingly in Switzerland' (1935, p. 35).

[13] In a very interesting passage, showing his skill as an experimental pedagogue, Bovet discusses other possible means the bureau would have had for analysing the figures, such as the median, and discusses the reasons for not using them.

[14] For this presentation, we take as a basis the presentation of Lustenberger (1997). Bovet, curiously, does not develop the proposition of Duvillard, crucial according to Lustenberger. Could this be due to the quarrels between Duvillard and the ISE in the 1930s?

References

Barth, A. (1919) *Die Reform der höhern Schulen in der Schweiz. Untersuchungen und Vorschläge über die Maturitätsverhältnisse und andere Mittelschulfragen, von Dr. Albert Barth ... Im Auftrag des Schweiz. Departements des Innern.* Basel: Spittlers.

Bovet, P. (1935) *Les examens de recrues dans l'armée suisse. 1854-1914.* Neuchâtel and Paris: Delachaux et Niestlé.

Briod, E. (1920) Examens de recrues et education, *L'Educateur*, XXX.

Crotti, C. & Kellerhals, K. (2007) 'Mögen sich die Rekrutenprüfungen als kräftiger Hebel für Forschritt im Schulwesen erweisen!' PISA im 19. Jahrhundert: Die schweizerischen Rekrutenprüfungen – Absichten und Auswirkungen, *Revue suisse des sciences de l'éducation*, 29, 47-64.

Duvillard, E. (1922) La réorganisation des examens pédagogiques des recrues. *L'Educateur*, XXX.

Herzog, W. (2008) Unterwegs zur 08/15-Schule? Wider die Instrumentalisierung der Erziehungswissenschaft durch die Bildungspolitik, *Schweizerische Zeitschrift für Bildungswissenschaften*, 30, 13-33.

Hofstetter, R. (in press) *Emergence des sciences de l'éducation. A la croisée de champs professionnels et champs disciplinaires. L'exemple de Genève de la fin du 19e siècle au milieu du 20e siècle.* Geneva: Droz

Hofstetter, R. & Schneuwly, B. (Eds) (2006) *Passion, Fusion, Tension. New Education and Educational Sciences – end 19th-middle 20th century* [Education nouvelle et sciences de l'éducation – fin 19e-milieu 20e siècle]. Berne: Peter Lang.

Hopmann, S. (2007) Epilogue: No Child, No School, No State Left Behind: comparative research in the age of accountability, in S. Hopmann, G. Brinek & M. Retzl (Eds) *PISA zufolge PISA* [PISA according to PISA], 363-393. Vienna: LIT-Verlag.

Lustenberger, W. (1997) *Les examens pédagogiques des recrues. Une contribution à l'histoire de l'école suisse.* Chur: Rüegger.

Monroe, P. (1931) *Conference on Examinations.* New York: Columbia University.

The Battle of the *Baccalauréat*: the long forgotten story of a divided committee

MARC ZARROUATI

SUMMARY The French Committee attended the three general conferences of International Examinations Inquiry (IEI) at Eastbourne, Folkestone and Dinard, while its chairman, Auguste Desclos, also attended all intermediate meetings. France even hosted the last general meeting of 1938, at Dinard. This committee should have played a key role in this international inquiry. However, this committee failed in sustaining the international efforts to improve European countries' way of examining. It did not contribute to releasing any French innovative methods or ideas abroad, nor did it convince French educational circles to adopt the modern views on examinations discussed at these conferences. Although it had carried out seminal studies on the *baccalauréat* examination, the Committee disappeared at the dawn of the Second World War and its work sank in the deep waters of indifference and oblivion. Considering the history of the French Committee is nevertheless of great interest to understand why and how French leading teachers, namely secondary school teachers, were predominantly opposed to new methods of examination in the 1930s, while these methods were broadly released and experimented with in many other European countries. We see that the French Committee was divided between those who promoted '*Culture générale*' based education and traditional examinations and those who wished to introduce testing within French primary and secondary schools. The latter carried out the scientific work, while the interpretations and discussions of the results were led by the former, during the Carnegie conferences. This latent conflict was detrimental both to scientific exchanges between French experimental psychologists and foreign scholars and to the introduction of experimental methods and psychometric views on examination within the French education system, as well.

'[Among] the national committees formed at Eastbourne in 1931, only the English and French committees carried out experimental researches. These researches were presented at Folkestone (1935) then at Dinard (1938) and led to significant publications ... The [experimental] investigations carried out by the [Carnegie] French Committee were published in 1936 in *La correction des épreuves écrites dans les examens*' (Commission Française, 1936), Henri Piéron wrote, at the beginning of his *Examens et docimologie* (Piéron, 1963, p. 16). A few lines further, he added: '[this publication] caused some commotion, although it had not been released widely ... When the war came, the results of [this] fundamental investigation ... were getting little coverage'.

Nowadays in France, few are those who ever mention the investigations of the Carnegie French Committee, and fewer are the copies of *La correction des épreuves écrites dans les examens* available on university libraries' bookshelves. This episode just seems so forgotten that it is hardly believable it caused any commotion, even as far back as the remote 1930s.

Did these investigations on examination lead to some concrete modification of the French education system? If not, why? Were these alleged commotion-causing results used later in the various fields of research and applications where the examination is at stake? Why is this story relatively unknown within French education circles? Did these series of international conferences and joint investigations enable French scientists to create or improve new international scientific collaborations on education?

To answer these questions even partly, I intend to present the ideas and work of the French Committee from Eastbourne to Dinard, and underline the causes of its internal tensions as much as the matter of its investigations. Indeed, the differences in the conceptions of education among the members of the committee had entailed some divergences about examinations in general, and hence about the scope of the Carnegie Inquiry and the interpretation of its results. It also had some consequences on the position of the French Committee as regards this international Carnegie project.

I. The Desclos Committee

'There undoubtedly is a need for an inquiry into our examinations' (Monroe, 1931, p. 12), Auguste Desclos [1] claimed, on behalf of the French Committee, at the outset of the first session of the Eastbourne conference. Before wrongly coming to the conclusion that he was welcoming some substantial mutation of the French system of examination, let us set out the French ideological context in which this inquiry was considered.

Desclos first explained that the French 'system of examination' 'is closely dependent on and related to [the] system of education' (Monroe, 1931, p. 6). He then described the latter as not entirely satisfying, as it 'lacks coordination':

> We have at the present moment three main systems of education existing side by side. [The] old traditional system coming down to us from the Middle Ages ... the *enseignement secondaire*, [which consists of] the *lycées* and *collèges* with the universities and the

Grandes Écoles at the top. This ... system is still the fundamental one.

By the side of that old system, circumstances ... have built up two new systems adapted to the present ... life. [The] *enseignement primaire* ... designed at first to teach the three R's to children up to about the age of eleven, it has gradually ... extended and transformed its subject matter, so that it has now come to take care of those same children until they are grown. Then later still we have ... the *enseignement technique*, preparing the children of the people for the carrying on of some ... practical occupation. It was at first limited to children of the age of about ten or eleven, and then it gradually extended its scopes and its program and took them on until they reached the age of eighteen or nineteen. Therefore we have co-existing side by side and until now with few co-relationships, three vertical systems of education. Each system has its separate administration, its separate staff ... with its separate program, its separate spirit.

[This] vertical division is not right ... . We are very much concerned in trying to bring those three parallels systems into one more direct and more efficient organization by grading the children by age and not according to type, by coordinating the programs so as to establish horizontal divisions instead of the vertical separations now existing. (Monroe, 1931, pp. 7-8)

This idea that sounded generous and democratic was gathering all reformers around a project that was necessarily vague, for it had obtained a universal agreement (Hugot, 2005). The *école unique*, Desclos said rightly, is 'a very convenient word, which is very much used in France although it is not always well defined' (Monroe, 1931, p. 8). For example, the *école unique* is not understood by Desclos as a tool to provide all children with the same education:

> We know that there are differences of minds and capacities, and we are eager ... that the best capacities shall be properly selected and shall be given a full and proper opportunity of reaching the maximum that they possess within them ... If we are going to reform ... our education according to the plans that have been sketched out under the title of the *École Unique*, there is no doubt that examinations will become ... the most important instrument of selection, of differentiation, of allocation to different tasks of young persons of the nation. (Monroe, 1931, pp. 10, 12)

In this still 'aristocratic' (Monroe, 1931, p. 10) though supposedly more equitable system, the selection had to remain. It is just that, instead of splitting up pupils at the first stage, once and for all, according to the fees that their parents could pay, the selection devices were now to be spread at each stage of the education process in order to guide any pupil toward the most suitable class level, according to his 'capacities'.

Auguste Desclos.

At this point, we should not expect Desclos to raise questions like 'how to properly assess the capacity of a pupil?' or 'who will be responsible for deciding which criteria have to be adopted to properly split up pupils into classes and courses?' According to him, there was indeed one non-polemic criterion that enabled teachers to assess pupils' capacities. There was one criterion upon which all French educators allegedly agree, from the schoolteacher to the university professor. There was one criterion that was expected to help programmes, scopes, methods and spirits of the side-by-side systems to converge towards a unique and equitable system of education: it was *Culture générale*.

> [The] idea inspiring the doctrine that you find dominating our whole system of instruction and our system of examinations ... is what we call *culture générale*. That general, broad, harmonious development of the faculties of the child, aiming not at the dogmatic acquiring of knowledge with a utilitarian purpose, of knowledge for knowledge's sake, but the quest of knowledge through a critical process of approach developing the spiritual faculties to the point of general fitness and alertness where they can best be specialized and applied to whatever particular task they may be called upon to perform. (Monroe, 1931, p. 10)

In his view, *Culture générale* was not only a conception of education (Desclos, 1935), but also a set of assessable and special qualities, such as subtlety, curiosity and rationality. From the most practical training to the highest intellectual lecture, this common feature was claimed to shape the spirit of lessons and examinations in a unique way. This was the keystone that gave strength and unity to French education, in spite of its old and complex and multilayered machinery.

Even the technical schools were more and more shaped by this conception of education.[2] Yet the best illustration of this doctrine remained the *enseignement secondaire* [3] for it was entirely – intrinsically – devoted to the acquisition of *Culture générale*.

> We have concentrated on that *enseignement* the experience of ages, and we think that both in the organization of that *enseignement*, in its curriculum, and especially in the spirit with which it is inspired, in the quality of the men who give that *enseignement*, we have reached the best of what we have in France. (Monroe, 1931, p. 11)

The *enseignement secondaire*, in so far as it was the cradle of every education based on the general culture, was raised at the pinnacle of the whole French education system by Desclos, and presented as a model to the other delegations. Any methods, programmes and examinations were valued depending on how close they were to the *enseignement secondaire*. It was the cornerstone of the educational system. It was the part that one needs to keep globally unchanged, for it is the core of the principles of French education. As far as it concerned secondary education, the reform was seen as a set of minor adjustments.[4]

Now we get a clearer view of the kind of inquiry Auguste Desclos planned to conduct: Desclos wanted the French Committee to help transform current examinations at any stage of education to organise them in a more rational way. However, 'rational' did not mean 'experimentally and scientifically tested', according to him. It meant 'reasonable' or 'according to reason', and 'thinking according to reason' was surely the most valued quality that an education based on general culture could instil into the pupils' minds. As the *école unique* reform was expected to recast primary and technical schools by reshaping them along the logic of education in use within the *enseignement secondaire*, Desclos wanted to help recast [5] examinations to implement a consistent series of examinations from the primary tests toward the secondary school exams, provided that the former were to be commensurate with the latter.[6]

II. Tact versus Test: the lonely committee

Were the other members of the French delegation in agreement with Desclos' views?

Célestin Bouglé, a prominent sociologist, was then deputy director of the *École Normale Supérieure*, the most elitist higher school in France and, incidentally, the secular temple, if any, of Desclos' beloved *Culture générale*.

Agreeing with Desclos, he praised French education and left little room for criticism, except on its lower stages. He expressed scepticism about scientific and quantitative tests when assessment of subtle abilities was at stake. He explained that traditional examinations were the natural way for the examiner to grasp some signs of the general culture that the student was supposed to have acquired.

Célestin Bouglé.

He defended oral examinations, and the discussion between student and examiner, as a special way to establish the intellectual complicity that could help the examiner to assess something as complex and subtle as the general culture mastered by the student, something that could be named 'tact' (Monroe, 1931, p. 45).

Charles Maurain [7] dealt with examinations as a way of recruiting high-ranking civil servants in France. No more than his colleagues did he question these examinations. He only consented to pointing out the complexity of the whole system of examinations, although he finally agreed that the diversity of ways of entering high public administration was an additional help for the deserving pupils of any origins who wished to serve the nation.

Following Desclos, Victor Cope, the President of the French union of secondary teachers, outlined the French educational system as one that was spiritually, if not logically, organised along the *enseignement secondaire* and its culture, which both formed the essence of the whole machinery.[8]

Paul Barrier was the only member of the French Committee who used different terms about the nature of examinations and the purpose of the Carnegie Inquiry on examinations. He spoke about 'aptitude' and 'child psychology'. As a chief education officer and deputy head of the primary school system at the Ministry of Education, Paul Barrier was familiar with the issues debated by primary teachers regarding the aims of examination. What was to be assessed by an examination? Knowledge or aptitude, or both? The *école unique* reform planned to allow primary school children to take an exam to possibly enter secondary school. 'Exam' means examiners. Who were to be examiners? What criteria were they to use? Who would control the entrance into the prestigious secondary education system? 'Who shall conduct the examinations?' Barrier asked. He gave some signs of agreement with the delegations that defended tests versus traditional examinations.[9] Yet he did not claim any divergence between his priorities and those of his French colleagues regarding this inquiry.[10]

At the end of the conference, Desclos still seemed to hesitate between his scepticism about tests and his obvious wish to take part in this international project. His final words were about statistics 'to be collected', tests 'to be applied right and left', interviews 'to be held' (Monroe, 1931, p. 255). He said that France would 'have to set up a new system of examination' and in order 'to set up that new system' the French Committee must collect material and experience brought by the other delegations. But, on the other hand, he claimed that the current system contained, nonetheless, 'a great element'. 'There is that element of tact, of which Bouglé spoke the other day. That process we have found to be a very excellent servant in the past; I do not think we shall be prepared to dismiss it' (pp. 254-255).

The key words were the following: rather than trying to 'dismiss' the tact-based traditional examinations, one had to 'add' to that process 'something newer'. The conference gave him some relevant ideas to supplement secondary school traditional exams with 'something that you gentlemen have been experimenting upon, that you have been discovering; and we shall be very glad if we can adapt some of that work to what we are doing' (p. 255).

III. Early Changes in the Committee

'While these [foreign] committees [that attended the Eastbourne conference] were made up of prominent specialists of psychological techniques of examination, [the French delegation] was only a reunion of administrators' (Piéron, 1932a, p. 237), Henri Piéron wrote in the Bulletin of the *Institut National d'Orientation Professionnelle* (INOP).[11] He had some good reasons to criticise the composition of the delegation so acidly.

In 1927, Henri Piéron, his wife and Henri Laugier co-authored a seminal paper presented at the 4th International Conference of Psychotechnique [12] and later published in *Pour l'ère Nouvelle* (Piéron et al, 1935). It expounded the results of a pioneer investigation about the *Certificat d'études* (the primary school final examination) concerning 117 pupils from three primary schools in Paris. The purpose of this investigation was to evaluate the selective capacity of the *Certificat d'études*, in comparison with a psychometric test. Mme Henri Piéron first mentioned this study as early as in 1922, in a paper she published in *L'année psychologique* (Piéron, 1922). Henri Piéron then claimed to have founded a new science, the *science des examens* (science of examinations) or *docimologie* from Greek *docime*, which means 'test'.

At that time, Henri Piéron was not really an unknown scientist. In 1907 he had been appointed director of the *Laboratoire de Psychologie expérimentale* (laboratory of experimental psychology/EHESS) by Edouard Toulouse, who founded it in 1900. He had been named director of the *Laboratoire de Psychologie Physiologique* at the Sorbonne in 1912, to succeed Alfred Binet who had suddenly died. The same year he became editor of *L'année psychologique*, a position he held for the rest of his life. In 1923 he was named to a newly created *chaire de physiologie des sensations* at the Collège de France, the most prestigious French academic institution.

Yet, surprisingly, when he was in charge [13] of forming the French Committee, Auguste Desclos did not resort to Piéron or another specialist of the examination techniques. Was he really unaware of the docimological researches? Did he believe that there were no specialists of the kind in France? He claimed at the opening session that 'never at any time in France [had] examinations been studied scientifically' (Monroe, 1931, p. 12), and at the closing session he said, 'the [French] processes of examination ... has never been studied in a systematic and scientific way' (Monroe, 1931, p. 254). Did it mean that he truly knew nothing about the researches led by Piéron and Laugier? It is hardly believable, for these were already prominent professors or researchers, and one member of the Committee, Paul Barrier, was a vice-president on the board of INOP (Piéron, 1953, p. 10). Rather, it is likely that Desclos and Bouglé had some suspicion, if not aversion [14], concerning works that they probably saw, at first, as the sign of a technical and utilitarian conception of education. Desclos presumably did not resort to them because he saw this alleged utilitarian conception as a marginal one, unsuited to give a correct picture of the unity of French education along the paradigm of general culture.

This raises some queries about the leadership in the French Committee. Why had Desclos been chosen to guide the formation of the French delegation and to chair it? A report [15] written by Monroe suggests that Desclos had been initially contacted by the Teachers College to facilitate the planned inquiry [16], not to chair it. The expected chairman was M. Belletête [17], the president of an international secondary teachers' union. Monroe reported that he met Belletête, who told him that 'several committees and members of his [union] [were] already engaged in studies on examinations'. [18] We don't know why Belletête had not formed then chaired the Committee and why Desclos had been chosen to replace him.[19] Monroe reported that Belletête 'could readily organise a committee of prominent schoolmen out of his organisation to sponsor such an investigation and secure the necessary expert help'. Had this idea become a reality, the face and fate of the French Committee would probably have been completely different.

Did Desclos realise during the Eastbourne conference that it was just his own traditional conception of education and examination that was marginal and inappropriate in regard to what Paul Monroe and the Carnegie funds had expected to support? Did he understand that he needed some experts to implement the tests that had 'to be applied right and left'? (Monroe, 1931, p. 255). Or did Paul Barrier and Charles Maurain put some pressure on him, after the conference, to reshape the Committee in order to give room to Piéron and Laugier's experimental approach, which was seemingly much in line with the concerns of the Carnegie project leaders?

However that might be, Maurain soon left the Committee and Laugier [20] came in. Piéron wrote early in 1932 that 'M. Maurain handed over to Henri Laugier' (Piéron, 1932b, p. 65) and he added in 1963 that 'Maurain asked to be replaced by Laugier' (Piéron, 1963, p. 16). Later, Hippolyte Luc, director of technical education at the Ministry of Public Instruction, who was to chair [21] the board of the INOP, came in and joined Laugier within the Committee, together with Georges Gastinel, a chief schools inspector and a former secondary school teacher in literature, who was also Célestin Bouglé's brother-in-law (Piéron, 1932a, p. 238). The Committee was definitely installed in January 1932, without Victor Cope, who had died just before. The official members were Auguste Desclos, Célestin Bouglé, Paul Barrier (the three of them had attended the Eastbourne conference), Henri Laugier, Hippolyte Luc and Georges Gastinel (who joined them afterwards) (Commission Française, 1936b, p. 6). Thus there were three members who promoted traditional examinations against modern tests (Desclos, Bouglé, Gastinel) and three members who had some experimental knowledge about testing processes, or at least, who had some inclination towards a modern conception of examination (Laugier, Luc, Barrier).

IV. The Committee at Work: unexpected results

Laugier's views quickly triggered deep changes in the directions of research. 'Laugier played a leading part in turning [the work of the French Committee] towards a rigorous and scientific experimental inquiry' (Piéron, 1963, p. 17).

> The work initially planned [by the Committee] was very ambitious, including some documentation, one sociological study (about the impact of examinations on society ...) and, at last, some technical – docimological – researches that aimed (1) to make a survey of public opinion about the common conception on aims and methods of examination, (2) to carry out experimental and comparative studies on examination in order to know whether the facts fit the common conception and whether the technique of

> tests is finalized, and (3) to work out whether it is desirable and possible to modify the current system. (Piéron, 1963, p. 18)[22]

With regard to documentation, the Committee edited and published a comprehensive description, including text and diagrams, of the complicated and multilayered French education system: *l'Atlas de l'enseignement en France* (Commission Française, 1933).

As regards the sociological concerns, the Committee released a collection of data provided by the Education Authority of Paris. The collection, prefaced by Bouglé, was made up of arrays and graphs displaying ratios of successful candidates to the *baccalauréat* regarding their socio-economic background (Commission Française, 1936a).

Concerning the survey, two questionnaires were elaborated. One of them, about the *Certificat d'études*, had come to nothing. Paul Barrier, who was charged to write a report on it, claimed in 1934 that the public consultation 'had already provided [the Committee] with precious hints' (Barrier, 1934, p. 44). Alas, no such written report was ever released, except the transcript of the general comments that Barrier made at Folkestone.[23]

The other one was about the *baccalauréat*. It was sent to no less than 3000 people, all of whom were teachers, presidents of educational circles or members of the teaching staff. The analysis of the (few [24]) answers had been carried out by Gastinel. The result of the survey was published in the first part of *La correction des épreuves écrites dans les examens* (Commission Française, 1936b), the key publication of the Committee. However, no striking ideas had arisen from it, for it was based on answers that were mainly conventional. Further, these answers expressed concerns that were quite off the point for the defence of this venerable exam. '[The public] had no doubt as to the impeccability of the findings of the examiners, no doubt that the examiners could be trusted to continue their work to the satisfaction of all concerned', Desclos commented (Monroe, 1936, p. 134).

Last but not least, Henri Laugier together with his collaborator Dagmar Weinberg carried out a statistical study on marking *baccalauréat* papers (Laugier & Weinberg, 1936). They intended to prove that the traditional examination process was far from being as reliable as it was commonly assumed. This study, which was published in the second part of *La correction des épreuves écrites dans les examens*, was the natural sequel to Laugier & Weinberg's previous researches about the subjectivity of examiners (Laugier & Weinberg, 1927). Before going into details to interpret their results, which were the very substantial part of the Inquiry, we need to know some basics about the *baccalauréat* examination.

According to Desclos, the *baccalauréat* was the most typical French examination (Monroe, 1936, p. 132). It was an examination set by the universities for those who had completed secondary school education.[25] It was then formed of two parts that were taken at a one-year interval, at the ages of 16 and 17, roughly. The first part was divided into three sections. The first, called A, was the classical section, including Latin and Greek subjects. The second was called A', with Latin and one modern language, but no Greek. The third was called B. It was the 'modern section', with two modern languages, and neither Latin nor Greek. French, mathematics, sciences, history and geography were common to the three sections. The second part of the *baccalauréat* had two sections. One was called 'Philosophy', with a major subject: philosophy and minor subjects: mathematics, science, history, geography and modern languages. The second section was called 'Mathematics' with mathematics and science predominating, and philosophy, history, geography and modern languages as subsidiary subjects (Commission Française, 1933, pp. 66-72).

The Committee selected one hundred scripts among six of the different subjects of the *baccalauréat* taken in Paris, in July 1930. These six sets of one hundred scripts were submitted to five different examiners, five for each subject, chosen from the panel of examiners. The subjects chosen by the Committee were (1) the French essay, the Latin translation, the English test and the mathematics test from section A', (2) the physics tests from the 'Mathematics' section, and (3) the mathematics test and the philosophical essay from the 'Philosophy' section. The examiners were asked to mark the papers exactly as they would have done in the genuine examination. They were requested, moreover, to send in a report explaining the method applied in marking the papers, the quality and defects they had looked for, the relative importance of the different qualities and defects, and what proportion of the total mark they allotted to the several qualities they had found.

One of the examiners in his report said, 'the scripts that are difficult to mark are those that are neither good nor bad; it is with those scripts that you can find divergences between different examiners that may go as far as reaching 2 marks out of 20'. This is a very fair sample of the opinion of the examiners, and also of the public, and, presumably, of Desclos and Bouglé as well, on the expected reliability of this examination.

However, the statistical elaboration of the numerical data made by Laugier and Weinberg provided results that were astoundingly different from what the Committee had expected (Laugier & Weinberg, 1936):

1. The range of the marks given to the same script by the various examiners reached 12 marks out of 20 in the Latin translation [26], 13 marks in the French essay, 9 marks in English, 9 marks in Mathematics, 12 marks in Philosophy and 8 marks in Physics.
2. The 'standard deviation' varied from 1.88 marks out of 20 in Physics, to 3.36 marks out of 20 in Philosophy.
3. The proportion of scripts whose mark reached or exceeded the 'arithmetic mean' of the marks of some examiners, and did not reach the 'arithmetic mean' of the marks of the others, formed 50 per cent of the scripts in the Latin translation, 70 per cent in French composition, 47 per cent in English, 36 per cent in Mathematics, 81 per cent in Philosophy and 50 per cent in Physics.

4. The various examiners show unequal standards of strictness (differences between 'mean marks') and use scales of unequal scope (differences between standard deviations); these two statistical indicators varied from one to two from one examiner to another in the case of the examiners at the extreme poles.
5. The coefficient of correlation between the marks given by the various examiners was as low as r = 0.112 in the worst case. The arithmetic mean of the coefficients of correlation between the examiners taken in pairs varied from r = 0.429 (Philosophy) to r = 0.888 (Mathematics). Consequently, in the most unfavourable case, the expectation (computed by means of the equation of regression) of the mark given by examiner B to a script S, according to the mark given to the same script S by examiner A, could reach 90 per cent of the error which would be committed if the marks of examiner B had been given at random.[27]

These conclusions sounded definitively devastating for Desclos, Bouglé and Gastinel's traditional conception of examination.[28] It seemed difficult to measure 'tact' and 'subtlety' according to such a quantitative tool as a scale of marking. This practice of marking appeared to be very unfair and put a veil of suspicion on the whole *baccalauréat* examination.

Considering the dramatic results of this experiment, we would have expected substantial changes in the conception of secondary school examination promoted by the 'traditional wing' of the Committee. Desclos and Bouglé could have remembered the numerous allusions made by Thorndike at Eastbourne in relation to similar studies (and similar conclusions) carried out in the USA many years before (Monroe, 1931, p. 23). Had this conceptual change happened, the Committee might have found an inner motivation to publicise these conclusions within the secondary school system and to support any political initiative to reform the whole set of examinations.

V. The Folkestone Conference: almost a confession

It is illuminating to follow the very moderate presentation that Desclos made of the dramatic research carried out by the French Committee.

Firstly, he explained that, after having faced at Eastbourne some important divergences of interpretation with the other delegations, the French Committee thought it indispensable to start by defining its terms: 'the members of our committee devoted their efforts to describing and defining our system of education and to showing how the ideals that it pursues are reflected in the examinations that it administers; and such is the consideration which explains the publication of our *Atlas de l'Enseignement en France*' (Monroe, 1936, p. 132). Secondly, he expressed his disappointment about the results of the questionnaire on the *baccalauréat*: 'among [the] few answers that we received the people who answered at once side-stepped the issue that was put to them, and started on the good old age long battle for the curriculum, dismissing in a few words the question of the technique of examination' (Monroe, 1936, p. 134). Thirdly, he gave a brief description of the *baccalauréat* examination.

The transcript of the presentation of these three items took up no more than three pages in the proceedings. These three pages should be compared to the eight pages of the rest of his presentation, entirely devoted to explaining and discussing what he called 'our experiment'. Of course, this was the experiment of Laugier and Weinberg, supplemented by the analysis of the criteria that the examiners said they had used in their marking. Even the discussion that followed his presentation dealt almost exclusively with the interpretation of this experiment. The unbalanced lengths of the two parts of his presentation could be seen as a sign of lucidity about what was really at stake in this series of conferences.

Alas, after Desclos confessed that when 'the result of the inquiry' would be published, 'there [would] be a certain consternation among the public' (Monroe, 1936, p. 136), he immediately tempered this impression:

> If we had been satisfied with these first brutal results of our inquiry, we should have been inclined to think, and everybody would have come to the conclusion, that our system of examination is just a matter of chance and should simply be scrapped. But when we came to look at it more closely, we did not think we could justifiably come to that conclusion. (Monroe, 1936, p. 136)

He did not acknowledge that, contrary to what he had said at Eastbourne [29], there were some good reasons to mistrust the *baccalauréat*. He even interpreted the general meaning of the discussion as a subtle denial of the general use of tests in favour of the old traditional examinations, hence in favour of his own views.[30] According to him, the key concept still is 'addition' or 'adjustment'. Desclos only wanted to implement some 'additional' processes to improve the quality of marking in the *baccalauréat* without thinking of any profound changes, and he enjoyed feeling a convergence between all delegations towards a mix of the two archetypical systems of examination: half test, half traditional examination.

Then Bouglé gave his personal experience as an examiner. Although he started by acknowledging that Laugier and Weinberg's experiment had shown 'the most discouraging results' (Monroe, 1936, p. 159), he desperately attempted to minimise its scope by pinpointing, for instance, that the examiners had been selected 'almost randomly', without taking into account their 'special qualifications' (Monroe, 1936, p. 160). Finally, he expressed the same scepticism about tests as he had already expressed at Eastbourne, making the same conclusion about subtlety, tact and tests as he had done four years earlier. Agreeing with Desclos, he suggested the same very poor, though relevant, ideas in order to improve this examination:

organising meetings of examiners to agree on common criteria of marking. No question arose from the audience about what Bouglé had said.

The rest of the French Committee's talks were devoted, first, to some technical explanations and discussion given by Laugier to answer the many questions that his analysis had brought up, and, second, to some general comments given by Barrier on the *Certificat d'études* and its projected improvements.

Desclos' hesitant presentation seemed at first to indicate his embarrassment about presenting a study that proved he had been wrong at Eastbourne. However, he did not explicitly pinpoint his earlier contradiction. He let the audience grasp it.[31]

At the end, there was no doubt concerning Desclos and Bouglé's will to minimise the work of Laugier and, maybe, to keep some leadership on the work of the Committee, at least in front of the other delegations. The problem was that, except for the brilliant, but quite unscientific and redundant, comments of Bouglé and the – still – in-progress report of Barrier, it seemed that no further scientific studies were going to be carried out, except for the promising developments of Laugier and Weinberg's analysis towards psychometrics. At the closing session, Desclos was quite vague about the future work of the Committee. At that moment, on account of the reactions of the audience, he had no doubt that Laugier and Weinberg's statistical work was to remain the key work of the Carnegie French Committee, but he did not mention it. He only delivered some conclusive and general considerations on examinations.

His behaviour seems surprising. It may be understood if we make the hypothesis that it was power, not controversial conceptions of education, which was at stake: the power to examine, namely the power to decide which criteria are relevant to assess pupils. Besides some general considerations on tact and test, it was the power to assess such or such knowledge that was seemingly at stake in Desclos and Bouglé's resistance towards any profound criticism of the secondary school traditional examination (Foucault, 1999, 2003). The same resistance would later appear in secondary education when some experts on docimology suggested introducing psychometric tests in traditional examinations. 'Who should conduct the examination?' Barrier asked. It was indeed the key question, although the actors of this story were obviously not fully aware of the underlying implications of this question.

VI. Wartime and the Committee: no legacy, except some 'unsettling' ideas

At Dinard in 1938, the threatening war already darkened the discussions and the near future of the international collaboration that had started seven years before. The French Committee was still chaired by Desclos, although he obviously had not been able to keep his French colleagues gathered around a common work since Folkestone.

Neither Laugier nor Luc attended the Conference, for they were in charge of strategic issues related to the growing international tensions with Germany.[32] It was Dagmar Weinberg who went to Dinard to present the only real work that the Committee claimed to have achieved since the Folkestone conference: *Recherches sur la Solidarité et l'indépendance des aptitudes intellectuelles* (Laugier & Weinberg, 1938). This research was to be published a few days later (Monroe, 1939, p. 22). It was a natural extension of Laugier and Weinberg's previous work about the *baccalauréat*.

Besides Weinberg, Gastinel, who was not at Folkestone, delivered some general thoughts inspired by his analysis of the reports of the examiners who marked (so divergently) the scripts of the Latin version. Bouglé left at mid-conference, after he had lectured (once again) in great detail on the examination entrance of the *École Normale Supérieure* and on the French spirit. Except for some additional considerations presented by Barrier on the reforms that were currently being implemented in the French school system, the French Committee presented no other specific items.

The fate of the Committee already rested on the shoulders of Dagmar Weinberg. Piéron, who hosted Weinberg's research in his INOP, wrote later that '[at that time ...] the French committee tried to persist, thanks to the participation of Dagmar Weinberg. But soon she had to go and live underground' with her old mother (Piéron, 1963, p. 26). She died just after the War at the age of 49 (Piéron & Weismann-Netter, 1946; Piéron, 1947). She was the only person who would have been able to revive the French Committee after the War, and help its publications to find an echo among teachers, and possibly to fuel further investigations. Laugier was appointed Assistant General Secretary of the New York-based United Nations Organisation in 1946 [33] and Desclos, profoundly affected by the Nazi barbarity, came out of war in desperation as regards the future of civilisation (Aury, 1999; David, 2006), not to mention the others, who had either died [34] or had long retired.

'The results of the Carnegie Inquiry had not the desirable release, for they seemed to be unsettling' (Piéron, 1963, p. 26). In 1937, the Minister of Education, Jean Zay, addressed the chief education officials about the *baccalauréat* examination. He asked them to organise meetings for the examiners to debate on the criteria of the examination (Piéron, 1963, p. 27). From an institutional point of view, this decree and its application were probably the most significant direct impact of the Carnegie conferences on the *baccalauréat*, and, more generally, on the French educational system.

Notes

[1] Auguste Desclos was born in 1876 in London, where he spent his childhood. His parents were French. They emigrated from Brittany to England after the war of 1870. When he was 15, he left England for France, where in 1906 he passed the highly competitive examination, the *agrégation*. He was an English

teacher in secondary school up to the First World War. Then he was appointed deputy director of the *Office National des universités et écoles françaises*. He travelled a lot, especially in English-speaking countries.

[2] 'When [*the enseignement technique*] was started, there was that tendency to put the boys into workshops and let them work there, doing nothing but what an ordinary workman carrying on a trade would do. Well, that first tendency has been definitely defeated.' Now, 'you find this conception of general culture even in [the] technical education, where we are teaching a boy to be, perhaps ... a locksmith. We are not concerned with trying to make of him, at the age of fourteen of fifteen ... a perfect locksmith, but we want to interest him in metals ... in the great ways in which you can work them. We are quite sure that with that interest, he will quickly acquire the necessary practical knowledge' (Monroe, 1931, p. 10).

[3] 'The system of education and examination [which is] the most characteristically French' (ibid., p. 11)

[4] This scheduled reform [of the *école unique*] had already been under discussion within the French community, explained Desclos. A discussion rightly centred 'on the best ways of readjusting this somewhat disconnected and disadjusted system, but, the principles themselves have not been put in question' (ibid.)

[5] Since 'our examinations are exactly adapted to our three parallels types of education and vary as those types vary ... like them they constitute three different systems and will have to be recast like the rest' (ibid., p. 12)

[6] Not surprisingly, as soon as secondary – or higher – school final examinations are under discussion, Desclos' prospective ideas about the Inquiry narrow to a few items, such as ergonomic-related issues, that could have been considered as marginal with respect to what was at stake. Further, his voiced concern for sociological studies, which might have led him to suggest the making of a sociological analysis of these examinations in themselves, was eventually diluted in his reflections on the general impact of exams on careers and in his criticisms on how bad the guidance of courses was, which was carried out at the early stages of the education system (Monroe, 1931, pp. 12-13).

[7] Dean of the Faculty of Sciences of the University of Paris.

[8] He went back to the description of the three side-by-side school systems. He explained that there are some good bridges from the 'higher primary system' to the university without passing through the secondary school. For example, the *agrégation*, the competitive examination that selects those who were to teach in secondary schools, was then open to any student who got a three-year graduation, including those who came from the 'higher primary school'. Thus, someone who had not been a pupil in the secondary school could nonetheless teach within it. Further, 'those teachers form excellent additions', for 'they have a genuine faith in culture and in the desire for knowledge' (Monroe, 1931, p. 207).

[9] Far from minimising the range of application of tests, he claimed to know experts in psychological or physiological tests who would be able to carry out

'an inquiry of this kind' (ibid., p. 85). He also mentions vocational guidance as an issue that should be of growing interest for those who were to carry out this Inquiry (ibid., p. 76).

[10] He did not really contest the prominence of General Culture as a desirable end, either (ibid., p. 74), even if almost all of his words intended to mean that this end couldn't govern alone the aim, methodology and process of the inquiry.

[11] The National Institute of Vocational Guidance, or INOP, was set up in 1928, by Henri Piéron, Édouard Toulouse and Henri Laugier. At that time, the INOP was hosted at the Musée Pédagogique, rue Gay-Lussac, in Paris. Cf. Piéron, 1953, p. 14. The French Committee was initially hosted there, too (Piéron, 1932a, p. 242).

[12] Martin, 2002, n. 1, p. 188.

[13] Maurain 'was particularly happy that Desclos invited him to join the French Committee' (Monroe, 1931, p. 204).

[14] Piéron wrote that there had been initially a 'curious and regrettable attempt to exclude any technical competence from the Committee' (1932b, p. 65), and later in the same year he claimed that there were 'some resistances to introduce [within the Committee] the psychotechnical point of view, some resistances we are accustomed to find with some literary sociologists who seem to be afraid of the rise of the experimental mind' (Piéron, 1932a, p. 238).

[15] I express my thanks to Professor Martin Lawn who communicated this instructive report to me.

[16] 'I have since conferred with M. Desclos representing the ministry of education with foreign contacts. He agrees on the importance of the question ... and, if undertaken, that the government and his office would be sympathetic and would cooperate. That is quite essential as the investigation would involve extensive use of the schools and of records' (Paul Monroe, undated typewritten document).

[17] 'In France the key man is Monsieur Belletête ... He could readily organize a committee of prominent schoolmen out of his organization to sponsor such an investigation and secure the necessary expert help' (Paul Monroe, ibid.)

[18] Ibid.

[19] The presence of Victor Cope at Eastbourne was perhaps related to these preliminary contacts made by Monroe.

[20] Henri Laugier was a professor at the *Conservatoire National des Arts et Métiers*.

[21] In 1933. Cf. Piéron, 1953.

[22] See also, Commission Française, 1936b, pp. 6-7.

[23] Desclos mentioned incidentally this projected work, wishing to publish 'the large amount of data that had been collected' (Monroe, 1931, p. 281).

[24] 'I do not think we got more than two hundred in all' (Monroe, 1936, p. 134).

[25] It occupies in the scale of French education a middle ground between the elementary school certificates on the one hand, and the great competitive examinations of higher university level on the other. It has two goals: first, it is

an assessment of the courses studied in secondary education and, second, it has a predictive character in that it qualifies for admission to higher studies.

[26] The scale of marking in these tests is from 0 to 20.

[27] Some comments on these five items for non-specialists (1) show how widely different the marks given to the same script are. The widest difference between two examiners reaches 12 marks out of 20 in Latin translation; (2) after the widest difference, the standard deviation gives the 'average difference'; (3) 70 per cent of scripts in French composition would have got a pass mark or higher from some examiners and would have got a mark below the pass mark from others, so, it means that 70 per cent of the pupils would have either failed or passed the French composition, depending on which examiner had marked their scripts; (4) some examiners did not use the whole scale of marking (0-20) nor did they put their 'average mark' around the middle of the scale; (5) although this fifth item may sound hermetic, it is undoubtedly one of the most interesting pieces of information to be extracted from this experiment: while the 'mean mark' and the 'standard deviation' give indication on the scale of marking really used by each examiner, they say nothing about the variation in the way the scripts are classified according to their marks by one examiner or another. The coefficient of correlation measures the range of this variation. If r is equal to zero, it means that the variation is similar to what it would be between one examiner and a 'random examiner' (someone who had marked scripts at random). The two examiners of philosophy who got a of coefficient r = 0.112 were not very far from this nightmarish case.

[28] As noticed by many members of other committees who had attended the Folkestone conference. See, for example, Judd, 1935.

[29] 'We have concentrated on that system of education and examination [namely the *enseignement secondaire*], the experience of ages, and we think that ... we have reached the best of what we have in France' (Monroe, 1931, p. 11).

[30] 'We are struck by a distinct change in the general point of view since the Eastbourne Conference. The traditional type of examination, the essay type, at Eastbourne seemed to be entirely discredited. This time it seems as if a respite had been given it, and that the question is now whether, by adding to it some improvements, it cannot continue to render good service in the field of education; and this time we are very happy to see and feel that the point of view of the French committee is no longer so very different from that of the other delegations' (Monroe, 1936, p. 132).

[31] The audience grasped it indeed. Some participants even understood this semi-confession as a radical change in the attitude of the French delegation, but it was not: 'Another international Conference on Examinations was held at the Hotel Metropole, Folkestone in June 1935. A salient feature of the Conference was the changed attitude of the French Committee. At the previous Conference they had seemed pretty well satisfied with their national system of education ... At the 1935 Conference their confidence in the exactness of examinations had vanished. They owned up that it had been misplaced. A preliminary inquiry which they had made elicited from some of the examiners an admission that divergences in the marks of examiners might go so far as to reach two marks out of twenty. When put to the test it was

found that they reached thirteen marks out of twenty. Indeed, one of the investigators came to the conclusion that divergence in the opinion of the examiners was normal and that coincidence was an accident. All this was disclosed by M. Desclos with an engaging candour that disarmed all criticism' (Ballard, 1937, pp. 208-209).

[32] Laugier had been appointed Chief Assistant of the French Minister of Foreign affairs two years before.

[33] Laugier spent the War in Canada, then in Algeria.

[34] Hyppolite Luc died in 1946.

References

Aury, D. (1999) *Vocation: clandestine*. Paris: Gallimard.

Ballard, P. (1937) *Things I Cannot Forget*. London: University of London Press.

Barrier, P. (1934) Le certificat d'études dans l'école unique, *Bulletin de la société Alfred Binet*, 31-45.

Commission Française pour l'enquête Carnegie sur les examens et concours en France (Ed.) (1933) *Atlas de l'enseignement en France*. Paris.

Commission Française pour l'enquête Carnegie sur les examens et concours en France (Ed.) (1936a) *Enquêtes sur le baccalauréat: recherches statistiques sur les origines scolaires et sociales des candidats au baccalauréat dand l'académie de Paris*. Paris: Hachette.

Commission Française pour l'enquête Carnegie sur les examens et concours en France (Ed.) (1936b) *La correction des épreuves écrites dans les examens: enquête expérimentale sur le baccalauréat*. Paris: La Maison du Livre.

David, A. (2006) *Dominique Aury: la vie secrète de l'auteur d'Histoire d'O*. Paris: Éditions Léo Scheer.

Desclos, A. (1935) The French Conception of Education, *The Modern Language Journal*, 19(4), 264-265.

Foucault, M. (1999) *Les anormaux, Cours au Collège de France, 1974-1975*. Paris: Gallimard.

Foucault, M. (2003) *Le pouvoir psychiatrique, cours au Collège de France, 1973-1974*. Paris: Gallimard.

Hugot, P. (2005) *La gratuité dans l'enseignement secondaire*. Paris: L'Harmattan.

Judd, C.H. (1935) The Third Conference of the International Inquiry on School and University Examinations, *The School Review*, 43(9), 653-663.

Laugier, H. & Weinberg, D. (1927) I. Le Facteur subjectif dans les notes d'examen, *L'année psychologique*, 28(1), 236-244.

Laugier, H. & Weinberg, D. (1936) Élaboration statistique des données numériques de l'enquête sur la correction des épreuves du baccalauréat, in Commission Française pour l'enquête Carnegie sur les examens et concours en France (Ed.) *La correction des épreuves écrites dans les examens: enquête expérimentale sur le baccalauréat*, 68-186. Paris: La Maison du Livre.

Laugier, H. & Weinberg, D. (1938) *Recherches sur la solidarité et l'indépendance des aptitudes intellectuelles: d'après les notes des examens écrits du baccalauréat*. Paris: Chantenay.

Martin, J. (2002) Aux origines de la 'science des examens' (1920-1940), *Histoire de l'Éducation*, 94, 177-199.

Monroe, P. (Ed.) (1931) *Conference on Examinations*, Eastbourne (England). New York: Teachers College, Columbia University.

Monroe, P. (Ed.) (1936) *Conference on Examinations under the Auspices of The Carnegie Corporation, The Carnegie Foundation, The International Institute of Teachers College, Columbia University, at the Hotel Metropole, Folkestone, England, June 8-10, 1935*. New York: Teachers College, Columbia University.

Monroe, P. (Ed.) (1939) *Conference on Examinations under the Auspices of the Carnegie Corporation*, Dinard (France). New York: Teachers College, Columbia University.

Piéron, H. (1932a) Une enquête sur le Certificat d'études, *BINOP*, 4(9), 237-242.

Piéron, H. (1932b) Un effort de Rationalisation des Examens, *BINOP*, 4(3), 65-66.

Piéron, H. (1947) D. Weinberg, *BINOP*, 3(2), 32.

Piéron, H. (1953) La place de l'Institut dans l'histoire de l'orientation professionnelle, *BINETOP*, 7-28.

Piéron, H. (1963) *Examens et docimologie*. Paris: Presses universitaires de France.

Piéron, H. & Weismann-Netter, D.R. (1946) Dagmar Weinberg (1897-1946), *Biotypologie*, 8, 117-119.

Piéron, H., Piéron, M.H. & Laugier, H. (1935) Étude critique de la valeur sélective du certificat d'études et comparaison de cet examen avec une épreuve par tests, *Pour l'ère nouvelle*, 105, 47-51.

Piéron, M.H. (1922) 'Étude psychotechnique de quelques tests d'aptitude, *L'année psychologique*, 23(1), 144-175.

Naïve, Expert and Willing Partners: the Scottish Council for Research in Education in the International Examinations Inquiry

MARTIN LAWN, IAN DEARY & DAVID BARTHOLOMEW

SUMMARY The Scottish presence in the International Examinations Inquiry (IEI) is substantial and fully involved. The IEI creates a strong international, financial and scientific opportunity for the embryo Scottish research network, the Scottish Council for Research in Education (SCRE). The power of the network is harnessed to a series of quantitative studies including wide school population testing. Carnegie recognised and strengthened the independent thinking of the Scottish network and SCRE formed itself within an American school of thought on educational research.

How did Scotland, a small country in the United Kingdom and often dominated by its southern neighbour, England, come to enter the International Examinations Inquiry (IEI) from its inception in the early 1930s?[1] Scottish educators had begun to look toward Teachers College, Columbia University, New York in the immediate post-war period, from 1918, as they turned away from their closer links with German universities where they had trained or visited earlier in the century. They recognised the power of the institution across the Atlantic and were ready for closer links with its researchers and their texts. Scottish education in the post First World War period was familiar to W.H. Kilpatrick and to Paul Monroe, both of Teachers College, and already beginning to be influential on education policy and practice. Kilpatrick had toured Scotland and its education sites in 1919, the year after the publication of his key book, *The Project Method*, and Monroe was made an Honorary Fellow of the Educational Institute of Scotland (EIS) (the main teacher association) in 1920. So a Scottish colleague like W.B. Inglis, who had been a student of Kilpatrick's in New York, and then worked with Philip Vernon, the Glasgow psychologist, and

Boyd, the leading Glaswegian educationalist of the time, and then later a deputy to Godfrey Thomson in Edinburgh, would become part of this virtuous circle of cross-Atlantic ideas and contacts. These kinds of links were to become important when knowing who to contact became an important element in the early stages in the IEI, when the conversations were taking place between Monroe, Thorndike and Keppel (at the Carnegie Corporation) in New York in the late 1920s. Just as important were the visits of Scottish academics to Teachers College. In 1924-25, Godfrey Thomson went from Armstrong College, Newcastle for a year's sabbatical, at Edward Thorndike's invitation, to research and teach classes and was finally offered a post there. Instead he returned back home and joined the University of Edinburgh the following year. Boyd, an enthusiast for modern education and a lecturer at Glasgow University, taught at Teachers College in 1930-31.

At the same time, links with the growing New Education Fellowship (NEF) began to link Scottish researchers and educationalists with a wider European and American community (certainly, Boyd and Rawson make this claim in their book [1965, pp. 73-74]). The growth of the NEF European meetings meant that a constant intercourse and exchange was happening in the 1920s and 1930s about new education practices:

> Throughout this period, the NEF provided members of the academy with an audience and an extensive international network. In turn, this enabled those of them with the requisite habitus to transcend their national boundaries and participate in the newly emerging international field of education and thereby gain social and cultural capital. (Brehony, 2004, p. 350)

Within Scotland there was a strong tradition of interest in the fairness of secondary school place allocation and with the needs of the brightest children. Unlike in England, this concern was less likely to be expressed as a question of private or elite grammar school provision, nor to be confused with social class and privilege. This context of Scottish education was important, as it drove the researchers on into new areas of work; within the NEF on examination inquiries and progressive pedagogies, and towards Columbia, on new methods of examining. Within Scottish borders, key members of the NEF and of the IEI worked on leading edge research and practices, such as Boyd and Drever's development of child guidance centres, Thomson's focus on intelligence testing, and McClelland's deep quantitative studies of a city and its education allocation. Scotland is a small country but it had advantages and interests which enabled a strong research network to develop easily within it, and its members to merge their individual experiences internationally with local networks and projects.

Scottish Contexts

Scottish involvement in the IEI actually began with a series of academic links (described above) but perhaps more importantly with a strong policy interest, shared by the recently appointed Directors of Education (although few in number) and the teachers in the EIS. Two issues came together after the First World War, the demand for education and the problem of examination (and so allocation in the education system). The role of the teaching profession, a community engaging with the purposes and practices of the education system in a new way, and supportive of inquiry into education, was central to this renewed interest in education.

In 1920, in Scotland, and unlike in England, there was a high proportion of graduate teachers, a figure which continued to rise in the next decades [2], and most of these teachers were in their national teachers' organisation, the Educational Institute of Scotland. The EIS represented them, but not in a narrow way; it began this post-war period with a strong interest in the nature and reform of education, and addresses to the EIS annual conference engaged with the idea of research as the basis for education reform. A Director of Education, Hepburn [3], pleaded for 'skilled, elaborate, scientific, statistical investigations' (Wake, 1984, p. 35) in the examination of pupils trying to qualify for limited places in secondary education. So, in 1919, the EIS formed its own research committee, a mixture of teachers and co-opted experts, chaired by William Boyd, its main motivator and support. Boyd was a member of the Glasgow University Department of Education, and soon to be President of the EIS. In its first statement of intent, Boyd's report of the committee proceedings lays out the particular nature of the project. It could manage without funding because of the support it could call upon:

> But provided the inevitable restriction of its activities by the lack of special funds is recognized, and that there is no illusion about its limitation, the Committee is willing to do all that can be done to make research work a vital concern of the Institute. The one condition of success is that it should be able to count on the cooperation of the whole profession. Realising this, the first question to which it has addressed itself has been – what can be done to get teachers all over the country interested in educational experiment, and willing to give what help they can? (Boyd, 1919, p. 772)

This call to teachers included several features. Research work meant educational experiment, defined as empirical investigation. It obligated their professional association, the EIS, to support research activity; for example, the creation of a research library, new research fellowships and regular reports in its journal about teachers' research. It begins the organisation of a community of teacher-researchers in Scotland, classed as Educational Scientists.[4] The Committee intended to advise on best procedures, supply information about work in scientific journals, and make comparative country reviews. By 1925, they were offering a prize to teaching college students for an essay of 5000 words on 'some aspect of school work involving personal observation or/and experiment'.[5]

Within two weeks, the *Scottish Education Journal* carried an article on the Qualifying Examination (QE), the final school examination of the primary stage to decide those pupils able to attend secondary education. The QE was an explosive subject, apparently, involving many kinds of issues: examination drills, inspector power (as the final arbiter of marks and allocations) and a fair type of examination. The argument, briefly, was that

> So long as the number of pupils allowed to go onto the enjoyment of higher education is restricted, there must be some method of separating out the favoured minority for whom there is accommodation in our secondary schools. That means that there must be an individual examination in some shape or form.[6]

Acknowledging that an 'intelligent membership of a democratic community' should involve all children in secondary education eventually, this argument was about fairness in selection. Discussing the problems of examination, and variations in judgements and marking, the writer suggests that 'American experience' should be used. There:

> educational experts have been experimenting with a view to determining fixed standards of attainment on the various subjects. Suitable tests are worked out, say, in Arithmetic. These tests are given to a large number of pupils, and on the basis of the results, the accuracy and speed to be expected ... can be established in definite figures.[7]

Within four months, the EIS Research Committee had invited interested teachers, of QE classes, wishing to use arithmetic tests to apply for them, and about 6000 were sent out. At the same time, a scheme to devise marking data using pupil compositions sent in by teachers (and about 3500 had been sent in) was created.[8] Boyd invited teachers, in the EIS journal, to communicate with the Committee if they were doing 'experimental work – however simple or unsystematic' and promised that the journal would publish records of research from Scotland and other countries, and the Committee would try to begin 'classes in Educational Sciences' (and a summer school).[9]. In the following year, 6000 arithmetic tests were sent out to the teachers who wanted to use them for their own assessment of the QE (for entry to secondary school). At the same time, 2500 essays were received to begin work on examining procedures. Boyd argued about the value of educational research, teacher experiments and their value in realising professional power. In the early 1920s, the *Scottish Educational Journal* (the EIS journal) had regular essays and comments about educational research, particularly on the comparison of examinations and testing, trying to face the question, 'Will those who have felt the difficulty of getting reliable marks let us know how the problem has presented itself to them, and what they themselves try to do to ensure satisfactory results?'[10]

In a paper written in 1920 for the *Scottish Education Journal*, Boyd argued at length the case for an experimental research which should yield results, and eliminate wasted pupil and teacher time, and public money. As soon as the aims of the research, determined by public policy and opinion, could be decided, then the methods, means and organisation of it could be managed amenably. Individual differences, specific capacities, (in effect) baseline assessment, and deviancy (misfits) could be researched by means of a logical process of objective measurement, taking due care with questions of sampling, of calibration, of norms and the final determination of the units of measurement. Exact stages of mental development in the individual, numbers to be classified as mentally deficient and the discovery of gifted children were all possible. Although Boyd was knowledgeable about American work, he felt that Scotland should take the lead in this area (and not merely follow others). In an address to the National Union of Teachers in England in 1921, his contention was that in America mental tests were used as the 'devices of supervisors, the men above, who were telling the teacher what to do and how to do it'.[11] So, Boyd walked a line between developing a research culture in education, which, while using American knowledge, used it within national cultures. Mental testing could help in the goal of achieving an 'educated democracy', which in the Scottish context meant differentiation by merit. Once the tools, established scales of measurement allowing comparison, were in place, then teachers could begin to experiment with different forms of action or different distributions of time in their work.

Teachers, collectively, were the key for Boyd. It is this call to teachers which was to shape the form of Scottish research. Boyd asks for teachers to contribute, to provide services or materials, and even work for the Research Committee, and in this way, 'make a substantial contribution to the sum of assured knowledge about education'.[12] From the first, and quite reasonably given the level of education among teachers, the educational researcher was not seen as a funded worker or as a university employee but as a collective worker, a networker, and as a part of an integrated scheme. An apposite metaphor, used by Boyd, was that the relation between the Research Committee and the teachers could be:

> compared to the work of the units of the army in the front line, without which no victories could be won. But just as in the case of the army, so also here we need a headquarters for staff work and especially organization.[13]

Ideally, experiment needed controlled conditions and customarily this meant laboratories. Yet Boyd argued that the normal conditions needed for experiment were only to be found in the classroom and that what was required was that the teacher became 'imbued with the necessary ideals of exact adherence to the conditions of the experiment' [14], then all would be well. The power and control of the teacher in their work was treated as an essential factor in the ability to do experiments, and possibly, a professional bias as detrimental to their ability to research. In effect, what Boyd was trying to achieve was a network of laboratories, all naturally occurring in classrooms across the country, with skilled teachers, able to use the new measurement tools, applying them to their practice but in a coordinated manner.[15] Yet there is a strong common interest, an eagerness to engage and experiment, and regular flows of information coming from the teachers, and in localities and conferences, shared amongst them.

In 1923, the *Scottish Education Journal* carried an announcement from the Research Committee about 'an ambitious programme of work' to be undertaken on examinations and tests [16], and inquiring into the use of intelligence tests in school work and on the level of reliability of examinations. Every branch was encouraged to explain their local QE conditions: who sets the papers, how are the examinations conducted and supervised, how are the papers marked and standardised, and what weight is given to the teachers' estimate of the pupil compared with exam results. In addition, individuals were asked how they managed the problems of examinations in their school work, for example, the problem of reliability of marking or how to get satisfactory results. What was required were 'the many fruitful ideas to be garnered out of the various experiences of Scottish teachers'.[17]

This system of experimentation in Scotland was connected by Boyd and others to the New Education Fellowship inquiry into examinations, the results of which were edited by Boyd and Wyatt Rawson, with a preface by Michael Sadler. By the time of the SCRE Report to the IEI, for the Dinard meeting in 1938, it recognised that 'there had been a considerable amount of experiment with different methods of carrying out this injunction'.[18]

Organising Nationally

The impetus in Scotland for experiment and inquiry in education, and its academic links with Columbia, and the NEF in Europe, turned into an agreement between the Directors of Education (in the local authorities) and the EIS to create a research council in Scotland, funded by their contributions. It was an ambitious idea produced on weak financial foundations: in its office, there was one part-time Director (Dr Robert Rusk), a secretarial assistant and a clerk. (Dr Rusk was a graduate of the University of Jena, Prussia, and was the SCRE Director from the start in 1928 until 1958.) In fact, SCRE was not an office or a hierarchical organisation. Its organisation combined the benefits of a small country with its poor finance; that is, it was able to use interest, enthusiasm, local knowledge and collegiality, and expertise in a wide network. Its engine was twofold, its expert enthusiasts like Boyd and Rusk, and its teacher volunteers; these gave the Council a 'phenomenal vitality' (Thomasson, 1978, p. 20). In 1930, it had no research workers or statisticians of its own but it drew upon a wide group consisting of

> a number of teachers, head teachers mostly, some directors of education, some university people, but very largely people from [the four] training colleges – in Jordanhill, Moray House, Aberdeen and Dundee. Although we tend to think of universities as the bases for educational research, the real strength of educational research in Scotland, in the early days, in the 30s, came from the training colleges. The Universities were involved ... but the main workers in it were the people in the training colleges. That is one of the main differences between Scotland and England, the colleges contained some quite outstanding research people. (Nisbet, 2003)

Godfrey Thomson provided the overall technical planning within the experimental and statistical paradigm, which was influenced by American innovations in mental testing. The SCRE network organisation allowed it to work more 'intensively and extensively' (Craigie, 1972, p. 7) than any one individual was capable of, ensured that a project became a national project, and could undertake long-term investigations:

> The Council helped the lone researcher by affording him expert guidance, supplying him with literature and test material, subsidizing his investigations and publishing his results [within their University of London series of Monographs. (10th Annual Report, reported in Craigie, 1972, p. 7)

SCRE was an early scientific knowledge network in education, linking together professional and lay expertise across the country in such a way that it acted as a single, consistent disciplined effect. This was a national but not a governmental initiative. The Scottish Office, the UK government office for Scotland in this period, did not enter into any formal relation with SCRE and nor was it represented on its Council.

> The Scottish Office [in the 1930s] took [no part] at all [in the Research Council meetings]. They thought that these researchers were trying to tell 'us' what to do, and wanted no part of it. (Nisbet, 2003)

Although SCRE did not engage in the sale of tests, it acted as the leading edge of the developing expertise about testing. From the outset, it had used Binet tests, revised for Scottish use. As early as 1931, it devised tests for types of ability to 'enable pupils to be directed into the appropriate secondary school course', and did so for English, modern language, mathematics, engineering, science and technical subjects (SCRE, 1948, p. 18). The school leaving age was to be raised and tests were seen as a useful way of managing this process of fitting the pupil to the curriculum and teaching. By 1936, the SCRE had been able, by extensive testing of ability and attainment, to promote 'the best combination' (Craigie, 1972, p. 15) of intelligence tests, examinations and teacher estimates to standardise the forecasting of the post-primary course best suited to the individual pupil.

Godfrey Thomson.

However, although SCRE was heavily involved in the new field of intelligence and ability, a key partner, Godfrey Thomson, a Professor of Education at Edinburgh and Principal of Moray House from 1925 to 1951, and a key writer on intelligence in the 1930s, actually produced the tests used and sold them profitably. These Moray House Tests were devised and sold by Thomson and his team at Edinburgh's Moray House Training College. The large profits from the tests were channelled back into further test development and research support.

The 1932 Scottish Mental Survey was a considerable achievement by the young research institute, a model of extensive fieldwork, a research partnership with teachers and an exemplar of policy-focused research work.

> The 1932 Mental Survey arose out of a proposal to hold an investigation into the incidence of mental deficiency in Scotland to match one in England on which a report has been submitted to the Board of Education and the Board of Control. It was early realized, however, that the amount of mental deficiency in the country could be assessed even approximately only if the distribution of intelligence was known for a whole age group. (Craigie, 1972, p. 17)

The proposal came from the Professor of Psychology at the University in Edinburgh, James Drever, and the test used was a version of the Moray House Test No. 12, produced by Godfrey Thomson. So, the scientific resources for this test were already contained in the university at Edinburgh but the SCRE offered a consolidating network of teachers and administrators and a flexibility of operation, which the University could not.

James Drever.

The contact with Columbia and Carnegie was described in an SCRE account as if it was selected from afar due to its international reputation. This seems unlikely at such an early stage of its development.

> The Council was at an early stage recognized abroad as a body of national and international standing, and in 1931 was invited by the International Institute of Teachers College, Columbia University, New York to undertake for Scotland investigations into various aspects of examinations for the International Examinations Inquiry. (SCRE, 1947, p. 10)

But it was the case that Thomson was invited to London, with J.C. Smith (the Chief Inspector of Schools, Scotland), to meet with Keppel 'to discuss the wisdom of starting a rather careful comparative study of examinations' (the letter suggesting also that a regular correspondence with Thomson took place about related matters) (Carnegie Corporation, 6 March 1931. FPK/G, Keppel memo).

Within a year of its creation, the Council received a letter from America:

> the first contribution to the new Council from philanthropic sources appears to have come from New York, in 1930, in the form of a solitary invitation from the Carnegie Corporation for SCRE to become one of the five European participants in an international study of examinations. (Watson, in SCRE, 1978, p. 14)

The importance of this invitation at first was that it helped to stabilise the finances [19] but it is clear that Carnegie was the third partner in SCRE during the 1930s, something that is not fully acknowledged in the national narrative around the ground-breaking institute. Indeed the IEI and its funding was used to develop a range of Scottish studies and it was essential to the 1932 Mental Survey (of every child in a single year group across Scotland) and the 1935-37 Survey. The 1947 report makes this clear: 'Without these generous subsidies [from Carnegie] the major investigations of the Council could not have been undertaken' (SCRE, 1947, p. 11).

Morris (1994) highlights this problem for SCRE, which is not represented in its histories, and which is overlaid by talk of its international standing (within two years of its foundation). Morris argues that in early 1932, 'the Council had reached a plateau. Finance was critical and the absence rate of members at committees was exceeding fifty per cent' (Morris, 1994, p. 86). And, luckily, on 14 January, they received a letter from professor Paul Monroe, the Director of the International Institute, Teachers College, Columbia, offering them $2500, paid through the Carnegie Corporation, for SCRE to join the IEI. Carnegie could not help them outright, like it was doing with Australia, because Scotland had its own Carnegie Trust, but Monroe was a trustee of the Carnegie Corporation and overcame this problem. Professors Thomson and Drever followed up the letter with Monroe: Drever is regarded in the official history as proposing the Mental Test Survey. Morris concludes by suggesting that 'the Council's acceptance saved it from possible liquidation' (Morris, 1994, p. 86). This can't have been easy; even though the secondary school entry exam (the Qualifying Examination) was causing problems throughout Scotland and the new problem of the secondary school examination was the subject of the IEI, it was the financial inducement that pushed them along (Morris, 1994, p. 87).

This institutional version of events does not use an informal history of network contacts, for example, by Thomson or Monroe, but another local version was offered by Rusk, a key member of the IEI and SCRE. The suggestion that there should be an inquiry into examinations had been made by Dr William Boyd to the New Education Fellowship. This had come to the notice of Professor Paul Monroe of Teachers College, Columbia University, who, on one of his visits to Europe, called on Tom Henderson, General Secretary of the EIS. Robert Rusk, who was in the building at the time, was called in, and an outline plan was devised. As the Carnegie Corporation could not by reason of its Charter subsidise an investigation in Europe,

Monroe arranged that the International Enquiry should be sponsored by Teachers College (Rusk, n.d., *Autobiography*).

Robert Rusk.

The general impression gained by SCRE's official histories or reports is a lack of curiosity about Carnegie and its desires. This may be because they felt they knew Carnegie, in the sense that the UK Carnegie Foundation was based in a small Scottish town. It was viewed as just philanthropic and that it recognised a body of international standing when it looked for one. Yet, in this wonderfully naïve view, there is little room for an analysis of Carnegie's motives and mission.

Most of the SCRE Council in 1928-29 became members of the IEI Scottish group, for example, W.A.F. Hepburn (representing the Directors of Education), Boyd, Glasgow and McClelland, St Andrews (representing the universities), Rusk, Jordanhill (the colleges) and Drever (British Psychological Society).

The following year new colleagues were added (Kennedy, Walker and Dawson), each of whom took part in the IEI work. In other words, there was no real distinction between SCRE and the IEI Scottish group in this period; they were almost homologous. The principle upon which SCRE was founded, and the Scottish IEI worked, especially in the Mental Survey, was clear from the beginning:

> results so far attained are highly satisfactory considering that the work has had to be carried out in the spare time of teachers, lecturers, directors etc at a time when their own commitments were exceptionally strenuous and serious. The outstanding feature displayed in the Council's efforts is the cooperation of all the

> interests participating, which even apart from the outcome of the work, must influence and increase the efficiency of Scottish education as a whole. (SCRE Annual Report 1929-30, p. 7)

William McClelland.

The new Council began work with a project on the problems of standards in the Qualifying Examination for post-primary or secondary education and the pupil failures in achieving the final secondary examination (SCRE Annual Report 1928-29, p. 10). So, from the outset, examinations and the use of tests were the core interests, reflecting a national policy problem and growing expertise in the new technology of testing. Indeed for the next few years, their enthusiasm for testing meant that inquiries into environment and mentality, a school mental survey, city/rural test experiments and school feeding and intelligence, were all taking place.

SCRE reported that its first works for the IEI were actually on the Prognostic Value of University Entrance Examinations and minor investigations on 'Time Devoted to Examinations' and 'Teachers' Estimates' before they began work on the Mental Survey and an annual city sample test. The Scottish Mental Survey of 1932 (SCRE, 1933) was a phenomenon. Almost all pupils born in Scotland in 1921 (nearly 100,000 pupils) in state or private schools or 'institutions', were tested on Wednesday 1 June in 1932.This was a remarkable logistical feat, undertaken by an inexperienced Council with its new network of voluntary support from the teachers and local authorities. The tests were administered and marked by the teachers, who also compiled the marks and sent them back to the Council. Another feature of the Scottish Mental Survey of 1932 was the large, personal contribution of senior academics and others. The SCRE archives in the

University of Glasgow hold materials in Thomson's handwriting demonstrating his large time commitment to the compilation and analysis of Survey data. Further, to validate the group test scores of the Moray House Test used in the 1932 Survey, 1000 children were tested later in the summer on the Stanford revision of the Binet scale. Almost 200 of these were tested by a single individual.

The need to test a further, smaller yet representative sample of pupils, within an individual testing process, was submitted to the third IEI Folkestone Conference in 1935. After devising a way of randomising the sample, the children were to be found throughout Scotland, in the cities and the Highlands and Islands. The process of 'locating the children' was a complicated affair. It needed a set of permissions, complex transport arrangements, and intricate labour plans.

> With the aid of Directors of Education, Education Officers, County Clerks, Education Committees, Headmasters and Teachers, the children were traced. (MacMeeken, 1939, p. 6)

A letter to a director or officer or clerk was sent out, explaining the necessity of the sampling process, how it would work, and its confidential nature. In each case, across the country members of the 34 Education Committees would receive the request, and in each case, after deliberation, gave assent. The single greatest number came from Glasgow (185) and then Edinburgh (76) but then some counties would be supplying only a single boy and girl, or perhaps four boys (Bute) or seven boys and two girls (Kirkcudbright). The tester prepared a testing programme and then, with permission, communicated, probably by letter, directly with the head teachers on the suitability of days and times of testing. Each county was approached separately and then arrangements to coordinate the work were made. Included in the sample were children from the county schools, special schools and private schools.

It has been argued that the key to understanding the logistical efficiency and effective management of the testing programme on intelligence was due to 'a widely diffused dedication to, and understanding of, empirical research in the Scottish profession' (Hope, 1978, p. 23). This point is echoed in the SCRE report in 1947, talking about the support from the teachers' union, the EIS; it refers to the 'active cooperation of its members' and the 'offers of help from teachers in applying tests or supplying data are never lacking' (p. 38).

The consequence of this involvement with mental testing meant that SCRE became a major source of expertise on mental testing and promoted their use in the training of teachers and in the armed forces. Inferences were drawn about intelligence and on occupation and housing:

> The sophisticated techniques which Thomson, Kennedy-Fraser and their colleagues employed in the *Intelligence of Scottish Children* 1933 placed them in the forefront of social research. (Hope, 1978,

> p. 24) (*The Intelligence of Scottish Children* was the published report of the Mental Survey.)

and

> But for sheer hard thinking, lucidity of research design, and credibility of findings there is really nothing in modern survey work which comes up to the standard of these studies. (Hope, 1978, p. 24)

Nisbet argued that many of the standard research procedures used since were pioneered in Council projects (SCRE, 1978, p. 7), including the standardisation of research instruments, such as the wide range of tests for ability and attainment. It was easy for a director of SCRE to state that

> Throughout its existence, the Council has had a distinguished record of research. The authors of the Council's early publications make up a Who's Who of the greats in this field – Drever, Vernon, Thomson, McLelland and Boyd. These people influenced educational thinking throughout the world. (SCRE, 1978, p. 10)

To undertake this research, a big undertaking, teachers were made the core of the process; in effect, they would be a resource as educational testers and researchers across Scotland for the next generations.

Reporting about 1936-37, SCRE said that the 1932 Mental Survey was being used in different ways across Scotland, and requests are made for the use of data for special investigations (SCRE, Annual Report, 1936-37, p. 11) and the Binet Thousand was returned to in 1937 to inquire into their school records, finding, to their surprise, that

> the type of employment upon which the pupils enter at this early stage [14-16 years] bears but slight relation to their intelligence level [and] the Council is alive to the fact that at the present time no administrative control can be exercised over the occupations selected by young people. (SCRE, Annual Report, 1936-37, p. 12)

and

> [in one county] it appears that ... children of superior intelligence do not as a body remain at school longer than their less gifted fellows. (p. 12)

In the following year, they expressed their disappointment in a society which, though believing in meritocracy, and now able to make more accurate judgements about the intelligence of its youth, still did not allow or recognise the social consequences of being able to turn the discourse of a meritocracy into a practice, through testing and close records:

> the records show that there is an apparent failure to utilise to the full the ability of individuals of the higher intelligence levels. (SCRE Annual Report, 1938-39, p. 17)

There was concern that intelligent children were leaving school in some areas and going to exactly the same jobs as the less intelligent. The 1939-40 Report, referring to a further analysis of the Binet Thousand Follow Up Study, continued this project of trying to map intelligence and connect it to occupation, trying to fit the person, the IQ and the job, into a Scottish reference grid:

> Educational and occupational histories are being compiled for groups belonging to different intelligence levels, for the sexes separately, and taken together, and for urban and rural groups ... an attempt is being made to construct an occupation-intelligence scale for use with 14-18 yr olds (SCRE, Annual Report, 1939-40, p. 7)

Conclusion

Kandel, the comparativist who played such a key role in the deliberations of the IEI, described national education systems as being determined by the 'cultural, social and political traditions' of the people they are designed for (Kandel, 1936, p. 52). This was the view taken by the historians of SCRE, who have tended to treat SCRE as a bounded Scottish phenomenon, created out of the genius of its theorists, blessed by the skills and willingness of a well-trained teaching force, and supported by its local education managers: in addition, in a small country they had an opportunity to network together and benefited from a silence from the four Scottish universities who were generally either indifferent or hostile to educational studies and their education professors (Bell, 1975, pp. 12-13). Without question, SCRE was a highly significant agency in the institutionalisation of the new technologies of selection and differentiation in Scotland. SCRE can be seen as a specific fusion of two research traditions; the older Germanic tradition of experimental research, always attempting to rationally and pragmatically engage with 'problems', was melded with the contemporary American influence and experience on testing and measurement (part of a general approach to practical action, described as a 'functional reality' [Nisbet, 1999, p. 6]).

> Scotland was a meeting place of that Germanic experimental tradition and the American measurement tradition and the way that it differed from England was that there these matters did not arise – the content and methods of education were to be decided by authority, by people who could write about it like Percy Nunn. A whole lot of English writers, who influenced English education, did it as philosophical writing in which they went to first principles

> and tried to decide what should be done. In Scotland, an empirical approach, linked to the Scottish enlightenment of the 18th Century ... directly drew from the Germanic tradition, because Thomson and Rusk and all the others went to Germany for their doctoral studies. (Nisbet, 2003)

This 'meeting of minds' would surely have helped the way that SCRE acted as an indispensable agent in the internationalising of American education and its methods and concerns (Smith & Hamilton, 1980). It was part of the expansion into new markets of the American experience with testing and surveying. It was sustained in part by Carnegie finance, provided with additional international contacts and travel, and treated as a skilled and resourceful partner by much more powerful forces than itself. Its histories only broadcast the myths of Scottish excellence, which serve to weaken the very real successes it had. Like all myths of course, they reflect real circumstance as well as imagined qualities. Although it was not intended to be a testing bureau, its lack of finances, as well as a Scottish interest in new ways of selection in its meritocracy, forced it to act like one, in a small way, selling on converted American tests. It became part of what can be discerned in retrospect as an American sphere of influence, concerned with educational efficiencies, differentiation and the new technologies of research in a new internationalism. It was in a subtle zone, which respected its scientific and educational independence but nevertheless influenced hugely its methods, tools, texts and ideas.

So, SCRE was a 'Scottish' research institute, and possibly a kind of prototype organisation for educational research, one which transformed the subjects and modes of inquiry of research, and which acted as a new form of governance, connecting research and policy. It was more than a site or a cluster of experts, it was an early knowledge-producing network, which looks increasingly modern in structure.

Notes

[1] This work on SCRE within the IEI forms part of the research undertaken in Edinburgh as 'A Scottish School of Educational Research', 1925-1950 (ESRC Award RES-000-23-1246) (Deary, Lawn and Bartholomew).

[2] 1920: Men 49%, Women 12%; 1938: Men 70%, Women 32%.Corresponding figures for England: 1920: Men 15.5%, Women 5.3%; 1938: Men 16%, Women 14% (in Wake, 1984, p. 80).

[3] Hepburn, Director in Ayrshire, was a member of the IEI and attended their national and international meetings. His education authority was one of the first in Scotland to use the new pupil tests from Moray House in 1935, a year after Edinburgh local authority. Previously, he had worked with Drever in his Psychological Laboratory in Edinburgh and, as a local head teacher in Northumberland, with Thomson.

[4] 'Classes in Educational Sciences should be instituted for teachers under the auspices of the Institute or of the Provincial Committees or of the Authorities. A summer school for instruction in regard to research work would be of the greatest value. It should also be considered whether the classes for the new Education Degrees (which include experimental work) could not be held at hours suitable for teachers engaged in the schools' (W. Boyd [1919] Educational Research, *Scottish Education Journal*, 14 November, p. 772).

[5] Anon. (1925) The Week: research in the history of Scottish education, *Scottish Education Journal*, 9 October, p. 1081.

[6] W. Boyd (1919) The Qualifying Examination, *Scottish Education Journal*, 28 November, pp. 800-801.

[7] Ibid., p. 800.

[8] Anon. (1920) The Week: research, *Scottish Education Journal*, 23 April 1920, p. 305.

[9] Ibid.

[10] Anon. (1923) The Week: research work, *Scottish Education Journal*, 28 December, p. 1000.

[11] W. Boyd (1921) Conference, *Scottish Education Journal*, 18 April, p. 264.

[12] Ibid.

[13] D. Kennedy-Fraser (1920) Research in Education, *Scottish Education Journal*, 9 January, pp. 24-25.

[14] Ibid.

[15] In fact, not only did individuals become directly involved in this work but branches of the EIS organised their own local research groups, and all branches were encouraged to (Anon. [1923] The Week: research work, *Scottish Education Journal*, 28 December, p. 1000).

[16] Ibid.

[17] Ibid.

[18] Scottish Council for Research in Education – International Examinations Inquiry Note (1938) *The Qualifying Examination Inquiry (Confidential)*, pp. 1-2.

[19] In 1931, the (Carnegie Corporation) of America paid direct to the Council the sum of £723 towards the cost of the Examination Enquiry and a further £4334 through the agency of the International Institute, Teachers College, Columbia University towards the same end (Craigie, 1972, p. 8).

References

Bell, R.E. (1975) Godfrey Thomson and Scottish Education. Unpublished paper.

Boyd, W. (1919) Educational Research, *Scottish Education Journal*, 14 November, p. 772 *Scottish Education Journal*, 14 November, p. 772.

Boyd, W. & Rawson, W. (1965) *The Story of the New Education*. London: Heinemann.

Brehony, K. (2004) A New Education for a New Era: the contribution of the conferences of the New Education Fellowship to the disciplinary field of education 1921-1938, *Paedagogica Historica*, 40(5 & 6), 733-755.

Craigie, J. (1972) *The Scottish Council for Research in Education 1928-1972*. Edinburgh: Scottish Council for Research in Education.

Hope, K. (1978) The SCRE and the Teacher, in Scottish Council for Research in Education *50th Anniversary, 1928-1978*. Edinburgh: SCRE.

Kandel, I. (1936) The International Examinations Inquiry, *The Educational Record*, 17, Supplement No. 9.

MacMeeken, A.M. (1939) *The Intelligence of a Representative Group of Scottish Children*. SCRE Publications XV. London: University of London Press.

Morris, J.G. (1994) The Scottish Council for Research in Education 1928-1993. PhD thesis, University of Edinburgh.

Nisbet, J. (1999) How it All Began: educational research 1880-1930, *Scottish Educational Review*, 31, 3-9.

Nisbet, J. (2003) Interview, Banchory, Scotland, 13 March.

Rusk, R. (n.d.) *Autobiography*. Glasgow: SCRE Archives, University of Glasgow.

Scottish Council for Research in Education (SCRE) Annual Reports 1922-1950. Edinburgh: SCRE.

Scottish Council for Research in Education (SCRE) (1938) Qualifying Examination Inquiry – IEE Meeting Dinard (Unpublished).

Scottish Council for Research in Education (SCRE) (1947) *The Scottish Council for Research in Education – its aims and activities*. SCRE Publications XXIV. London: University of London Press.

Scottish Council for Research in Education (SCRE) (1978) *50th Anniversary, 1928-1978*. Edinburgh: SCRE.

Smith, J.V. & Hamilton, D. (Eds) (1980) *The Meritocratic Intellect – studies in the history of educational research*. Aberdeen: Aberdeen University Press.

Thomasson (1978) The SCRE and the Teacher, in Scottish Council for Research in Education *50th Anniversary, 1928-1978*. Edinburgh: Scottish Council for Research in Education.

Wake, R. (1984) *Events Antecedent to the Founding of SCRE*. MEd thesis, University of Edinburgh.

Laurin Zilliacus and the 'War' against the Finnish Matriculation Examination

MINNA VUORIO-LEHTI &
ANNUKKA JAUHIAINEN

SUMMARY In this chapter the activities of the Finnish Carnegie Committee are reviewed. The first part establishes the social and educational context within which Zilliacus and the Carnegie Committee operated in Finland in the 1930s. In the second part the Finnish secondary school system (*oppikoulu*) is reviewed and Zilliacus's experimental secondary school is described. The chapter then examines the members of the Finnish Carnegie Committee and the outcomes of the enquiry. The last section evaluates the impact of the Committee for Finnish educational policy.

Introduction

> The International Institute Examinations Enquiry in Finland has been conducted by a Committee jointly appointed by the governing bodies of the Pedagogical Society of Finland and the Finland Section of the New Education Fellowship. This Committee has adopted as its official name 'The Finland Examinations Enquiry'. The Committee wishes to record its warm gratitude to the Carnegie Corporation, the Carnegie Foundation, and the International Institute of Teachers' College, Columbia University, who have launched and supported an enquiry on an international scale into the question of examinations and who have included Finland in that Enquiry.
> (Committee report, 1939, p. 5)

The committee, which in its preface expressed its gratitude towards the American Carnegie Corporation for its support of educational research, was a rather peculiar phenomenon in the Finnish educational sector in the 1930s. Although international pedagogical and educational discourse was followed –

at times quite closely – even in Finland throughout the twentieth century, being included in an international research group was a rare occasion. Nevertheless, a committee consisting of seven members – the 'Carnegie Committee' [1] – carried out a research effort in Finland from 1935 to 1939 which was linked to those of the International Examinations Inquiry.

The establishment and work of the Carnegie Committee are inseparably intertwined with the life and work of Laurin Zilliacus, an interesting pedagogue and undoubtedly the central figure of the International Examinations Inquiry in Finland. His network of international contacts and experience in comparative research were key factors in explaining Finland's inclusion. Zilliacus was involved in the Finnish pedagogical community from the mid-1920s to the early 1940s. During this period he contributed actively to Finnish pedagogical discussion – particular the debate on the matriculation examination.[2]

In this article we will review the activities of the Finnish Carnegie Committee. Since official histories of the Finnish educational system contain few references to the Committee, the search for clues and references to the Committee's activities has seemed a task suitable for a private investigator. Our sources include the two Committee reports published by the Finnish Carnegie Committee; we have also reviewed debates carried on in the principal Finnish pedagogical journals from the late 1920s until the early 1940s. We have had access to the archives of Tölö Svenska Samskolan, which was Laurin Zilliacus's school, and to material related to Laurin Zilliacus in the Svenska Litteraturskällskapet's archives and at the University of Helsinki library. Furthermore, the pedagogy researcher Mary Zilliacus-Söderhjelm kindly assisted us by making her private archives available to us and also agreed to an interview. She had personal recollections of Laurin Zilliacus as both teacher and relative. Despite several attempts we failed to discover the archives of the Finnish Committee or Laurin Zilliacus's personal correspondence. Thus we were not able to accurately identify his network of contacts within the Nordic region, the members of which apparently maintained lively contact with each other.

The first part of the article establishes the social and educational context within which Zilliacus and the Carnegie Committee operated in Finland in the 1930s. In the second part we review the Finnish secondary school system (*oppikoulu*) and describe Zilliacus's experimental secondary school. We will then take a look at the members of the Finnish Carnegie Committee and the outcomes of the enquiry. The last section evaluates the impact of the Committee for Finnish educational policy.

The Finnish Educational Sector and International Influences in the 1930s

The first half of the twentieth century was a time of transition for Finnish society, the Finnish education system and educational research. Finland had become independent from Russia in 1917 and the young nation began to emerge. On the other hand, the civil war which followed on the heels of World War I left a deep social tension in society, which contributed to the polarisation of Finnish society and stood in the way of reforms.

The school system faced great expectations: it was to harmonise the Finnish nation and restore its integrity. However, in the first half of the twentieth century, the school system was comprised of two very separate systems: the elementary school (*kansakoulu*, also called 'folk school'), which provided public education in the form of compulsory basic education, and the secondary school (*oppikoulu*), which provided academic education. Compulsory education and its enforcement promoted educational equality by extending the elementary school to all citizens. Education available to the children of the poorest families and in remote districts still remained more limited, which kept up the regional inequality in this respect. However, the real obstacle to educational equality was the continued existence of the parallel school system. At the end of the 1930s, an average of 12% of children attended secondary school. The parallel school system thus divided the 11 year-olds into two classes with regard to educational opportunities: those attending elementary school and those attending secondary school (Jauhiainen, 2002, pp. 130-131; Ahonen, 2003, pp. 99-102).

In Finland, the parallel school system remained in place for longer than in western and northern European countries in general, and in international comparison the educational level of the majority of the population remained relatively low. The great majority never achieved a vocational qualification (Ahonen, 2003, pp. 103, 203).

Bilingualism was another aspect typical of the Finnish school system, school administration and educational research. In the early years of Finnish autonomy, the small educated class was fully Swedish-speaking. In the first half of the nineteenth century, secondary education was only available in Swedish. The Finnish language only began to gain ground in the latter half of the nineteenth century (Salminen, 2002, pp. 40-42, 48).

The pedagogical community saw educational science as a way of promoting the scientific dimension of education, and the 1910s and 1920s were characterised by dynamic and experimental educational thinking. In the background we can see a number of new international – progressive – trends in research and education, which reached Finland via Germany or Britain and Scandinavia. The activity school in particular attracted keen initial interest, yet other pedagogical trends of new education also gained followers in time (Lahdes 1961, pp. 93-94).

The Swedish-speaking sector of the Finnish pedagogical community was particularly active in calling for school reforms. International events were closely followed at elementary schools and secondary schools alike. Swedish-speaking teachers were fewer in number and in many ways a more homogeneous group than their Finnish-speaking counterparts, and there were no language barriers hindering contact with the Swedish reformists. In the 1930s, the Swedish-speaking private secondary schools in particular applied Decroly's pedagogical thinking (Committee report, 1939, p. 23; Lahdes, 1961, pp. 95-96).

The intelligence tests developed by the German researcher Ernst Meumann and his French colleagues Alfred Binet and Thomas Simon were also known in Finland. Professor Albert Lilius became particularly interested in differential psychology and psychometrics. The enthusiasm for measurements covered a wide range of different educational issues. Almost anything was regarded as capable of being measured, and the results were used to justify both pedagogical decisions and educational policy measures. In many Finnish towns, children were subjected to a range of tests in an attempt to affect their educational careers. Empirical research was employed in the search for scientific methods that would give reliable information on the children and their differences. This reflected the belief that different groups have different capabilities. The separation of children of limited intelligence into special remedial schools was seen as particularly necessary. This desire was based on social-hygienic thinking (Ahonen, 2000a, pp. 403-405, 2003, pp. 105-106).

The Finnish Secondary School System in the 1930s

The interwar period was a time of plans and pedagogical reforms for the Finnish secondary school system. The secondary school was facing a need for reform: numbers of pupils were increasing markedly, particularly in towns and other settlements near railway junctions. The national education project also had sparked demands for equal education opportunities for everyone, and Finnish-speaking families started to demand equal education opportunities compared with Finland's Swedish-speaking population (Pietiäinen, 1995, p. 95; Salminen, 2002, p. 8). Pedagogically, the secondary school was in need of reform. The old Herbartian pedagogical approach based on discipline, obedience and absolute authority of the teacher received continuous criticism, and it was no longer seen to satisfy the requirements of modern secondary school education (Kiuasmaa, 1982, pp. 284-290). The planned reform sparked lively discussion on topics such as the structure of the new secondary schools and how elementary education could in the future be linked with secondary education. Various school experiments were also launched (Isosaari, 1973, p. 74; Kiuasmaa, 1982, p. 297).

In the 1930s, the Finnish secondary school system comprised state secondary schools and private secondary schools. Pupils could seek entry to a secondary school after four years at elementary school, at the age of 11. The secondary schools could be roughly divided into two types: five-year and eight-year schools. Pupils attending a five-year secondary school only completed the five forms of the intermediate school (*keskikoulu*, also called 'middle school'), after which they received a general secondary school certificate which gave them eligibility to certain vocational schools. These pupils did not continue to upper secondary school or take the matriculation examination. The eight-year secondary schools, know as *lyseo* (lyceum), included the intermediate school and upper secondary levels. Having completed upper secondary school, the pupils took the national matriculation examination, which gave eligibility to university studies (Isosaari, 1973, p. 77).

The matriculation examination was a national examination organised at secondary schools each spring. The purpose of the examination was to determine whether the pupils had achieved sufficient maturity for university studies and whether they had mastered the syllabuses taught. The examination included both written and oral tests, both of which the pupils could take at their own school. Tests in the pupil's first language (Finnish or Swedish), the second national language, a foreign language, mathematics and humanities and science subjects were compulsory. Only matriculated students were eligible for university studies. Although internationally renowned, the Finnish matriculation examination was subject to continuous public debate and reform demands. Secondary school teachers in particular felt that the examination limited their work. Since both teachers and parents wished to have the pupils prepared for the examination as thoroughly as possible, the focus of education shifted to learning by rote, which placed a great strain on the pupils. In the 1930s, the matriculation examination was also discussed at two official state committees: the Secondary School Committee (Committee report, 1933) and the Committee against the Torrent of Matriculated Students (Committee report, 1935). This latter committee in particular demanded that the nature of the examination as a preliminary demonstration of academic prowess was to be moderated and its cultural value reduced. The Committee was particularly concerned with reducing the number of examinees, since otherwise Finland would inevitably be facing a torrent of matriculated students (Vuorio-Lehti, 2006, pp. 57-59).

Laurin Zilliacus and the Dream of a School of His Own

In the 1920s, the Finnish secondary school community received an enthusiastic supporter of the new education when Laurin Zilliacus moved to Finland and founded his own school, the Tölö Svenska Samskolan. Zilliacus's family background and personal history were unique.[3] He was born into an important family originating from Vyborg, the members of which held prominent public positions at the end of the nineteenth century and the beginning of the twentieth century. His father emigrated from Finland at the end of the nineteenth century, and he grew up a multilingual cosmopolite whose home was sometimes in Japan, at other times in the USA or Britain. Studying at Bedales School in Britain, which applied the new pedagogical thinking, was of particular importance for Laurin Zilliacus's later career as pedagogue.

Zilliacus returned to Bedales School as a teacher, having first obtained a degree in engineering (chemistry) at the Massachusetts Institute of Technology. During his years as a teacher he became increasingly interested in both pedagogics and social and political issues. He attended several international New Education Fellowship (NEF) conferences, finding there a sounding board for his own pedagogical thinking (Zilliacus, 1993, pp. 19-20).

Laurin Zilliacus.

Despite his international background Zilliacus cherished his national roots and planned to move to Finland. In 1925, he carried out his plan and moved to Helsinki with his family. Zilliacus's dream of a school of his own was fulfilled when his own private secondary school opened its doors in the autumn of 1928 (Zilliacus, 1993, p. 21). Zilliacus intended to apply and integrate several pedagogical reforms at his school. The classes were smaller than in most Finnish secondary schools; another special feature was that the school housed both elementary and secondary levels under one roof. Zilliacus himself described the school as follows:

> The school at Helsingfors where I am employed is a school for all stages, from beginners of six and seven to those about to enter the university at the age of nineteen and twenty. We have no nursery stage, but all others, which means in terms of our Finnish education system, two schools, primary and secondary. (Laurin Zilliacus, 1988, p. 22)

Heading his own school brought Zilliacus face to face with the examination problems within the Finnish educational system. The matriculation examination in particular restricted the work at secondary schools, and Zilliacus was not able to apply the new pedagogics as extensively as he desired (Therman, 1934, p. 14; Furuhjelm, 1977, p. 10). In 1937, Zilliacus gave a presentation about his own school and its special characteristics in New Zealand, taking this opportunity to criticise the traditional secondary school and its heavy load of homework for being extremely taxing on the children:

> As a step towards the new education we have adopted an individual system, based on the Dalton Plan, which replaces homework entirely except for children who have fallen behind through absence, or for the slowest one, or the interested ones who give a great deal more time to study than do the others. The children in my country, as in most countries of Europe, are undoubtedly overworked at school, the matriculation taking care of that. (Laurin Zilliacus, 1988, p. 23)

Zilliacus's criticism of the traditional secondary school and the matriculation examination is understandable in the light of his own educational principles. He placed great emphasis on physical health during the first seven or eight years at school. Since physical health was the foundation of everything, school was to bear its share of the responsibility for promoting the health of children. School hours were to include a sufficient amount of physical activity, and children were not to be overburdened with homework that would require them to stay at their desk for long periods (Zilliacus, 1930, p. 3; Therman, 1934, p. 15).

The second principle was guiding a helpless child to grow into a person in control of his/her surroundings. School was to help children gain an understanding of their environment and develop their practical abilities. Thus, Zilliacus was an advocate of functionality. It was the school's task to replace some of the homework by offering meaningful activities that serve true life. Third, Zilliacus emphasised communality and public education: people should learn to live as part of the community and accept their share of responsibility (Zilliacus, 1930, pp. 3-4, 5)

With regard to older schoolchildren, the goals were slightly different: now, the school was to spark an interest in aesthetic, ethical and religious issues and direct the intellect of the young towards the heritage of human knowledge. Zilliacus considered it important for everyone to learn how to discover their own interests (Zilliacus, 1930, pp. 5-6).

Zilliacus wanted to offer feelings of success and competence also to children who were not particularly successful at school. He hoped they would find their own strengths through interests such as sports or drama, or through practical subjects. The school offered a line of practice-oriented studies for those not aiming at the matriculation examination. These pupils attended school as usual, except that they had been exempted from the subjects that were compulsory in the matriculation examination. Instead, they studied more practical subjects such as home economics, economic geography or social studies (Furuhjelm, 1977, p. 10; Zilliacus, 1993, p. 55).

Laurin Zilliacus served as headmaster until 1940. During this period he took an active part in pedagogical debate among the Swedish-speaking community in particular. Zilliacus wrote articles for journals and periodicals, was actively involved in a number of pedagogical associations and maintained an extensive network of contacts. He was continuously in search of inspiration and ideas for the pedagogical development of the school. His own school and its teachers formed a community that was very important for him. For example, in 1930 Zilliacus and his fellow teacher, Rachel Furuhjelm, visited Belgium together, meeting Ovide Decroly and visiting his school. Based on this visit they published a book about Decroly's pedagogical ideas (Furuhjelm & Zilliacus, 1931).

The New Education Fellowship and those interested in New Education formed another important collaboration network for Zilliacus. In the next section we will look at how Finnish pedagogues joined the new education movement.

International Networks and the Examination Issue

Zilliacus was familiar with NEF from the very beginning. He attended the first NEF conference in Calais in 1921, which made a great impression on him. NEF offered Zilliacus an opportunity to make the acquaintance of the central figures of New Education, and he was an enthusiastic delegate at various conferences. He also contributed several articles to *New Era*, a journal published by NEF (Zilliacus, 1993, pp. 22, 28).

After moving to Finland Zilliacus also encouraged other Finns to join NEF. While Finnish educational journals made note of the Heidelberg (1925) conference, Zilliacus was the only delegate from Finland. The Helsingör conference (1929) was the first one to actively invite representatives from the Nordic region in particular to attend the conference. In Finland, *Kasvatusopillinen aikakauskirja* (Journal of Education) discussed the conference and its themes well in advance. Zilliacus also encouraged other Finns to attend. He wrote about the conference in *Yksityiskoululehti* (Journal of Private Secondary School) in 1928-29, noting that the conference offered a rare opportunity for meeting colleagues from other countries and for learning about education systems from both near and far (*Kasvatusopillinen aikakauskirja*, 1925, p. 67, 1929, pp. 84-88, *Uudistuva kasvatus- ja opetustyö* [Innovative Education and Teaching], 1926, p. 35, *Yksityiskoululehti*, 1928-29, pp. 125-129; see also Brehony, 2004, pp. 748-749).

All of these efforts were not in vain: according to the list of delegates, a total of 63 Finns attended the Helsingör conference in 1929. Ten of them – Carin Rosenius, Aksel Koskenjaakko and Laurin Zilliacus among them – received a travel grant from the Pedagogical Society of Finland. All three of them would become members of the Finnish Carnegie Committee a few years later. Since Zilliacus was a member of the organisation committee for the Helsingör conference, he had a chance to assist in drafting the programme. Oskari Mantere, later the Chairman of the Carnegie Committee, also attended the Helsingör conference – he was a member of the Nordic honorary committee, along with (Counsellor of Education) Ralf Saxen. (*Kasvatusopillinen aikakauskirja*, 1929, 84-88; *Opettajain lehti* [Teachers' Journal], 1929, pp. 682-684).

Among Nordic representatives there were at least Johan Hertzberg, a headmaster from Oslo, Norway, and Nils Hänninger, a Counsellor of Education from Sweden – both became members of the International Examinations Inquiry. NEF conferences probably offered a useful forum for establishing relations and networking (*Kasvatusopillinen aikakauskirja*, 1929, pp. 84-88; *Uudistuva kasvatus- ja opetustyö*, 1929, p. 132).

The Nordic New Education movement gained momentum at the Helsingör conference. A decision was made to establish the Finland section of the New Education Fellowship [4] (Lahdes, 1961, pp. 75-76). Nordic cooperation was also reinforced, and the idea for organising pan-Nordic New Education conferences saw light in Helsingör. Nordic pedagogues were keen to review the application of reform-pedagogical theory within a Nordic context, as this was seen to differ from that of the British or German countries, for example. In the 1930s there were three New Education conferences held in the Nordic region: one in Widtsköfle, Sweden in 1931, the second in Lillehammer, Norway in 1933 and the third one in Helsinki, Finland in 1938 (*Kasvatusopillinen aikakauskirja*, 1931, p. 221).

The idea of an enquiry related to the examination issue first emerged at the New Education Conference at Locarno in 1927. A decision was made to appoint an examinations enquiry comprised of representatives from some 20 countries, which would collect comparative data on examinations in the various countries. The enquiry presented reports on its work at the Helsingör (1929), Nice (1932) and Cheltenham (1936) conferences, and individual members published less extensive reports in various journals. Zilliacus compiled a summary of the enquiry for the report 'The Examination Tangle and the Way Out', which was published in 1935. According to Zilliacus, the investigations carried out by NEF specifically proved that the problems associated with examinations were global (Zilliacus, 1943, pp. 430-431).

The examination issue was a key theme also at the pan-Nordic NEF conferences. Examinations were one of the two main themes discussed at Widtsköfle. Several presentations were made around this theme, including one by Hänninger. The conference issued a resolution to the effect that examinations should not be allowed to direct school work to the extent that was the case (*Kasvatusopillinen aikakauskirja*, 1931, p. 221). The Lillehammer conference (1933) dedicated one whole day to the examination issue. Zilliacus gave a presentation in which he reported the work of NEF's examinations enquiry (*Yksityiskoulu*, 1933; *Kasvatusopillinen aikakauskirja*, 1936, pp. 41-43;).

Zilliacus joined the NEF board in 1930. In a letter to *Kasvatusopillinen aikakauskirja* from the Nice conference (1932) Zilliacus waxed almost lyrical when describing how the delegates had held both official and unofficial meetings to work and discuss matters, and how they had felt a great unity in their approach to pedagogical questions. Zilliacus particularly mentioned evenings spent in discussion with delegates from other Nordic countries (*Kasvatusopillinen aikakauskirja*, 1932, pp. 179-182). This letter contains an aside which indicates that Zilliacus was at times frustrated with the sluggish attitudes the New Education movement met in Finland. Having noted the presence of official delegates from Turkey, Iran and Palestine and many other countries, Zilliacus remarked that if NEF were to organise a few more international conferences, it might finally merit official attention also in Finland (*Kasvatusopillinen aikakauskirja*, 1932, p. 181).

According to Erkki Lahdes, who has studied the New Education movement in Finland particularly from the perspective of the elementary school, the movement, which emphasised international interaction, lost part of its driving force in the late 1930s. In 1936, the Cheltenham conference still attracted a total of 12 Finnish delegates, and Finland also hosted its own exhibition stand at the conference. From the Finnish perspective, the conference was also important because Zilliacus was elected to follow Beatrice Ensor as President of NEF. The internal cohesion of the Fellowship had nevertheless weakened due to Germany, Italy and the Soviet Union withdrawing from the Fellowship. The repercussions affected Finland as well (*Kasvatus ja koulu* [Education and the School], 1936, pp. 167-173; Lahdes, 1961, p. 104).

The Finnish Carnegie Committee

Finland joined the International Examinations Inquiry in its second stage in the mid 1930s. The Enquiry was extended to Finland and Sweden following the withdrawal of Switzerland and Germany, with Norway invited to join the Enquiry four years later (Zilliacus, 1943, p. 431).

The decision to include Finland was made at the second general assembly of the International Examinations Inquiry in Folkestone, which Zilliacus attended at the invitation of Paul Monroe. In his report to the National Board of Education Zilliacus explained that he had, together with his Nordic colleagues Hertzberg (Norway) and Hänninger (Sweden), prepared an investigation into the examination issue in the Nordic region. During the conference Zilliacus received a guarantee from Paul Monroe concerning research funding and thus Finland joined the Enquiry.

The Finnish Carnegie Committee was a mixture of influential officials in the field of education, experienced secondary school teachers and school reformers. The group was united by an interest in New Education and the pedagogical opportunities it offered. Interest in international issues and school conditions abroad was another uniting factor. The Finnish Educational Research Association was also well represented, as three of the committee members had acted as Chairman of the Association at various times (including the current Chairman). The most important factor bringing the members together was Laurin Zilliacus, who acted as secretary to the Committee. He is likely to have influenced the composition of the Committee, which consisted largely of Swedish-speaking representatives from the Finnish educational sector.

The Chairman of the Carnegie Committee, Oskari Mantere, PhD, represented a prestigious authority – the Board of Education, of which he was President. His contemporaries describe Mantere as a cheerful, enlightened and optimistic cultural personage. He was actively involved in politics as member of the National Progressive Party, which represented the liberal centre ground, and served as Member of Parliament and in several ministerial positions, including Minister of Education and Prime Minister. Mantere was the long-standing Chairman of the Finnish Educational Research Association in the 1930s and a member of the Private School Teachers' Association, acting as its Chairman in 1918-19. Mantere was interested in the New Education movement and international pedagogical discourse (Autio, 2001). Mantere's role in the Finnish Carnegie Committee was to steer its work. He was not involved in the sub-investigations.

Another important and influential figure in the Finnish Carnegie Committee was Dr Aksel Koskenjaakko. Headmaster of a secondary school, Koskenjaakko served as Chairman of the Finland section of the New Education Fellowship in the 1930s and later also as Chairman of the Finnish Educational Research Association. Koskenjaakko began his career as a teacher at the Helsinki Agricultural Lyceum, which aimed at combining general education with practical studies. This fact testifies to his reformist aspirations. He was also the editor-in-chief of *Oppikoulu*, a nationally important journal targeted at secondary school teachers. Koskenjaakko supported New Education and made several visits abroad to learn about education in different countries (Heikari & Sandelin, 1933, pp. 292-293). In his role as headmaster and editor-in-chief, Koskenjaakko was able to promote the ideas of New Education among a large number of pupils and teachers. As member of the Finnish Carnegie Committee he carried out one sub-investigation related to the matriculation examination together with Carin Rosenius.

Albert Lilius, Professor of Education, represented the academic circles in the Committee. One of the main figures of experimental education in particular in Finland, Lilius published ground-breaking work in the field of child and youth psychology as early as the beginning of the twentieth century. He was also one of the first Finnish pedagogues to introduce the New Education trends in Finland. Lilius was Mantere's predecessor as Chairman of the Finnish Educational Research Association. He had an extensive network of contacts within German academic circles, and he studied in Germany under Professor Ernst Meumann during the first half of the twentieth century (Ahonen, 2000b, pp. 1-2). Lilius's role in the Carnegie Committee seems to have been that of a specialist, as he did not participate in the enquiries himself. He resigned from the Committee in the autumn of 1936 due to ill health.

Aksel Koskenjaakko.

Yrjö Ora and Carin Rosenius were both teachers who participated in the phase I enquiry of the Finnish Carnegie Committee, the results of which the Committee reported in 1939. Rosenius was also one of the leading figures of the Finland section of the New Education Fellowship and served as its librarian. She attended the Helsingör (1929) and Nice (1932) conferences, as well as the pan-Nordic conference in Vidtsöfle in 1931. Rosenius held a full-time position as an English teacher. She published several articles on the new pedagogical trends in Finnish pedagogical journals (*Kasvatusopillinen aikakauskirja*, 1930; Heikari & Sandelin, 1933, p. 521).

Eemil Saarimaa and Ernst Tegengren each represented particular interests in the Carnegie Committee: Saarimaa the State Normal Lyceum, and Tegengren the Swedish department of the National Board of Education. They were not involved in the actual investigations.

The actual research team appointed by the Finnish Carnegie Committee included Erik Falck, Bertel Hedström, Anna-Liisa Jatkola, Carin Rosenius, Kaarle Sorainen and Tor Therman. Falck and Hedström in particular worked with the sections requiring mathematical processing and carried out the statistical analyses (Committee report, 1939, pp. 6-7).

Therman was one of Zilliacus's closest colleagues at Tölö Svenska Samskolan.

With regard to testing expertise, the Finnish Carnegie Committee relied on Dr Matti Koskenniemi, a prominent name in Finnish intelligence research. The Committee employed the Moray House Test 21, obtained from the Scottish Council for Research in Education.

When the Finnish Carnegie Committee was established, its secretary – Zilliacus – was assigned to draft the enquiry programme and hire researchers for the separate enquiries. He was actually able to steer the work, as he met the researchers weekly during the school year. Although each member was responsible for his/her own research area, the entire group communicated continuously during the project. The Finnish Committee met every 4 to 5 weeks to review the researchers' intermediate reports and to discuss the progress of the enquiry (Committee report, 1939, p. 5). The Finnish Committee maintained amicable relations with the pedagogical community. The Finnish Educational Research Association, the Finnish section of the New Education Fellowship, various teachers' organisations for private and state secondary schools, individual secondary schools, the National Board of Education, the Ministry of Education and the Matriculation Examination Board all provided assistance at different stages of the project, which made it possible for the Committee to conduct comprehensive investigations.

The Carnegie Committee's Research in Finland

When the Finnish Carnegie Committee was first established in 1936, the Finnish pedagogical journal *Kasvatusopillinen Aikakauskirja* published a detailed plan prepared by headmaster Laurin Zilliacus. The journal informed its readers that the work would begin with a basic enquiry into the number of secondary school pupils, their social background and achievement levels at school. Next, information would also be required concerning how well they did in examinations in various subjects and the extent to which it would be possible to standardise such examinations. The technical organisation of examinations would also be looked at, and an investigation would also be carried out concerning how different teachers graded the same tests or what kind of differences there were between the marks given by the teachers and those given by the matriculation examination board. The latter half of the plan also included an investigation into the later success of high achievers in life (*Kasvatusopillinen aikakauskirja*, 1936, pp. 154-157).

The Finnish Carnegie Committee published two reports. A third report was originally planned but never appeared. The first report was published in March 1939 under the title 'The School and Examination System of Finland with Some Investigations into the Secondary School'. The report was quite extensive. The first chapter gave an overview of the structure of the Finnish secondary school: its history, administration and structure, the teachers' qualification requirements, school fees and overall school attendance in

Finland in the 1930s. The second main section explained the principles of admission, the general secondary school certificate and the matriculation examination institution. The actual enquiry was not addressed until page 50. The enquiry included an empirical study on the average length of school attendance in secondary school in Finland, how often pupils had to repeat a year and the amount of additional work pupils had to do in the summer to satisfy the course requirements and move to the next grade.

The first committee report gave a thorough overview of the status of secondary education in Finland and its problems. It seemed that secondary school was not the appropriate seat of learning for a large proportion of the 11 year-olds admitted to the school. According to the investigation, 75% of those accepted into the school completed the intermediate school, and only 25% completed the matriculation examination. The average duration of attendance at full-length secondary schools was 9.1 years, although the school was only supposed to take eight years. Only 58% of the pupils were moved up unconditionally. One in five pupils had to repeat a year at some stage, and one in five had to resit examinations annually before being allowed to move up to the next year. Requirements were set so high that approximately half of the secondary school students took private lessons after school, particularly in languages and mathematical subjects (Committee report, 1939, pp. 83-84).

The second Committee report was also completed in 1939, but its publication was delayed due to the Finnish Winter War. The report only appeared in May 1940 when interim peace was declared. The second report focused on the matriculation examination, which was the national final examination at the secondary education level. Like the first report, the second committee report was also very thorough, detailed and critical towards the matriculation examination. The first part of the report contained a detailed overview of secondary-level examinations in other European countries. Such comparisons were typical of the work of Finnish committees at the time, which shows that the school administration and education authorities were familiar with European education systems and practices.

The authors next addressed the investigations. The first investigation compared the pupils' marks in various subjects with the marks they obtained in the matriculation examination, as well as the consistency of marks awarded at different times. Naturally, the results were also reviewed in relation to gender. Next, the authors reviewed the distribution of marks awarded for the matriculation examination in different years. Did the difficulty level remain unchanged from one year to another? The data was extremely extensive, consisting of the marks for all pupils participating in the matriculation examination in 1935-37.

The third sub-investigation focused on the correlation of marks awarded by the teachers with those awarded by inspectors of the matriculation examination board, i.e. it tested the consistency and validity of the matriculation examination. The Finnish Carnegie Committee used study designs developed in the USA and Britain to determine whether having different readers grade the matriculation examination would affect the marks awarded for the Finnish essay. A total of 32 graded essays were given to new readers and the marks they gave were compared with the original marks. In addition, teachers were sent an interesting open questionnaire concerning the tests in humanities and science subjects. The results clearly showed marked differences between different readers performing the grading. Even highly experienced teachers found it difficult to give exactly the same marks. The conclusion of the Committee was very clear: 'there is thus strong evidence that the marks given in our matriculation papers (with the exception of mathematics) do not possess the objective validity generally ascribed to them' (Committee report, 1940, p. 161).

The Finnish Carnegie Committee collected more data than is included in the first two Committee reports. A third report was planned concerning the entrance examinations of Finnish secondary schools. These results were never published. Apparently the Committee also carried out some intelligence tests, since the committee report made reference to the expertise of Matti Koskenniemi, a prominent figure in Finnish intelligence research, having been employed. It is also known that the Committee had access to the Moray House Test. In an article he wrote in 1943, Zilliacus also states that the Committee had collected material concerning the matriculation examination results and later success at studies. No mention of this issue is made in the reports, however (Zilliacus, 1943, p. 433).

The Impact of the Carnegie Committee

The issues addressed by the Finnish Carnegie Committee were of urgent interest to the Finnish educational sector in the 1930s: the structure of the secondary school, pupil intake, teaching and the pupils' success at school, the examinations used and their capacity to measure achievements accurately. The secondary school reform was an important issue for the young republic. Here it must also be noted that, in addition to national interest, these issues also had an extensive international dimension. From an international perspective, secondary-level education faced a totally new situation in the early twentieth century, as an increasing number of countries were forced to make this avenue of education – originally reserved for small privileged groups – available to new groups, realigning it in a less elitist direction (see McCullogh, 1998, pp. 44-46).

The investigations conducted by the Finnish Committee clearly pinpointed the problems associated with the secondary school and the matriculation examination. Finding a solution was a different matter. The issues were linked to fundamental policy definitions – educational policy included– which affected the entire education system and would have required a consensus between the various interest groups. In the 1930s an overall reform of the education system failed to win sufficient support, even though Oskari Mantere, President of the National Board of Education, was willing to integrate the elementary school and secondary school into a comprehensive school that would serve as large a majority as possible.

For Finland, inclusion in the extensive International Examinations Inquiry offered a unique opportunity to conduct an in-depth investigation into the secondary school, which probably would not have been possible on national funding alone. Membership in the Enquiry also meant significant international interaction between Finland, the Nordic region and other European countries. An international dimension was much appreciated in the 1930s, but seldom did such good opportunities present themselves.

Regarding the impact of the Finnish Carnegie Committee's research, it can be noted that the Committee produced comprehensive reports and accurate criticism, which nevertheless failed to have an impact on the matriculation examination, which remained relatively unchanged until the 1990s. In the 1970s, it did seem for a moment that the entire examination would be abolished; such thoughts were soon discarded, however. The matriculation examination has always enjoyed an immense cultural respect in Finland. It has been associated with strongly nationalistic connotations and embodies many elements that are intrinsic to Finnish identity, which makes it difficult to carry out any kind of reform (Vuorio-Lehti, 2006).

The work of the Carnegie Committee was not wholly without effects. We believe that the published results at least contributed to the revision of the secondary school entrance examination in the 1950s. After all, the Committee had found that as teachers had an understanding of the overall capacities of their pupils, their evaluations should be given more value. Scientific studies had also clearly demonstrated that school grades were a better indicator of future success than the final examinations. The number of pupils seeking entry to secondary school exploded in the 1950s. The selection system, in place since the 1930s, was inefficient, and in the course of public debate the whole issue was declared to be more difficult than any problems related to the matriculation examination. Moreover, the system had sparked an unofficial preparatory institution to coach pupils for the entrance examination. The entrance procedure was reformed and practices which had also been found commendable by the Carnegie Committee were introduced (Meinander & Aattonen, 1965, p. 76).

As was the case many in other European countries, World War II put a stop to peacetime plans for development in Finland as well. Although many issues were taken up after the war, the atmosphere, pedagogical desires and objectives had changed. The social climate was much more pessimistic after a major war than in the dynamic 1930s.

In Finland, educational policy sought new alignment immediately after the war, aiming at a total reform of the education system. A general understanding to the effect that the various forms of schools could no longer ignore each other began to win ground; the education system was seen to merit rethinking as a unified system taking the interests of the entire age group into account. Decisions concerning the basic structure of the comprehensive school system were not reached until the early 1960s, however. It should be noted, though, that the curricula of the comprehensive school integrated many pedagogical ideas which the New Education movement had promoted three decades earlier.

Finland's inclusion in the International Examinations Inquiry was closely tied to the person of Laurin Zilliacus. He had been actively involved in the work of NEF since the 1920s, establishing contacts with other NEF members, and also made the acquaintance of several members of the International Examinations Inquiry. Zilliacus seems to have played an active role in the creation of pan-Nordic networks. Under the shadow of the Second World War he nevertheless withdrew from the Finnish educational sector, leaving the alternative school he had created in the hands of his successor, Tor Thermann. Zilliacus himself embraced major international challenges as President of NEF. He was a highly exotic and original addition to the Finnish secondary school and the education it provided. While he failed to bring about the abolition of the matriculation examination, his ideas and thoughts inspired and encouraged his contemporaries to carry out a reform of secondary schooling.

The members of the International Examinations Inquiry seem to have applied a variety of educational policy perspectives to their review of examinations. In an evaluation report he wrote in 1943, Zilliacus noted that the French members in particular had voiced conservative views, emphasising the selective function of examinations and their importance in guaranteeing a sufficient intellectual level. At the other end of the scale was the American system, which emphasised the right of all pupils to a longer period of education. Instead of having a selective function, examinations were aimed at discovering the examinee's capabilities and inclinations. In our opinion, Zilliacus leaned towards this latter view. He wanted to develop secondary school education in a direction that would help all kinds of pupils to benefit from it. It was not the purpose of the school to educate examinees but to produce functional citizens.

Notes

[1] The official name of the Finnish committee was 'The Finland Examination Enquiry'. Among their contemporaries the committee was known more informally as 'the Finnish Carnegie Committee'. We use this name in this article due to its more succinct character.

[2] The matriculation examination is the final examination taken at the end of general upper secondary education.

[3] Laurin Zilliacus was born in Yokohama on 4 October 1895. His father Konni Zilliacus was a well-known political author and activist. Laurin's grandfather served as the Mayor of Helsinki, as deputy to the Procurator General and as Senator. Laurin's father, however, turned out to be a restless and adventurous

character who, unlike many of his relatives, refused to settle down on a steadily progressing career as a public official. He abandoned his first family, drove his wealthy father to the verge of bankruptcy and roamed restlessly around the world. He was employed as a journalist in Chicago and as a reporter to the US Indian wars. Laurin was born of Konni Zilliacus's second marriage to Lilian Graef, the daughter of a German-American businessman (Klinge, 2007).

[4] After the Helsingör conference, *Opettajain lehti* published an article by A. Liukko, one of the Finnish delegates. Liukko was disappointed at the failure of the Finnish delegates to cooperate in the conference, as well as their having had few opportunities for getting acquainted with one another. According to Liukko, the Swedish-speaking delegates from Finland failed to pay enough attention to their Finnish-speaking counterparts. Invitation to the meeting held for the purpose of discussing the establishment of a Finnish association was only published in Swedish. According to Liukko, this explains why there were hardly any Finnish-speaking pedagogues present at the meeting (*Opettajain lehti*, 1929, pp. 682-684).

References

Archive References

Kansallisarkisto [National archive in Finland]: Oskari Mantereen yksityiskokoelma [Private collection of Oskari Mantere]. Kansio 10: Koululaitokseen liittyviä asiakirjoja

Svenska litteraturskällskapet i Finland [The Society of Swedish Literature in Finland]. Historiska och litteraturhistoriska arkivet. U – Övriga handlingar. Klippböcker SLSA 882:Ua1-Ua3.

Mary Zilliacus-Söderhjelms private archive.

Newspapers

Helsingin Sanomat 1936

Hufvudstadsbladet 28 August 1929

Uusi Aura 26 February1934

Periodical Journals

Kasvatus ja koulu 1936

Kasvatusopillinen aikakauskirja 1925, 1929, 1930, 1931, 1932, 1936

Opettajain lehti 1929

The New Era November 1936

Uudistuva kasvatus- ja opetustyö 1926, 1929

Uusi Suomi 26 February 1934

Yksityiskoulu- Privatskolan 1928-1929; 1933

Committee Reports

Committee report 1933. Oppikoulukomitean mietintö marraskuun 3 päivältä 1932 [The Finnish secondary school – report 3 November 1932]. Helsinki.

Committee report 1935. Ylioppilastulvan vastustamiskomitea [The committee against the torrent of matriculated students]. Helsinki.

Committee report 1939. The Finland Examinations Enquiry. The school and examination system of Finland with some investigations into the secondary school. Helsinki.

Committee report 1940. The Finland Examinations Enquiry. The matriculation examination in Finland. Helsinki.

Research Literature

Ahonen, Sirkka (2000a) Kasvatustiede. Teoksessa, in P. Tommila (Ed.) *Suomen tieteen historia. Osa 2: Humanistiset ja yhteiskuntatieteet* [Educational sciences, in P. Tommila (Ed.) The history of sciences in Finland], 396-437. Helsinki: WSOY.

Ahonen, Sirkka (2000b) *Lilius, Albert. Kansallisbiografian verkkojulkaisu* [Online publication of the National Biography of Finland]. Helsinki: Suomalaisen Kirjallisuuden Seura. http://artikkelihaku.kansallisbiografia.fi/artikkeli/7012/ (accessed 8 January 2008).

Ahonen, Sirkka (2003) *Yhteinen koulu. Tasa-arvoa vai tasapäisyyttä?* [The Common school – equality or uniformity]. Tampere:Vastapaino.

Autio, Veli-Matti (2001) *Mantere Oskari. Kansallisbiografia-verkkojulkaisu* [Online publication of the National Biography of Finland]. Helsinki: Suomalaisen Kirjallisuuden Seura. http://artikkelihaku.kansallisbiografia.fi/artikkeli/550/ (accessed 7 January 2008).

Brehony, Kevin (2004) A New Education for a New Era: the contribution of the conferences of the New Education Fellowship to the disciplinary field of education 1921-1938, *Paedagogica Historica*, 40(5 & 6), 733-755.

Forsberg, E., Lundahl, C., Román, H. & Waldow, F. (2006) International student assessments, national assessment culture and reform history. *D-nr: 2006-2447.* Stockholm: The Swedish Research Council.

Furuhjelm, Rachel (1977) *Laurin Zilliacus och hans skola. I Tölö svenska samskola – ulsåsa – 1928-1975* [Laurin Zilliacus and his school, in Tolo Swedish co-educational school 1928-1975], 8-15. Helsingfors.

Furuhjelm, Rachel & Zilliacus, Laurin (1931) Decroly-skolan. En omgestaltning av läroplan och undervisningsmetod [The school of Decroly. The new curriculum and educational method]. Helsingfors: Söderström & C.O. Förlagsaktiebolag.

Heikari, Toivo & Sandelin, Armas (Eds) (1933) *Suomen opettajisto* [Secondary school teachers in Finland]. Turku: Polytypos.

Isosaari, Jussi (1973) *Suomen koululaitoksen rakenne ja kehitys* [The structure of the Finnish school system]. Helsinki: Otava.

Jauhiainen, Annukka (2002) *Työväen lasten koulutie ja nuorisokasvatuksen yhteiskunnalliset merkitykset* [The schooling pathway of working-class children and the social significance of the education of youth. The question of continuation schools for elementary school leavers from the late 1800s to the 1970s]. Turku: University of Turku.

Kiuasmaa, Kyösti (1982) *Oppikoulu 1880-1980* [The secondary school in 1880-1980]. Oulu: Kustannusosakeyhtiö Pohjoinen.

Klinge, Matti (2007) *Zilliacus, Konni. Kansallisbiografian verkkojulkaisu* [Online publication of the National Biography of Finland]. Helsinki: Suomalaisen Kirjallisuuden Seura. http://artikkelihaku.kansallisbiografia.fi/artikkeli/3698/ (accessed 7 January 2008).

Lahdes, Erkki (1961) *Uuden koulun vaikutus Suomen kansakouluun* [The New Education in Finland]. Helsinki: Otava.

McCulloch, Gary (1998) *Failing the Ordinary Child? The Theory and Practice of Working-Class Secondary Education*. Buckingham: Open University Press.

Meinander, Ragnar & Aattonen, Toivo (1965) *Oppikoulun hallinto* [The administration in Finnish secondary schools]. Helsinki: WSOY.

Pietiäinen, Jukka-Pekka (1995) Yksityisoppikoulut nuoressa tasavallassa 1917-1944 [Private secondary schools in Finland in 1917-1944], in J. Teoksessa, J-P. Salminen & J. Teperi Pietiäinen *Yksityisoppikoulujen historia 1872-1977* [The history of the private secondary schools 1872-1977]. Helsinki: Painatuskeskus.

Salminen, Jari (2002) Alamainen sivistysprojekti, tasa-arvo ja edistys. Suomen yksityisten oppikoulujen rakenteellinen kehitys, 1872-1920 [Equality and progress – the Finnish Education Project under Russian rule. The structural development of private secondary schools in Finland 1872-1920]. Helsinki: University of Helsinki.

Therman, Tor (1934) Den 'nya' skolan [The New Education]. A.K.Ottelin: Pedagogical profiles (offprint). Helsingfors.

Vuorio-Lehti, Minna (2006) Valkolakin viesti. Ylioppilastutkintokeskustelu Suomessa toisen maailmansodan jälkeen [The message of the white cap. Public discourse concerning the Finnish matriculation examination after the Second World War]. Turku: University of Turku.

Zilliacus, Laurin (1930) Min uppfattning om skolans mål [My view about the purpose of school], *Privatskolan*, 8 (journal offprint). Helsinki.

Zilliacus, Laurin (1943) *Examenundersökningar. Psykologisk Pedagogisk Uppslagsbok* [The inquiry about the examinations. Psychological pedagogical ideas], 430-435 Stockholm: Natur och Kultur.

Zilliacus, Laurin (1988) *The School in Finland. The Lecture Laurin Zilliacus Gave in New Zealand in 1937*. 60th Jubilee book, 21-25. Helsingfors.

Zilliacus, Mary (1993) *Fostran till aktivt medborgarskap. Laurin Zilliacus som reformpedagog 1920-1940* [Active citizenship – Laurin Zilliacus as a representative of reform pedagogy]. Vasa: Åbo Akademi.

Inter/national Assessments as National Curriculum: the case of Sweden

CHRISTIAN LUNDAHL

SUMMARY The use of assessments and the use of the international scene are two strategies to change the national curriculum that are typical in modern educational systems. This chapter illustrates how a progressive movement in Sweden used participation in the International Examinations Inquiry to promote and establish a very specific institute in Sweden: the State Psychological Pedagogical Institute (SPPI). By the realisation of the SPPI the progressive movement won an important position on the Swedish educational field, from which they could distribute discourses on and for comprehensive schooling. These discourses became, contrary to the intentions, more and more psychology laden over the years to come.

Introduction

The use of assessments and the use of 'the international scene' are two available strategies to change the national curriculum that are typical for modern educational systems.[1] Comparing students' achievements in education and comparing countries' education, often by student achievement, is possible through the production and the mediation of knowledge about education and its outcome. A general tendency in the history of modern societies is the development of specific institutions to reflect the progress of society. Modern societies differ from traditional ones by, among other things, their 'institutional reflexivity' (Giddens, 1991). This chapter is about using international assessments, and more specifically participation in the International Examinations Inquiry (IEI), to promote and to actually organise such a reflexive institution in Sweden: the State Psychological Pedagogical Institute (SPPI). This is also the story of how a group of progressive educationalists travelled abroad and brought home perspectives to an argumentation for new ways of organising the national educational system and its curriculum. They used these perspectives in discursive coalitions to challenge representatives of traditional education. The goal was to reach greater unification of the educational system; a comprehensive school.

The purpose of this chapter is to empirically shed light on the Swedish participation in the IEI project and the possible connection to the pre-history and development of the SPPI.[2] Thereby it will also be possible to raise analytical considerations about the use of an international model in the national curriculum work, i.e. to elaborate on the effects of national and international discourses on specific national historical events. After further developing this point of departure, the chapter has the following structure. In a brief introduction to the Swedish participation in IEI and to the main conclusions of the reports from the Swedish team, the specific national discourse on assessment will be brought to the fore. The next section places this discourse within a progressive movement in Swedish education and illustrates how the progressive movement (1) tried to strengthen their position on the educational field, and (2) what changes of the system they tried to accomplish. The last empirical part illustrates in more detail how participation in IEI functioned to strengthen this position and what different effects it had on Swedish education. In the concluding section the fact that 'the international' in this case consisted of ideas about assessment, is further elaborated.

Using the 'International' – departure and analytical considerations

The Swedish Committee joined the IEI in 1936, about the same time as two other Scandinavian countries: Norway and Finland. The group representing the Swedish Committee at the IEI conference in Dinard two years later consisted of one official administrator, one headmaster and one expert on statistics. This group was backed up by a larger team of researchers, teachers and other official administrators (see Table 1). The Swedish Committee published three reports though none of them was written by the persons attending the Dinard conference. Two of the reports were written by the most influential Swedish researcher on assessment at that time, Frits Wigforss, and the third one by head teacher Stellan Orrgård (with assistance from Professor in Psychology and Pedagogy, Rudolf Anderberg).

A common approach when analysing effects of internationalisation is tracing international influences on national discourses in terms of borrowing (cf. Steiner-Kamsi et al, 2004). Reviewing the Swedish reports, or briefly looking at what the Swedish representatives said at Dinard, clearly shows, though, that the Swedes stayed within a national discourse that had quite a long history. They did not really borrow any ideas from other countries in the IEI project. Still it is possible to find traces of IEI in Swedish policy documents and teacher journals from the 1930s and 1940s. So if not using IEI for borrowing ideas one must ask if the participation in IEI had other effects not obvious in the immediate discourse. Were references to the international scene made in other ways and for other purposes?

From a Swedish historical research perspective the most interesting fact about the Swedish participation would not be the reports published by the Swedish team. The discourse the reports relate to is well known, and more importantly, it developed in Sweden before Sweden joined the IEI. Of greater interest, then, is the organisation under which name these reports were published: the Society for a Psychological Pedagogical Institute The State Psychological Pedagogical Institute (SPPI) founded in 1944 is fully recognised in contemporary historical research for its reflection of, and influences on, the national curriculum, but the Society behind such an institute has hitherto not been investigated. The empirical question that serves as a guide through this article is if and how the Swedish participation in IEI had any relation to the SPPI through the Society for a Psychological Pedagogical Institute. Departing from a neo-institutional perspective (Meyer & Rowan, 1977; Schriewer 2000, 2004), it will be argued that references to IEI functioned as a strategy to legitimise a progressive position within the national educational field.[3] Strengthening this position within the field then had quite far going consequences – not only intended ones.

Taking the National Perspective Abroad: a brief introduction to the Swedish participation in IEI

As mentioned, one should hesitate before using the concepts of borrowing to understand the impact of IEI on Sweden. Still, IEI had impacts. Representing Sweden at Dinard we find Dr Nils Hänninger, Dr Tor Jerneman and headmaster Hugo Grimlund. The chair of the Swedish team, Nils Hänninger, was a former member of the State Board of Education and director of a publishing house. Jerneman, an expert on statistics, worked at the State Social Board and Grimlund was the headmaster of one of the largest secondary schools in Stockholm. While Hänninger also attended the Folkestone conference 1935, the Dinard conference was the first occasion where the Swedish Committee presented itself and its work to the other members of IEI.

Already in his introduction to the team's presentation Hänninger connects the Swedish work in IEI to a national context and 'essential problems for the time being within our educational world in Sweden' (Monroe, 1939, p. 207). He presents, as the first aim of the Swedish investigation, the work of Frits Wigforss where he points out that Wigforss 'is also engaged in another investigation of the same kind, on the basis of a wider material'. Hänninger mentions that this other investigation is a high-stakes governmental report (SOU 1938:29) on abolishing entrance testing and instead letting elementary school marks work as instruments for selection (Monroe, 1939, p. 208). A prerequisite is that the marks can be made equal for equal student achievement, i.e. standardised. In the IEI report, Wigforss shows that the correlation between entrance test result and later school achievement is generally quite low (Wigforss, 1937; Monroe, 1939, p. 210). If standardised marks could show better correlation with school success, then entrance tests would be unnecessary.

Dr Nils Hanninger.

Also in introducing the second aim of the Swedish investigations, Hänninger departs from a current problem in Swedish educational system, the matriculation examination in secondary education. He says that the question of determining fitness for different kinds of practical vocations as well as suitability for continued studies at university is 'the most central point in the whole complex of problems, from the standpoint of Swedish conditions' (Monroe, 1939, p. 208). One, for the time unusual, methodological approach to that problem was to carry out a survey on teachers and school leaders' attitude towards, and experiences of, the matriculation examination (Orrgård, 1937). When briefly pointing at the third and final aim of the Swedish investigation, the problems of intermediate school examinations (which, by the way, were never reported), Hänninger once again refers to typical Swedish conditions. He claims that the marking as such in the matriculation examination, either written or oral, is not of first grade importance 'as these things are arranged in Sweden' (Monroe, 1939, p. 209).

In presenting the results of the Swedish investigation, Tor Jerneman exposes what can be claimed to be the main object in the Swedish discourse on assessments during this period. He said that the major difficulty in standardising how teachers give marks was 'the fact that the individual teacher does not like to drop his own judgment of the pupils' ability in order to base the marks on the test' (Monroe, 1939, p. 211). This was the clear outcome of Wigforss's study (1937). The study that Orrgård carried out did not just find similar results but also showed the same kind of respect for teacher judgement in its methodological approach and research questions (Orrgård, 1937; Monroe, 1939, p. 213).

Tor Jerneman.

The two studies reported by the Swedes both put teachers and, one can say, instruction in the foreground of assessment problems. This also holds true looking at Hugo Grimlund's inquiry, at the time ongoing and only tentatively presented at Dinard, in which the Committee followed up complaints from teachers about the national examinations in modern languages. The tests used in language 'compel teachers to exercise a grammatical drill for years before the examination' (Monroe, 1939, p. 265). In other words, the problem seen from a Swedish perspective was not mainly about fairness in students' life chances (meritocracy) but about the effects of assessments on teachers' work. In this respect, and compared to what especially Hänninger and Wigforss had written before, it is possible to claim that the participation in IEI did not lead to any change in the Swedish discourse on student assessment and examinations. Another way to put this conclusion would be to say that the participation in IEI did not affect the textual discourse. No ideas were borrowed and none were, as it seems, impressing the other participants, considering the general discussion on the Swedish team's presentation.[4] As I will try to show, the effects were of another kind. The experience of working in this international framework was used to strengthen a particular progressive Swedish discourse and its representatives on the educational field. The roots to that discourse and the 'need' for change embedded in it can partly be explored in the history of the Society for a Psychological and Pedagogical Institute and among the people forming this network, and partly from an investigation of the Swedish educational field at large in the 1930s.

Hugo Grimlund.

After discussing these two themes and the need for educational change in Sweden I try to extract more explicitly the effects IEI had on the Swedish curriculum.

Change in a Small Country – the fieldwork of a progressive network

> The work of the Swedish Committee has not proceeded as far as in certain other countries. This in the fist place depends on the fact that we were not able to take up our work at the beginning of the International Institute Examinations Inquiry but entered it about 1936. It is also because of the situation in a small country where there are not so many persons who are at the same time qualified for a certain investigation and unprevented from other occupations to take it up. (Nils Hänninger, cited in Monroe, 1939 p. 207)

This statement by Hänninger at the Dinard conference illustrates one circumstance representative of the Scandinavian countries in IEI. The competence necessary for the project was distributed over quite a few individuals, preoccupied also by other obligations. In Sweden there are some names that constantly pop up when reviewing texts and occurrences from the 1930s and 1940s, for example, Nils Hänninger, Frits Wigforss, Hugo Grimlund and Stellan Orrgård. They were all part of a progressive force in

Swedish education, informally, as it seems, led by a woman named Anna Sörensen, principal at the Teachers' College in Stockholm. Sörensen and Hänninger wrote textbooks together and they participated in several educational societies. They were both editors of a well-known journal called *Skola och Samhälle* (School and Society). Hänninger, Wigforss and Grimlund also shared an interest in participating in other international communities; for example, they went together with Sörensen to the 14th Nordic School meeting in 1935 (*Svenska folkskolans historia* [*SFH*], vol. V, p. 406). The four of them were also frequent writers in another very influential journal (cf. Elgqvist-Saltzman, 1993, p. 93), *Rostads elevförbunds årsskrift (RÅE)* (The Yearbook of Kalmar Teachers' College).

If we pay Nils Hänninger and Frits Wigforss some additional attention it becomes clear that they represented a kind of progressivism as a programme for teacher professionalism. This perspective was rooted in what has been called the Spirit of Rostad: a philanthropic belief in the self-regulating, responsible youth. The upbringing of such a youth required a teacher that by himself had experienced great responsibility and autonomy (cf. *RÅE*, 1930, pp. 8-9). This point of view was of course shared by a larger group of people, but had in Rostad Teachers' College (in Kalmar) a strong institutional base. Wigforss was an appreciated lecturer at Rostad.

Hänninger and Wigforss were also influenced by recent international trends on teacher training. While Wigforss in his work on standardised tests was more inspired by German writers (especially Johannes Kühnel's classic text *Neubau des Rechenunterrichts*; see Kilpatrick & Johansson, 1994, p. 10), Hänninger has been named as one of the persons that made American ideas available to the thinking on education in Sweden (*SFH*, vol. V, p. 488). Hänninger went to America in1921 on a state scholarship. In his book *The World of American Upbringing* one can see his fascination for non-traditional methods and perspectives on education; project work, student responsibility, supervised teaching, the abandonment of homework, etc. (Hänninger, 1922). One other thing that came to Hänninger's notice was what he called 'Americanisation' (p. 80) – how to use education to create the unification of a fragmented society. The progressive movement in Sweden had the same vision for Swedish education (Lindensjö & Lundgren, 2000), but saw as a prerequisite to first accomplish unification in the educational system (see further below). It was during this visit to the USA that Hänninger first met Paul Monroe, who personally introduced Hänninger to Teachers College at Columbia (Hänninger, 1922, p. 16). It is reasonable to believe that they kept in contact through the years to come and also that this personal contact was the major factor in Hänninger becoming chair of the Swedish Committee, but it has not yet been possible to find either first-hand or secondary sources. The first time Hänninger publically refers to IEI is in a critical essay on examinations in 1932.[5] An investigation in Nils Hänninger's personal archive, though, reveals that Hänninger was appointed as Isaac Kandel's guide when he visited Sweden in 1933 for the IEI project.[6] In a letter dated

9 November 1934, Kandel informs Hänninger that he had told Paul Monroe about Hänninger's interest in the examination inquiry. On 20 May 1935 Paul Monroe wrote a letter to Hänninger from Istanbul, inviting him as a guest to the Folkestone conference in June. On 4December 1935 Monroe wrote to inform Hänninger that the Carnegie Corporation Board agreed to grant Sweden and Finland 3000 dollars if they were willing to initiate the work of IEI in Scandinavia.

If Hänninger promoted American unification and comprehensive schooling in general, Wigforss's main interest was using tests as a means both to accomplish a more effective school system and, of more importance, increased teacher professionalism. He had already in an article in 1931 scrutinised and criticised well-known testing methods for not promoting teacher and student development but only measuring past achievement.[7] When it comes to student examination, Hänninger and Wigforss were both very critical of the existing tradition and the stress it caused in the everyday life of students and teachers (Wigforss's governmental reports: SOU 1938:29, 1942:11; Hänninger, 1932). At the same time they relied on teachers' ability to accomplish fair judgements. Wigforss's idea was to develop standardised test with an overarching purpose to aid teachers in their instruction. In his first longer article about these tests, he wrote:

> It is important, though, that standardized tests become what they are supposed to be: a measuring-rod in every class teacher's hand and not one in the hands of a controlling school agency.
> (Wigforss, 1933, p. 222, my translation)

The solution was, in other words, not to replace teachers' judgement with the 'objective' judgement from intelligence tests, but to improve the teachers' judgement. Wigforss argued that school tests and scientific tests could be merged together and offered to the teachers as a methodological tool to use in their everyday work (*SFH*, vol. V, p. 175).

This points to an all-embracing issue at that time – the necessity of an organisation that could introduce scientific methods and perspectives to the teaching profession, fusing theoretical and practical knowledge (cf. Lundahl, 2006). In 1934 Hänninger and his network of other progressive thinkers took the initiative to try to realise such an organisation and formed the Society for a Psychological Pedagogical Institute. A majority of the people involved in the Swedish IEI Committee were also members of this society (see Table I).

The Society for a Psychological and Pedagogical Institute – a discursive coalition

In 1929 a committee appointed two years earlier to suggest a new structure for teacher education produced its final report (SOU 1929:10). Hänninger, at the time a member of the National Board of Education, enclosed a reservation about the Board's general comment on the committee suggestions. In this he proposed a central institute responsible for bringing the theoretical and practical parts of teacher education closer together. His idea was met with half-hearted interest from the Government (cf. SOU 1938:50, pp. 33f., 224ff.) This did not stop him from forming a society together with people in his personal network with the aim to establish such an institute. The society was formally constituted on 14 December 1934 (*SLTG* [*Svensk lärartidning* (The Swedish Teachers' Journal)], 1934, p. 1202). In November 1944 the State Psychological Pedagogical Institute became reality (*Skola och Samhälle*, 1944, pp. 189-202). The question is to what extent the participation in IEI was used by the Society to promote the establishment of the institute.

The first step to answer that question is to establish a further connection between the Society and the participation in IEI. Table I lists the people involved in the Swedish IEI committee on the left side and members of the Society to the right.

As we can see, a scarce majority of the people involved in the Swedish IEI work were also members in the Society for a Psychological Pedagogical Institute. Of 13 people involved in the Swedish participation in IEI, seven were also members of the committee (n = 21) for the realisation of this institute. We can also see that members of both committees included both practical and theoretical pedagogues (teachers and headmasters as well as scholars), and to some extent with political influence. It is possible to talk of a discursive coalition (Wagner et al, 1991; Schriewer, 2000) between researchers, practitioners of education and politicians. As well as Mr Wagnersson on the list, a member of parliament, others were politically involved or connected.

National Research Team, IEI 1938	The Society for a Psychological Pedagogical Institute, 1934
*Chair – Nils Hänninger, Former member of the National Board of Education, Stockholm	R. Anderberg, PhD, Professor (in Psychology and Pedagogy)
*Hugo Grimlund, Headmaster, Vasa Secondary School, Stockholm	H.J. Berg, former member of the National Board of Education
Tor Jerneman, Sec, State Social Board, Statistics Expert	M. Björkquist, Headmaster
**Bror Jonzon, PhD, Chief Inspector of Elementary Education in Stockholm	E. Edén, Medical officer of health
Gustaf Lagercrantz, Bank Director	H. Grimlund Headmaster
Nils Lundqvist, PhD, Headmaster	C.W. Herlitz, Assistant Professor
*Anna C Petterson, Headmistress	O. Holmdahl, Director General, National Board of Education
*Karl Steenberg, Headmaster	N. Hänninger, Member of the National Board of Education, Stockholm
Erik Wellander, PhD, Professor (in Swedish Language)	G.H. von Koch, Deputy Director

Gustaf Mattsson, Headmaster	A. Lichtenstein, PhD, Professor (in Pediatrics)
* Frits Wigforss, PhD, Lecturer, Teachers College, Kalmar	K. Nordlund, Chief Inspector of Elementary Education
Stellan Orrgård, Head Teacher	N. Persson, Inspector of Elementary Education
*Rudolf Anderberg, Phd, Professor (in Psychology and Pedagogy)	A.C. Pettersson, Education Officer
	T. Ramer, Doctor of Medicine
	K. Steenberg, Head Teacher
	A. Sörensen, Headmistress, Teachers College (Chair) (d. 1943)
	S. Tunberg, Professor (in Cultural History?)
	R. Wagnersson, Member of Parliament
	V. Wigert, Professor (d. 1942)
	F. Wigforss, Lecturer, Teachers College
	J. Wintzell, PhD
	Additional members 1944
	B. Jonzon, Chief Inspector of Elementary Education
	D. Katz, PhD, Professor (in Psychology and Pedagogy)
	H. Nygren, Headmistress, Member of Parliament
	G. Kaleen, PhD student

*, ** Also members of the Swedish Society for a Psychological Pedagogical Institute (**SLTG* 1934, p. 1202, ***Skola och Samhälle*, 1944, p. 193).

Table I. List of people involved in the Swedish IEI committee and in the Society for a Psychological Pedagogical Institute

It is possible to illustrate how this discursive coalition could work in practice. When Wigforss worked on one of his research studies within the IEI project he turned to a municipality in Sweden, Gävle, to gain access to teachers who could help him investigate the difference between primary school teachers' student certificate and secondary school teachers' entrance examinations. Hildur Nygren, who Wigforss acknowledges in the introduction to one of his IEI reports (Wigforss, 1941, p. 6), was a headmistress in the municipality of Gävle. She was also a member of the Society for a Psychological Pedagogical Institute. When, some years later, forming the actual Psychological Pedagogical Institute, the Government decided that it should be state-owned – and not, as the Society had suggested, half private and half state-owned (Hänninger, 1935; *Proposition 1944:207*, pp. 61-78) – Hildur Nygren tried to affect the Government's decision preventing any member of the Society from being part of the board of the institute. She wrote, now as a Member of Parliament, a bill to the Government in which she pointed out that:

> it is of some value, that the Society [of PPI] becomes represented in the board of the proposed institute. The Society has ... not only promoted the thought of a Psychological Pedagogical Institute but has also taken initiative to and carried out investigations that shown themselves of practical pedagogical importance to the ongoing reforming of our school system. In this matter one could especially direct the attention to the investigations on entrance testing and examinations that the Society carried out ... with financial support from the Carnegie Cooperation in the United States. (*Motion 470 AK* [Bill no. 470, second chamber 1944, pp. 11-12]; my translation)

Nygren's suggestion was initially rejected by the Educational Committee (*RD prot AK 24:68d*, 1944).[8] But in the end her plea was heard When the Government finally proposed and the Parliament decided on the budget of the State Psychological Pedagogical Institute in 1945, not only was the yearly funding raised from initially 15.500 SEK to 85.500 SEK, Frits Wigforss was selected as a member of the board (*Proposition 1945:232*, pp. 63-66; *RD prot AK 30:35d*; *Skola och samhälle*, 1944). One may add that the Minister of Finance, who gave his approbation to this proposition, was named Ernst Wigforss and was the older brother of Frits Wigforss.

The discursive coalition was built up by peple knowing each other due to the fact that Sweden is a small country. Another fact is that it was well hidden. Coming this far in the process of realising the SPPI, its origins from the Society and the international work the Society carried out are not mentioned in the proposition that led to the final decision on the establishment of the SPPI (*Proposition 1944:207*).[9] This can be compared with the governmental reports and propositions that were published earlier (*SOU 1938:50*; *Proposition 1942:255*, pp. 87-101), where the work of the Society is richly acknowledged. Below, this will be discussed as a politicisation of the discourse observed in similar situations where politicians 'forget' the origins of ideas (Spreen, 2004). In other words, even if the participation in IEI helped in establishing the SPPI, it was not acknowledged in the constituting political documents.

So far we have an example of an actual discursive coalition, but to get a better picture of how it shaped Swedish educational discourse one needs to look at the Swedish educational field in the 1930s and 1940s.

The Swedish Educational Field of the 1930s and 1940s – in need of unification

In his article 'Educational Studies in Europe' (2000) Jürgen Schriewer illustrates how German scholars from the faculties of philosophy during the mid-war period entered a discursive coalition with the Prussian administration and leading representatives of secondary school teachers, to suppress a disciplinary and practical threat. This threat came from left-wing politicians, experimental psychology/education researchers and primary school teachers (p. 75). By joining forces and using arguments that a development of the educational system was a matter of socio-historical reflection based on sophisticated epistemology, the former coalition could stop the advancement of a comprehensive school based on ideas about equality and on psychological investigations. In doing so, the faculties of philosophy could safeguard their social reproduction as responsible for teacher training (p. 78). In Sweden, during the 1930s we find the same two kinds of coalitions, but the outcome of their struggle was the direct opposite (cf. Lundgren 1979/1989). It is possible to argue that the Society for a Psychological and Pedagogical Institute used their participation in IEI as a power resource in this struggle over the educational field and that the realisation of the SPPI can be seen as a materialisation of the discourse entertained by a progressive coalition. The SPPI was produced by this discourse on purpose to re/produce it, i.e. to re/produce a new type of language in and about education.

One way to understand why the outcome could be different in Sweden compared to Germany is to consider the fact that the faculty involvement in respective coalitions was weaker in Sweden. The psychological and pedagogical discipline had split away from philosophy in the early 1900s (Fransson & Lundgren 2003). This and the fact that Sweden at the time lacked philosophers of the same calibre as the German ones, made the educational field less important from a disciplinary perspective. The discipline of Psychology and Pedagogy already owned it. But for understanding the Swedish case the tensions between the political sides and between the different teacher groups are of greater importance. As in Germany, secondary teachers and conservative parties relied on teacher tradition while primary school teachers and left-wing politicians wanted to extend the influence of psychological and pedagogical research. In Sweden the struggle between these positions was not so much about educational content as in Germany. Instead it was focused on organisational matters and especially on at what age it was proper to differentiate the students to the different educational tracks.[10] This issue had already been raised in the late 1920s but due to economic regression in Sweden, school problems were not really dealt with under the social democratic governance during the 1930s. During the Second World War Sweden had an all-party government and in this government a right-wing politician, Gösta Bagge, became Minister of Education for the fist time in decades. Bagge thought that many of the problems in the educational system were the same for the different types of school (Sweden had at that time 12 different school forms within the primary and the secondary sectors). Bagge was able to unite the different political parties in this view and in that they should seek one solution – comprehensive schooling. But agreeing on merging primary school with secondary school reinforced the discussion about the right age for differentiation for working life or secondary schooling. On this matter the different political parties disagreed, as did the two major teacher unions. Secondary school teachers and conservative politicians wanted an early differentiation since they thought that it would enhance the intellectual development of the students if most of their training took place in secondary education. Mrs Alva Myrdal, famous in Sweden for her commitments within the social sector [11], tried to settle the discussion by claiming that the question of differentiation was a matter of scientific proof rather than of political and professional opinions. In so doing, she introduced a way of dealing with political and pedagogical controversies that set the path for future disputes – turning to science (see, for example, Lindensjö & Lundgren, 2000, pp. 40-48). Since knowledge production in the educational field was owned by the discipline of Psychology and Pedagogy the solutions were sought within the dominating epistemology of this discipline; that of experimental and differential psychology.[12] Since primary school teachers had most to win by showing that late differentiation was 'objectively' better, they were also the ones embracing the introduction of experimental and differential psychology in the practical curriculum.

In Sweden, Psychology and Pedagogy became a discipline of its own in 1907 and influenced teacher training at both primary and secondary level more and more during the years to come (Fransson & Lundgren, 2003; Askling, 2006). But it was with the question of differentiation that the psychological discourse really came to dominate within the field, especially in relation to primary school and in the area of assessing and judging student achievements. In primary school teacher journals from the 1930s and 1940s, the use of psychological language and the spreading of results from psychological research increased and replaced a pedagogical language and perspective on schooling. This was not the fact in secondary school teacher journals (Lundahl, 2006, part 3). That relationship holds true also when looking at comments in these journals on the Swedish participation in IEI, the Society for a Psychological and Pedagogical Institute and on the SPPI. These occurrences are never mentioned in the largest journal for secondary school teachers at the time, *Tidning för Sveriges Läroverk* [Journal for Upper Secondary Schools], while getting, if not much, at least some attention in primary school teacher journals.

Reviewing these articles, a complex picture appears in relation to the educational field and the need for a psychological discourse and an institution re/producing it. From the articles in which first, the formation of the Society (*SLTG*, 1934, p. 1202), and second, the realisation of the SPPI (*SLTG*, 1944, pp. 11-12; *SLTG*, 1944, p. 1216; *Skolan & Samhälle*, 1944, pp. 189-202), were described/presented, it is possible to draw a picture of a fragmented field and to illustrate the unifying function of the SPPI (Figure 1).

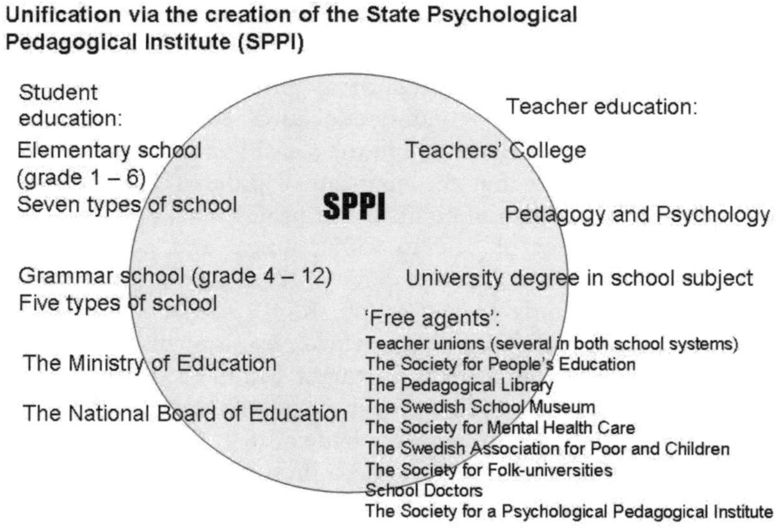

Figure 1. The unification purpose of creating the State Psychological Pedagogical Institute.

The formal Swedish educational system and the field surrounding it was fragmented and filled with vested interests. If we look at the proposed function of the SPPI from the perspective of Hänninger and Wigforss it is actually possible to talk of two different unifying functions. Hänninger was mostly preoccupied with the needs of a coordinating organisation. In the article 'Do We Need a Psychological-pedagogical Institute?' Hänninger elaborates his idea of an institute at length:

> On the whole there is a need for a joint platform for discussion and deliberation – and investigation – of the many different problems concerning the upbringing raised by the school of today. They are about for example the relationship between doctors and teachers, between medical-psychological and pedagogical practice ... A pedagogical institute would create a meeting spot for the medical and the pedagogical interests. (Hänninger, 1935, p. 61; my translation)[13]

In other words, it was thought possible to unify the fragmented, ineffective and polarised Swedish educational system if the SPPI could work as a meeting point for different educational actors. Following Wigforss it is possible to add one function, that of a *shared language*, offered by assessments. Standardising assessments would reduce the complexity of the communication between different types of school and the different agents in the system. In the second of Wigforss's IEI reports he discusses the possibility of normalising teachers' certificates with the aid of standardise tests [14]:

> Uniformity in [arithmetic] would obviously have been gained if the certificates had been awarded according to the verdict of the standard tests, but the question is whether such a method would be justified. To what extent can one be sure that the verdict of the tests is the right one? The trustworthiness of a test depends on how well the test is related to that which is the object of testing (i.e. the curriculum) and the suitability of the test as a measuring instrument. (Wigforss, 1941, p. 127)

Adapting tests to curriculum (or vice versa), and ensuring that teacher certificates are verdicts along the same standard, would reduce the complexity of the system enormously, since entrance testing then could be abandoned. Developing these tests was ascribed as one important task for the SPPI, and during the first years of the SPPI, Wigforss had chief responsibility over the construction of standardised tests with the overall purpose of calibrating the curriculum to the 'normal' child.

This takes us back to the main purpose of this article. It is obvious that the Swedish educational field was fragmented. The development of unified institutions has been typical for modern societies. The SPPI was one, among other organisations, that could help in unifying the Swedish educational field. So, specifically, how did the participation in the IEI project help in realising the SPPI?

The Effects of the Swedish Participation in IEI on the Swedish Curriculum

There is no doubt that the SPPI and especially the investigations carried out by Frits Wigforss on and with assessments have affected the development of the Swedish curriculum (Kilpatrick & Johansson, 1994; Lundahl, 2006). In this chapter I have shown how the Society for a Psychological Pedagogical Institute worked for the realisation of the SPPI and how the SPPI could serve certain needs in modern Swedish education. To answer the question to what extent the participation in IEI helped realise the SPPI one must be reminded that even if there was not any direct opposition against the formation of the SPPI, there were strong interests against the kind of modernisation of the educational system that the SPPI represented. Most of all the teachers at secondary school were about to lose their right to decide which students they should teach. They were also about to lose their autonomy. Psychologists, medical doctors and educational researchers entered the field to an extent not seen before (cf. Lundahl, 2006). They could also see that a long tradition of a certain way to 'do school' was threatened. To convince people with these kinds of fears, international trends and experiences from international conventions could be used as a powerful strategy – without any actual borrowing taking part.

In different teacher journals and in the governmental reports and propositions it is possible to trace two major ways of using the participation in IEI in arguments for curriculum changes. The first one relates to examinations and entrance testing. Wigforss referred at quite some length to the Swedish experience from the IEI project in his governmental report on standardised grading. Orrgård's survey, especially, was given a lot of attention (SOU 1938:29, pp. 43-60). The Swedish results, but even more the situation in other IEI countries, were used in influential journals when arguing against examinations and entrance testing (Hänninger, 1935, p. 60; *SLTG*, 1936, pp. 4-5; *SLTG*, 1938, p. 1046; *Psykologisk pedagogisk uppslagsbok*, 1943, pp. 430ff.; *Skola och samhälle*, 1944). In an interview after coming home from Dinard, Hänninger commented on the problem experienced by several countries with external examination boards, a theme thoroughly discussed at the conference (see Monroe, 1939). Hänninger said:

> Here in Sweden we don't have this kind of board; it is for example not the supervising examiners that decide the grades in the upper-secondary final examination but the teachers. In relation to the last student examination committee there came proposals on establishing such boards. I objected to those proposals bearing in mind the experiences made in other countries [referring especially to England, France and Finland]. (SLTG, 1938, p. 1046; my translation)

Clearly, some alternatives could be dismissed from the agenda with help from the experiences of IEI countries. But other than this, the results referred to from these countries can hardly have surprised the Swedish delegation. Earlier and parallel national investigations had often drawn the same conclusions on, for example, the subjective bias in entrance testing (cf. Hänninger, 1932), or about the overrated usefulness of intelligence testing (*Skolkommissionens betänkande*, 1921-1923; Hänninger, 1922; *SLTG*, 1931, pp. 1179-1180). Still, it seems that it was important to report on the experiences from IEI and one may wonder why. Two reasons are obvious; there is an attraction in strengthening their own discourse with help from, or in contrast to, experiences from other countries. Secondly, the people involved in the Swedish IEI team and in the Society owned the means to print their experiences (whatever they were) as, in several cases, they were members of editorial boards. In other words, the first effect related to the participation in IEI can be said to be a strengthening of an existing progressive discourse and at the same time an exclusion of threatening alternatives.

The second impact of the participation in IEI relates to the need of a Psychological and Pedagogical Institute to re/produce this discourse – a modern institution bringing science and educational practice closer together. Here IEI was used as an example of work that could be carried out by the SPPI. References to the results from the Swedish Committee were, for example, made in the first governmental proposal for the establishment of a Psychological Pedagogical Institute (*Proposition 1942:255*) together with the notion that one important task for the Institute should be to develop new forms of test that could substitute the entrance tests. The participation in IEI also affected the participants' knowledge about similar institutes in other countries: Zentralinstitut für Erziehung und Unterricht in Berlin, Teachers College in New York and the Scottish Council for Research in Education served as inspirational sources (Hänninger, 1935, p. 62; SOU 1938:50, p. 224; *Svensk skoltidning*, 1944). References to these institutes were also made in the governmental proposals for the establishment of the SPPI (*Proposition 1942:255*, p. 95). The impacts of these references are of course difficult to measure. A more accountable effect was the not negligible amount of money involved. Sweden received 3000 dollars from the Carnegie Foundation (*SLTG*, 1936, p.5), which was about the same amount that the well-established SPPI received from the Swedish Government during its first year in 1944. The Carnegie dollars were used to pay, for example, Frits Wigforss to carry out his investigations (see also Kilpatrick & Johansson, 1994) and to print and publish the results (Wigforss, 1941). The Society for a Psychological Pedagogical Institute was also promised funding for their courses from the Swedish Government if they could show that they had external financing (*SLTG*, 1936, p. 1384). The participation in IEI helped establish the Society as an economically strong actor in the educational field, which in the long run probably contributed to the realisation of the SPPI.

Concluding Remarks

This chapter began by claiming that the participation in IEI did not affect the Swedish discourse on assessments, at least not looking at its basic ideas. But it did affect the discourse in several other ways. The Swedish participation in IEI helped a reform-friendly network to systemise and publish results that gave support for abandoning entrance testing. It helped this network to strengthen its position on the educational field in the capacity of acting as 'travellers'; people with perspectives. The participation also functioned as an argument for the establishment of a Psychological Pedagogical Institute in Sweden which, among other purposes, aimed at bringing pedagogical practice and psychological theory closer together, thereby creating a sense of greater unification in Swedish education. In claiming this conclusion, it is of course important to remember that almost all sources available on the Swedish participation in IEI are contaminated by a close kinship between members of the Swedish Committee and/or of the Society for a Psychological Pedagogical Institute.

It is tempting to interpret the story of IEI as yet another story of how American and English psychology colonised educational thinking here and there. For the Swedish case that would be an exaggeration. What the Swedish travellers were probably most eager to import was rather the idea of what Hänninger called 'Americanisation', i.e. unification. In reaching unification a need emerged to reduce the complexity of the system, a need that could be met by the quick, unambiguous language of 1940s psychology. The use of psychology, in other words, worked as a means to reach the goal of unification and was not a goal in it self. Hänninger and Wigforss were both keen to stress that the import of psychological thinking should always depart from the needs of the teachers.

But the picture of a colonising psychology would fit the descriptions of the 1950s and 1960s quite well. As stated above, the educational discourse in Sweden soon became more political and in relation to that more scientific. When realising the SPPI, its origins from the Society and the influences from abroad seem to have vanished in the political documents. As Carol Ann Spreen noticed on the contemporary scene, international borrowing at some point no longer is viable to legitimate reform:

> It is precisely when ideas begin to take hold and become national policies that they must confront cultural beliefs, practices, and local understandings; then the international argument loses weight. (Spreen, 2004, p. 112)

It is important for politicians to make ideas appear as their own. That is a matter of gaining legitimacy but it is also reasonable to suspect that when all the decisions are made and when reform is to be implemented; it is of greater importance to show the effects, the outcomes with facts and figures, than it is to elaborate alternatives with help from international perspectives. In Sweden and for decades after World War II, a psychology-laden pedagogy turned the scope inside the educational system rather than looking abroad. This led to a curriculum philosophy bearing the marks of social engineering:

> Swedish behavioural research at the outset of the 1950's, irrespective of whether it carried an educational or psychological label, was essentially marketed as social engineering, which more or less amounted to telling people what they were good for. It could help to predict who was going to be able to cope with higher education or demonstrate aptitude for certain occupations. (Husén, 1972, p. 234)

In the years to come the Swedish Government used the SPPI to promote psychological tests and to intensify teacher training in psychology. Wigforss lost ground, and when he died in 1954 most of his spirit and beliefs in the possibility to develop, not replace, teacher judgement were forgotten

(Kilpatrick & Johansson, 1994). In 1949 the editor of one of the most important teacher journals wrote that they were disappointed at what had become of the SPPI, which they believed too theoretical to be able to support practical educational work (*Folkskolan*, 1949, p. 34).

Progressive pedagogues had laid the ground to – quite contrary to their intentions – a psychological colonisation of the educational field, and thus a deprofessionalisation of teachers. On the road to this development the participation in IEI had come to play a part.

Notes

[1] 'Curriculum' is used in the more philosophical sense as a set of thoughts on education that are dominating in a given society (cf. Lundgren, 1972).

[2] This article is based on an investigation of the appearance of IEI in governmental reports and propositions, and in six influential teacher journals between the years 1930 and 1950: *Svensk lärartidning (SLTG)*, *Tidningen folkskolan*, *Svensk skoltidning*, *Tidning för Sveriges Läroverk*, *Skola och samhälle*, *Rostads elevförbunds årsskrift*. The investigation has been carried out in relation to a Swedish–German project: International Student Assessments, National Assessment Culture and Reform History. A 2007-2009 Research Project Funded by the Swedish Research Council (Forsberg et al, 2006).

[3] 'Educational field' in this article refers to the discursive and political field and the positions held by three major educational actors: politicians and administrators, researchers, and teachers (representatives).

[4] The general discussion that followed the Swedish presentation was not at all about the results of the Swedish group or about examinations – the theme of the conference – but about problems in language education in small countries not native speakers of any of the world languages (Monroe, 1939, pp. 265-267).

[5] This was in the Journal *Skola och samhälle* (School and Society), where he ends his text 'Examinations and School Work' with the following words: '[I]t would be of most interest not only to get the question of examinations discussed by teachers but also from people standing on the outside of the schools. Such kinds of investigations have started here and there around the world, among other things, in Germany and in England. According to what I have heard, one large institution in America planned to carry out one widespread investigation on examinations that might even be expanded to some countries in Europe. I find it desirable that also our country took upon itself a similar task' (Hänninger, 1932, p. 194; my translation).

[6] The archive is available at Lund university library. See: http://www.ediffah.org/search/present.cgi?id=ediffah:lub:327421:1170862131

[7] Tests developed by, for example, P.H. Ballard (representing England at Dinard), W.S. Monroe and H. Meyer (Wigforss, 1931, pp. 86-88; cf. Kilpatrick & Johansson, 1994, p. 10).

[8] Protocol of decision in the Swedish Parliament (Riksdag), second chamber (AK) 1944.

[9] This also goes for an important suggestion from the National Board of Education concerning future assignments for the SPPI (*SLTG*, 1944, pp. 11-12).

[10] For example, in the influential Encyclopaedia of the history of the Swedish elementary school the part about what was called 'the outer organisation' is given around one-third of the 570 pages summarising the period between 1920 and 1942 (*SFH*, vol. V).

[11] Alva Myrdal also received the Nobel Peace Prize 1982 for her global engagement in issues of arms reduction.

[12] When looking at the epistemology and the qualities of the language of psychology, its 'facts and figures appearance' indicates that it could be perceived as a 'quick language'. A quick language is a highly codified self-referential language that not only seems faster in that it is *not* deliberative (objective), but also works faster in that it connects several interest groups with one another in an unambiguous lingua, which, once learned, is easy to decode (cf. Lundahl, 2006, ch. 12). Believing and working in this rationality reduces the complexity of the system (Forsberg & Lundahl, 2006).

[13] It is worth mentioning that Hänninger writes that the idea of such an institute was first formed in Sweden by the elementary school inspector Frans von Schéele in an article in 1913 (p. 60). He also mentions Zentralinstitut für Erziehung und Unterricht in Berlin, Teachers College in New York and the Scottish Council for Research in Education as inspirational sources.

[14] It is worth noticing that this report uses data collected by Wigforss and his colleagues between 1929 and 1937. In other words, the Carnegie Foundation did not initiate the investigation as such. As claimed above, the Swedish reports followed on a national tradition of investigating this topic, but, as also stated in the report, Carnegie helped finance it (Wigforss, 1941, pp. 3-6).

References

Askling, B. (2006) *Utbildningsvetenskap – ett vetenskapsområde tar form* [Educational science – the shaping of a scientific domain]. Stockholm: Vetenskapsrådet.

Elgqvist-Saltzman, I. (1993) *Lärarinna, kvinna, människa* [Teacher, woman, human]. Stockholm: Carlssons Förlag.

Forsberg, E. & Lundahl, C. (2006) Kunskapsbedömningar som styrmedia [Assessment as steering medium]. I. *Utbildning & demokrati*, 3, pp. 7-30.

Forsberg, E., Lundahl, C., Román, H. & Waldow, F. (2006) International Student Assessments, National Assessment Culture and Reform History. D-no.: 2006-2447. Stockholm: Swedish Research Council.

Folkskolan (1949) Rotel för pedagogisk försöksverksamhet [Division for experimental work], 33-35.

Fransson, K. & Lundgren, U.P. (2003) *Utbildningsvetenskap – ett begrepp och dess sammanhang* [Educational science – a concept and its context]. Vetenskapsrådets rapportserie 2003:1. Stockholm: Vetenskapsrådet.

Giddens, A. (1991) *Modernity and Self-identity: self and society in the late modern age.* Stanford: Stanford University Press.

Hänninger, N. (1922) *Den amerikanska uppfostringsvärlden* [The world of American upbringing]. Stockholm: P.A. Norstedt & Söners Förlag.

Hänninger, N. (1932) Examen och skolarbete [Examinations and school work], *Skola och samhälle*, 185-194.

Hänninger, N. (1935) Behöva vi ett psykologiskt-pedagogiskt institut? [Do we need a Psychological Pedagogical Institute?], *Rostads elevförbunds årsskrift*, 60-63.

Husén, T. (1972) Two Decades of Educational Research, in Social Science Research Council *Social Science Research in Sweden*, 225-239. Stockholm: Social Science Research Council.

Kilpatrick, J. & Johansson, B. (1994) Standardized Mathematics Testing in Sweden: the legacy of Frits Wigforss, *NOMAD, Nordic Studies in Mathematics Education*, 2(1), 6-30.

Lindensjö, B. & Lundgren, U.P. (2000) *Utbildningsreformer och politisk styrning* [Educational reforms and political governance]. Stockholm: HLS Förlag.

Lundahl, C. (2006) *Viljan att veta vad andra vet. Kunskapsbedömning i tidigmodern, modern och senmodern skola* [To know what others know. Assessment in education in pre-modern, modern, and late-modern times]. Stockholm: Arbetslivsinstitutet och Uppsala universitet.

Lundgren, U.P. (1972) *Frame Factors and the Teaching Process. a contribution to curriculum theory and theory on teaching.* Stockholm: Almqvist & Wiksell.

Lundgren, U.P. (1979/1989) *Att organisera omvärlden. En introduktion till läroplansteori* [Organizing the world around. An introduction to curriculum theory]. Lund: Liber.

Meyer, J.W. & Rowan, B. (1977) Institutionalized Organizations: formal structure as myth and ceremony, *American Journal of Sociology*, 83(2), 340-363.

Monroe, P. (Ed.) (1939) *Conference on Examinations (Dinard, France, September 16-19, 1938)*. New York: Bureau of Publications, Teachers College, Columbia University.

Motion 470 AK. Hildur Nygren (1944). (Bill by Member of Parliament).

Orrgård, S. (1937) *High School Entrance-Tests and the Work of the Primary-School: a Swedish nation-wide investigation in 1936.* Stockholm: Norstedt. Serie: Publications of the Swedish Society for a Psychological Pedagogical Institute, no. 2.

Proposition 1942:255 (Governmental proposition).

Proposition 1944:207.

Proposition 1945:232.

Psykologisk pedagogisk uppslagsbok [Encyclopaedia of psychology and pedagogy] (1943) Examensundersökningar [Examination inquiries], 430-436. Stockholm: Bokförlaget Natur och Kultur.

RD prot AK 24:68d (1944) (Parliament decision protocol).

RD prot AK 30:35d (1945).

Rostads elevförbunds årsskrift (RÅE) (1930) Rostad [Article about Rostad Teachers' College], 8-9.

Schriewer, J. (2000) Educational Studies in Europe, in E.S. Swing, J. Schriewer & F. Orivel (Eds) *Problems and Prospects in European Education*, 72-95. Westport & London: Praeger.

Schriewer, J. (2004) Multiple Internationalities: the emergence of a world-level ideology and the persistence of idiosyncratic world-views, in C. Charle, J. Schriewer & P. Wagner (Eds) *Transnational Intellectual Networks: forms of academic knowledge and the search for cultural identities*, 473-533. Frankfurt and New York: Campus.

Skola och samhälle [School and Society] (1944) Pedagogisk forskning. Specialnummer i anledning av upprättandet av Psykologisk-pedagogiska institutet [Pedagogical research. Special edition due to the establishment of the Psychological Pedagogical Institute], 13, 189-202.

Skolkommissionens betänkande, 1921-1923 [1918 års skolkommission]. Stockholm. (Government report).

SLTG (*Svensk lärartidning* [The Swedish Teachers' Journal]) (1931, 1179-1180) Inträdesproven till läroverken [The entrance tests to secondary school].

SLTG (1934, 1202) Pedagogiska institutet förverkligas [The Pedagogical Institute carried into effect].

SLTG (1936, 4-5) Hur stort värde har ett examensbetyg? Engelsk undersökning ger häpnadsväckande resultat [What value does an examination mark have? British investigations show prodigious results] (refers to Philip Hartog's study).

SLTG (1936, 1384) Föreningen för psykologisk-pedagogiska institutet [The Society for a Psychological Pedagogical Institute].

SLTG (1938, 1046-1047) Examensproblemet ventileras. Internationell konferens med svenska representanter [Airing of the examination problem. An international conference with Swedish participation].

SLTG (1944, 11-12) Psykologiskt-pedagogiskt institut blir verklighet? Intressant förslag av Skolöverstyrelsen. [A Psychological Pedagogical Institute becomes reality? Interesting suggestion from the National Board of Education].

SLTG (1944, 1216) Aktuellt på skolfronten: Psykologisk-pedagogiskt institut 1 november. [School news: Psychological Pedagogical Institute November 1].

SOU 1929:10. Utredning och förslag rörande praktisk lärarkurs för blivande lärare vid de allmänna läroverken m. fl. undervisningsanstalter. 1927 års skolsakkunniga [Investigation and suggestions concerning courses in practical teaching]. Stockholm: Ecklisiastikdepertementet.

SOU 1938:29. Betänkande med utredning och förslag angående intagning av elever i första klassen av de allmänna läroverken och med dem jämförliga läroanstalter [Intake of students in the first class of the lower secondary school]. Stockholm: Ecklesiastikdepartementet.

SOU 1938:50. Betänkande angående utbildningen av lärare vid de allmänna läroverken och med dem jämförliga läroanstalter. 1936 års lärarutbildningssakkunniga [Government report concerning education of secondary school teachers and of teachers in similar school forms]. Stockholm: Ecklesiastikdepartementet.

SOU 1942:11. Betänkande med utredning och förslag angående betygssättningen i Folkskolan [Government report on mark setting in the elementary school]. Stockholm: Ecklesiastikdepartementet.

Spreen, C.A. (2004) Appropriating Borrowed Policies: outcomes-based education in South Africa, in G. Steiner-Kamsi (Ed.) *The Global Politics of Educational Borrowing and Lending*, 101-113. New York and London: Teachers College Press.

Steiner-Kamsi, G. (Ed.) (2004) *The Global Politics of Educational Borrowing and Lending*. New York and London: Teachers College Press.

Svensk skoltidning 1944, 50, 7. Psykologisk-pedagogiska institutet sätter igång [The Psychological Pedagogical Institute starts up]. Sveriges småskollärarinnors förbund [The Society for Female Elementary School Teachers].

Svenska folkskolans historia (SFH), vol. V (1950) [Encyclopaedia of the history of Swedish elementary school]: Det svenska skolundervisningsväsendet 1920-1942 [The Swedish school system, 1920-1942], ed. V. Fredriksson. Stockholm: Albert Bonniers Förlag.

Wagner, P., Wittrock, B. & Wollman, H. (1991) Social Science and the Modern State: policy knowledge and political institutions in western Europe and the United States, in P. Wagner, C. Weiss, B. Wittrock & H. Wollmann (Eds) *Social Sciences and Modern States: national experiences and theoretical crossroads*, 28-85. Cambridge: Cambridge University Press.

Wigforss, F. (1931) Rostads standardprov i sifferräkning [The Rostad standardized test in numerical arithmetic], *Rostads elevförbunds årsskrift*, 28, 86-100.

Wigforss, F. (1933) Färdigheten i mekanisk räkning i folkskolan enligt Rostads standardtabeller [Skills in mechanical arithmetic in the elementary school according to the Rostad standard tables], *Skolan och samhälle*, 14, 191-122.

Wigforss, F. (1937) *The Entrance Examination in View of Later School Performances*. Swedish Society for a Psychological Pedagogical Institute. Stockholm: Norstedt. Serie: Publications of the Swedish Society for a Psychological Pedagogical Institute, no. 1.

Wigforss, F. (1941) *A Paper on the Awarding of Marks and Certificates in the Primary School and the Possibility of Normalizing the Awards*. Stockholm: Norstedt. Serie: Publications of the Swedish society for a Psychological Pedagogical Institute, no. 3.

Between Common Schooling and the Academe: the International Examinations Inquiry in Norway, 1935-1961

HARALD JARNING & GRO HANNE AAS

SUMMARY The major report from the International Examinations Inquiry in Norway was published in 1961. The last of the two books from the project was based on data and investigations from the second half of the 1930s. The Norwegian Carnegie Committee started its work in 1935 and managed to initiate a number of investigations done by a group of younger educational researchers, before the German occupation from 1940 to 1945. After the war the committee was re-established for some years. The investigations focused mainly on upper secondary general education. The main areas of concern were related to the pressure from a newly unified common basic school on post-compulsory education. Key investigations focused on the validity of marking and the national examinations as well as on the impact of examinations on pedagogy and everyday student life. Results were published in Norwegian, and with a delay of a decade or more. Documentation from the project would support the more general impression in the decades after the war that the national examinations had acceptable validity. Also important was a concern for national assessment as a main institution and caretaker of control of educational quality. In this respect the investigations did not support attempts to introduce test-based systems on a broad scale and as an alternative to the established system based on mandatory national examinations.

A Latecomer at the Folkestone Conference

When three of the Nordic countries, Finland, Sweden and Norway, were invited in to the International Examinations Inquiry (IEI) project from 1935 [1], Johan Hertzberg, an elderly progressivist secondary school headmaster, was the only participant from Norway. Hertzberg himself was no educational researcher, but participated as invited research organizer from a national project which was still to come. In national and international public exchanges of educational experiences and ideas in the 1920s and 30s he had been a visible participant, not least in the fifth world conference of the New Education Fellowship in Denmark in 1929. At the Helsingør conference Hertzberg gave the main presentation on new education in Norway (Boyd, 1930, *Towards a New Education*, pp. 55-57). He was a strong advocate of reform pedagogy also in general secondary education, and with the typical Nordic emphasis on common public schooling as the home ground for new education.

In his presentation at the conference Hertzberg made a brief sketch of the educational landscape surrounding secondary school examinations in Norway. He chose to focus on the two national secondary school matriculation examinations – the middle school examination taken at the age of 16 to 17, and the upper secondary matriculation examination, *examen artium*, taken at the age of 18 or 19. These national examinations were according to Hertzberg 'held in high esteem by the general public in Norway' and were taken by a high number of candidates, when one takes into account that the population is small.

However, Hertzberg pointed to the fact that one would also find a broad popular distrust in examinations. This could be seen not least in the support of the simple rural elementary schools that with an 18-weeks course and no kind of examination system had shown good results. In other respects than with regard to bookish learning, the country children were ahead: 'They have a clearer understanding of numbers, they write better compositions, they learn better to depend entirely upon themselves' (Hertzberg, in Monroe 1936, p. 247). He also raised questions about the paradoxical general cultural effects of modern examinations:

> It is a question, after all, whether there is not a connection between the markedly formalistic character of our Western civilization and the prevailing examination system. The examinations will also, as long as they remain essentially as they are, have a decidedly conservative tendency. They will, for instance, to a great extent, certainly prevent, or at any rate delay, educational reforms. This may suffice to suggest the importance of this one aspect of the examination problem, namely, the effect of the examinations on the whole intellectual development of the growing generation. (Hertzberg, in Monroe, 1936, pp. 248-249)

In more than one way, then, the Norwegian contribution at the Folkestone conference articulated some of the important national and Nordic concerns on the contributions of examinations and grading in the early expansion of modern common schooling and mass education. Some of these themes, but not all, were taken up and investigated by the IEI projects in Norway.

Early Development of a Non-stratified System of Education

The design and development of the examination inquiry in Norway was closely related to the educational policy agenda of the time. In this way the examination investigations also relate to long lasting lines of struggle over modern schooling that led to an early establishment of a comprehensive system of education. In a longer historical perspective one will see how these developments in the first part of the twentieth century took advantage of educational initiatives from the state church as well as from modern social and educational movements.

Before Norway got its own constitution in 1814, the state church was the cornerstone of educational initiatives in Denmark and Norway. Compulsory provision of mass primary schooling was a strong state pietist policy from the 1730s. Through reforms of the elite Latin school (1809) and of mass schooling (1827, 1848) compulsory attendance to basic schooling and a growing secular state control was established. In this way state control in primary and secondary education was consolidated before the educational modernization and expansion of the 1850s. Before 1900 an early form of a comprehensive educational system was established. A national reform of primary schooling in 1860 started a gradual move away from the wholly traditional curricula in primary as well as secondary schooling. In 1869 instruction in classical languages was delayed to the three last years of lower secondary schooling (*middelskole*) and the upper secondary, the *gymnas*, were divided into a classical track (*latinlinje*) and a modern track (*reallinje*) without Latin. After the following reform of 1896 the *gymnas* would normally consist of two modern tracks, a science-based track and a track based on modern foreign languages. All tracks had national and modern subjects – Norwegian language and literature, history, and modern foreign languages – as a common core. Together with these curricular changes the 1896 reform provided a systematic linkage between urban primary schools (*folkeskole*) and lower secondary (*middelskole*). After five years in primary school it was now possible to go on to four years of lower secondary, and then again further to the last three years of upper secondary (*gymnas*). At the same time co-education was made a criterion for state support of secondary schools. This partial abolishment of a stratified school system before the end of nineteenth century was taken further in the decades after the First World War. In 1920 the Norwegian parliament decided that secondary schools would have to recruit students from the fulfilled seven-year *folkeskole* in order to qualify for state support. In the 1920s and 30s this comprehensive organization was consolidated through legislation and curriculum reforms for primary schools – *folkeskole* – as well as for secondary general education – *realskole* (years 15-16) and *gymnas* (years 17-19).

Examination-Based and Examination-Free General Secondary Schooling

Table I indicates the relative place of the predominantly urban *examination-based* secondary schooling as well as the rural *non-examination-based* high schools (*folkehøgskoler*) in the years before 1940.

Year	Folkehøgskoler *One year examination-free courses*	Middelskoler *Lower secondary examination*	Gymnas *Examen artium*
1880	1857	865	176
1890	2091	1249	201
1900	2392	2151	350
1910	2996	2614	492
1920	5033	4670	988
1930	4554	4732	1325
1940	3968	7344	2992

Table I. Students in lower and upper secondary examinations, and in *folkehøgskoler* courses (Jarning 2002).

Of interest is the parallel expansion of examination-based and examination-free lower secondary schooling, as well as the almost exponential growth of the number of students with *examen artium* in the decades from 1910 and onwards. In the wake of the consolidation of unified basic schooling in the 1920s and 30s, the embryo of post-compulsory mass education, a main policy concern of the second part of the century, was already present. Still, examination-free secondary schooling showed a substantial recruitment throughout the first half of the twentieth century. Through this situation the pressure from a newly unified common basic school on post-compulsory education was a question that gradually would be of growing concern, not least among the secondary school teaching profession.

Norwegian Reform Pedagogy before 1940

In Norway, the heterogeneous discourse of reform pedagogy grew rapidly in the inter-war period and was connected to other central discourses in education: those of unified schooling, the turn to research-based knowledge and testing, and a broader politics of population that can be characterized by the slogan 'Every man in the right place' (Aas, 2006). The intertwining of these discourses can be illustrated by some examples.

In Norway, ideas of reform pedagogy could be set in practice on a larger scale more or less only in the public school sector. In the new national curriculum guidelines for the *folkeskole* that were issued in 1939 (Normalplanen of 1939), as well as in the national guidelines for general secondary schools from 1938 (Undervisningsplan), many educational approaches rooted in reform pedagogy and principles of unified schooling were united. With a unified educational system came also the requirement for a national system of examinations and a national system of marking to have a strong linkage between basic and secondary schooling and at the same time a fair selection process. It was proposed in the guidelines for the *folkeskole* that the marking on a national basis should follow a normal distribution (the bell curve). At the same time, the necessity for a limited use of marking was stressed to restrict negative influences on pedagogy and school life.

The principle of the normal distribution of marks was introduced with explicit reference to the scientific quality of tests, discussed in research leading up to the Normalplan by Bernhof Ribsskog and his collaborators. Ribsskog was a renowned reform pedagogue, active at the top level of Norway's largest national teachers' union, and from 1931 he was appointed school district leader in Oslo. For more than two decades he combined roles as a national educational policy maker, a top school administrator in the capital area, and a main educational research entrepreneur in Norway (Aas, in Thuen & Vaage 2004). He played an initiating role in two important initiatives taken to further research in pedagogy and teachers' work in 1933 and 1934 and was a driving force behind the establishment of the Committee for Educational Research for the capital region from 1935. The committee was financed by school district councils in Oslo and Akershus and cooperated with an established publishing house, and was the framework around the largest and most vital educational research network of the time. From the 1930s to the 1950s, then, Ribsskog wrote or contributed to a great number of books and reports based on research projects and development work from the Oslo area.

In other words, when a Norwegian group was invited to join the International Examinations Inquiry, there were relevant topics being both researched and discussed – not among the general public, but amongst teachers and others interested in the development of the Norwegian school system. Examinations, marking systems and testing were on the agenda as a part of this broad reform pedagogic movement for a decade or two (Aas, in Thuen & Vaage, 2004). Historically, the critique of a performance pedagogy centred on examinations and grading also had been a main issue in the search for alternatives for rural schooling, led for more than half a century by the *folkehøgskoler*. However, this nationally dominant research network was not included when the Norwegian project was developed.

Struggle over Examinations in the Development of Schooling for All

In a presentation at the Folkestone conference in 1936 Professor Isaac Kandel gave interesting comparative perspectives on education in the United States, focusing on reasons why examinations had not had the same dominant role as in the European systems of education. The dual system with the marked division between primary and secondary schools began to disappear in the nineteenth century. It developed gradually to the situation at the time of the conference with 'no selection of pupils for the secondary stage either by qualifying or by competitive examinations' (Monroe, 1936, p 83). This framework had contributed to a situation where selection issues were related less to documented performances and more to differentiation of abilities, and to testing rather than examinations.

Two Recurrent Topics – equality and differentiation

Also in the educational history of Norway, qualifying examinations were unquestioned knowledge institutions prior to the start of struggles for a modern, vertically integrated system of education. Through this interlinking of primary and secondary schooling, a national framework of examinations as well as a centralized educational state was consolidated. It is true that during the gradual growth of post-compulsory mass education, keywords in the discourses would be *likhet* (equality) and *enhetsskole* (unified schooling). However, from a historical and theoretical perspective, struggles over differentiating strategies will be of primary interest. The differentiation topic, in this perspective, is no less important for the development of national policies than the equality topic. Thus the selective and differentiating functions of marking and national examinations have often been at the top of agendas of policy struggles.

The core of the examination system at the time of the IEI project was composed of the three leaving examinations:

- *examen artium* – the upper secondary matriculation examinations were normally taken at the age of 19;
- *middelskoleeksamen* – the intermediate secondary examination was taken at age 16 or 17;
- *folkeskoleeksamen* – the primary school leaving examination was taken at the age of 14.

In its early modern form the *artium* goes back to a Danish reform in 1809. In the Latin school reform of 1809 the *examen artium* was established as the primary national academic examination.[2] Throughout the nineteenth century and most of the twentieth century the *artium* was the basic means for controlling admission to university studies in Norway, in the sense that the *artium* had the function of a certificate of academic citizenship and would, without further selection, qualify a student for any university studies. In this sense the *artium* was from the start a qualifying entrance examination rather than a competitive leaving examination. With the establishment of the University in Kristiania (Oslo) from 1811, the *examen artium* had the form of a collection of entrance examinations arranged by the university in the capital each spring.

From 1882 the *artium* became the centrepiece in a new nationwide system of external uniform secondary school examinations. The actual examinations were from this time, and are still today, held at local upper secondary schools, but under national control by a state-appointed examination agency. Main features in this national examination system have from that time included:

- assignments are uniform and constructed by the national agency;
- local examinations are arranged simultaneously at all certified secondary schools;
- marks are set by teachers from other schools appointed by an external agency.

The addition into this system of the intermediate examination at the secondary level – *middelskoleeksamen* – took place in 1869. From 1879 a separate kind of this examination for girls was added. From 1935 this examination level would be termed *realskoleeksamen*. All matters related to the assessment system, examinations and marking in the *folkeskole* were traditionally seen as questions the municipalities would decide.

Closely related to the strengthening of the unified basic school and the partly connected expansion of post-compulsory education, marking and examinations from the 1920s became national policy questions of growing importance. In 1923 the Medical Faculty at the University of Oslo for the first time would introduce *numerus clausus*. The proposal gained the necessary support from the University and the Government, but the Norwegian parliament then insisted on continuing the practice with open admission to all academic studies for anyone who had passed the qualifying examination. In 1939 the rector of the University pointed to the need for a broad reconsideration of the unregulated admission policies, and from April 1940, the use of *numerus clausus* by the medical faculty was accepted by parliament (Collett, 1999, p. 133). With these changes the *examen artium* would gradually develop into a competitive examination, with growing impact on the pedagogy in secondary schools. From the 1920s important supporters of unified schooling also would advocate stronger meritocratic competition to have the *folkeskole* accepted as the primary school for all children. With the national curriculum guidelines from 1939 marking for grade 4 to 7 was made compulsory and should follow a normal distribution. Altogether such changes in national policy agendas have been part of the background for the Norwegian project.

IEI in Norway – project and persons

In the last session at the Folkestone conference Johan Hertzberg in his expression of thanks at the same time shed light upon the process leading to the establishment of the Norwegian part of the international project. He expressed his particular thanks to 'Professor Kandel for picking me out as the one fortunate Norwegian', and then to 'Dr. Monroe for inviting me' (Monroe, 1936, p. 291). In this way he confirms the crucial role of the researchers in comparative education at Colombia University in the initiative to invite a Norwegian group to join the IEI project.

From the two contributions by Hertzberg referred in the conference proceedings it is also evident that actual investigations had not yet started, but that discussions about the design of the whole Norwegian project had led to a reasonably detailed plan for the national project. At an early stage of the development of the IEI in Norway, Hertzberg had then started to orchestrate the project, involving people with relevant competence and positions covering very different generations. In the absence of established institutions for educational research that the IEI project could be connected to, a first step was to establish an organisational framework, '*Den norske komite av den internasjonale Carnegie Examinations Inquiry*'. This committee was formalized by 1936 and active and visible from 1937. In this way the participation of Hertzberg at the Folkestone conference can best be seen as a prelude to the implementation of a national project.

The Key Persons – two academic generations

Three prominent academic and secondary school leaders made up the board of the Norwegian Carnegie Committee. Chairman was the rector of the University of Oslo from 1927 to 1936, Sem Sæland, with headmaster Anton Alexander as co-leader, and Hertzberg as secretary. In this group Sæland was the established researcher and professor in physics. He had started his academic career in the research group of the founder of modern meteorology, Vilhelm Bjerknes, and his background also included work as lecturer in science education at the Norwegian University College for Teachers in its founding years in the 1920s. Alexander had for more than three decades been connected to the teaching of science and mathematics in secondary schools. At a relatively early stage in his teaching career he had focused on the need for a more reliable system of national examinations. Earlier in his career he had also taken part in scientific work, including the establishment of the national journal for mathematical research, *Norsk Matematisk Tidsskrift*, where he was one of two editors in the early years. From 1921 Alexander was headmaster of upper secondary schools in three towns in eastern Norway. He was a member of parliament for the liberal-radical party, Venstre, from 1934 to 1936, and from 1938 until his death he was the leader of the state-appointed examination policy committee.

Hertzberg was secretary for the Norwegian Committee and chaired the Committee after the death of Sæland. In the introduction to his book from 1961, Piene confirms that Hertzberg was the one contacted by the Carnegie project and asked for help to set up a group that could establish a project in Norway. On the European side of the Atlantic the New Education Fellowship functioned as a public arena for early articulation of reform interests and the need for a thorough investigation of examinations and alternative forms of assessment. Though he himself was no researcher,

Hertzberg might very well have been a first choice for a liaison in Norway because he was a secondary school leader who was active in international educational cooperation, and not least within the New Education Fellowship.

Important contributions of these three men to the national project also seem quite obvious. A main advantage of having Sæland as the chair of the national committee was that he as university rector would represent academic support in a situation where education as a discipline was not yet institutionalized as part of the university programme. Only in 1936 had parliament voted for the establishment of an institute for educational research and a chair in Pedagogikk at the University in Oslo, and two years later Helga Eng was appointed professor and leader of the institute. Alexander has been pointed to as the one who set up the initial five-point plan for a Norwegian examination investigation programme. Through his leadership in the policy work on secondary school examinations, from 1938 a door was opened for broader social contributions from the investigations. From the start Hertzberg placed himself in the role as 'secretary', the organizer among the three. In the reorganisation after the war he took over as Chair.

The Young Researchers

None of the experienced board members had been active in educational research, but a main function of the board was to recruit researchers and set up a team of investigators. In doing this the board oriented themselves to a generation of academics about 30 years younger, and at the start of their professional career. The members of the research team all received their university education in the 1920s, and all had teaching experience from upper secondary schooling. Common for this academic generation in Norway was that they all would have a degree with a normal duration of six years or more, which included a post-graduate thesis, with a length and academic level between what today is the norm for a PhD and a master's thesis. The members of the research team were:

- Edvard Stang, Humanities
- Kay Piene, Science and mathematics
- Einar Høigård, Humanities
- Olav Sundet, Humanities

All the researchers worked for the project on a part-time basis, combined with their primary employment, mainly as secondary school teachers. Piene, in his 1961 book, says that he was engaged from 1937 onwards, until the Second World War and the German occupation made further active project work too difficult. Einar Høigård was the main researcher together with Piene in the early years and it was reasonable that the two then would represent the team at the Dinard conference in 1938.

From 1938 Høigård was the first researcher ever to have a scholarship position at the new Institute of Educational Research, and in this respect it is worth noting that his engagement in the Norwegian IEI project pre-dates this engagement. In recruiting Høigård the older members of the team then had secured a very promising younger educational researcher for the IEI work. Stang started the work on his part of the project a year later than Høigård and Piene, and he did not publish in relation to the project. In the reorganisation after the war his tasks and data were taken over by Olav Sundet. He continued and finished the investigations on the student related sub-project with the publication of the book on examinations and schoolwork in 1947. Sundet also took over the functions as secretary in the reorganized Norwegian Committee from 1946.

Einar Høigård.

In his presentation at the Folkestone conference of the preliminary ideas for an examination inquiry in Norway Johan Hertzberg focused on the intermediate and finishing examinations from the general secondary schools. He first pointed to the need for a historical investigation of the background to the main examinations of the time. Already at this early stage, and before the finishing of the organizational framework with the Norwegian Carnegie Committee (NCC), Hertzberg referred to a project plan. This plan was developed mainly on the basis of ideas from Anton Alexander. In addition to the historical dimension, the design would include the following five parts:

1. with the aid of school registers, examination lists and university registers, to follow the progress of a certain number of individuals from the beginning to the close of their studies;
2. it is intended to extend the inquiry mentioned in point 1 beyond the years of study, as far as it proves practicable, to find out how far the examinations may be considered safe methods for selection;

3. to make a comparison between the teachers' marks on the basis of the scholars' work during the terms, and the examination marks;
4. in order to throw light on the objectivity of examiners, to compare the judgements of a certain number of examiners;
5. to inquire into the effect of the examinations on the instruction, and on the work of the students.

A brief summary of investigations and reports will show that the project design was set into practice in all main areas. However, as already indicated, the investigations were affected heavily by the wartime situation. The sub-projects would meet a number of small disasters until reports were finished and accessible for public presentation.

Kay Piene.

Research Areas and Findings

Høigård was the historian of education in the research group. Already in his short presentation at the Dinard conference he had touched upon a few historical aspects. He proposed that in the material from a small nation like Norway it is easier than in most countries to see the reciprocal influence of schooling and society. In relation to the examination inquiry he focused on the interest of bourgeois society in formal examinations. Høigård never published separately on the history of the Norwegian examination system, but parts of his research are included in his *Oslo katedralskoles historie*, published in 1942 and in a book on the history of education in Norway published after the war.

Themes 1-4 outlined in the section above were mainly taken up in the research by Piene, but also in a couple of articles by Høigård. At the Dinard conference the large part of the presentations from the Norwegian group was done by Piene. While his final book comparing the marking of local teachers and assessment results from the national examinations was published almost 25 years after he started his investigations, the presentation from June 1938 shows that Piene already at that time was able to document that the correlation of marking was good when the results were compared with the marking from the local teachers' assessment (Piene, in Monroe, 1939, p. 290). This finding corresponds with the main conclusion from the final report from 1961 (Piene, 1961, pp. 280-282).

Due to the centralized leaving examinations for lower secondary as well as for upper secondary schooling it was relatively easy to collect and combine the information needed from school registers and registers from the central examination body in Norway, Undervisningsrådet. Analysis of the relations between the previous marking of teachers during term time and the results from the final examinations is a focal point in Piene's 1961 book. Parts of the results were also published earlier in articles from 1941 and 1945. Summaries of the investigations by Piene, Høigård and Sundet were also included in a textbook on educational psychology co-written by Høigård and Einar Østlyngen (Østlyngen & Høigård, 1941).

In a separate publication from 1953 Piene also made a similar analysis based on data from the primary schools in Oslo from 1946 to 1951. From his analysis of the marking in secondary schooling the general conclusion is that the teachers' marks as well as the examination marks can be recognized as more or less correct expressions of the performance of the students:

> Altogether my impression is that the marking of the local teachers and the results from the national examinations should be recognized as more or less correct expressions of the students' performances. There is a clear positive correlation between them due to that both measure subject based competences in the one and same subject. (Piene 1961, p. 281)[3]

The teachers' marks give predictions of later progress with a degree of accuracy very similar to that of the examination marks. A practical conclusion from Piene was that it is documented that 'by and large the whole examen artium apparatus functions quite acceptably' (1961, p. 282). At the same time he addressed the possibilities for considerable improvements in a number of areas.

The book by Olav Sundet, *Eksamen og skolearbeid* (Examinations and school work), published in 1947, is the main contribution in relation to part 5 of the 1935 plan, effects of examinations on instruction and on students' work. Research on this theme was started by another member of the research group, but was taken over by Sundet. General policy-oriented proposals from Sundet were that a rational system of examinations was of such major importance that it would be worth investing in the development of a form that could unite the threefold demands to an examination as follows:

> That the assignments give an acceptable basis for comparison (reliability), measure what they are constructed to measure, and have a positive feedback on school work. (Sundet 1947, p. 284)

Among the more specific findings were that the students had no real wish to abolish examinations altogether, but to reduce the influence of chance on examination results. Examinations were seen by students as more impartial than teachers' marks during term time. Many students also pointed to common national examinations and assessment as an advantage. Among the negative aspects of examinations, the unreasonable stress on luck or the lack of it on one specific test was the most frequent criticism. Quite a few also wrote in the negative about the possibility of getting a good result by cramming for examinations. Teachers made complaints in particular on the negative course of pedagogy that often would follow from the demands of examinations.

No Collaboration between Research on Primary and Secondary Schooling

In retrospect, one of the really puzzling questions to try to understand better is how it was possible in the work of NCC to have no active cooperation with the larger educational research milieu in the Oslo area. A small, but very visible and active research team around school district leader Ribsskog was engaged in quite similar investigations, but more or less only with data from the *folkeskole* sector. Norway is a small country, and Oslo is and was certainly no large city. In this respect a total segmentation between research efforts on basic and secondary schooling needs to be looked at more closely.

In Norway the 1930s was the pioneering decade in the institutionalisation of educational research, closely related to struggle for a seven-year unified *folkeskole* with a reform pedagogic approach to curricular content and teaching methods. These research strategies were mainly related to primary schooling and carried out by researchers starting their professional career as primary school teachers. It is interesting that, in relation to this, there is no evidence of contact or cooperation between the Norwegian secondary school examinations inquiry and the educational researchers that focused on primary schooling. This indicates that in spite of a more or less common struggle for unified schooling, relations between the two segments of educational research follow the very traditional division between academic and non-academic teacher education sectors. An indication of the strength of this segmentation of the education sectors can be found in the summary of IEI research by Piene (1961). When he refer very briefly to the publications from the project in Sweden, he stops with the conclusion that they 'cover a lower stage, the basic school and a lower secondary school starting earlier than our own' (Piene, 1961, p. 270).

In spite of the focus in the inter-war decades on the furthering of comprehensive schooling, neither the linkages between the *folkeskole* examinations and secondary schooling nor the possible impact of a strong examination-free sector on the secondary level was taken into account in the design of the IEI investigations in Norway. Also interesting in this respect is the exclusion of Denmark at the time when the Nordic countries were invited into the IEI in 1935. In the overview of the international project by Piene in 1961 there is a small comment on this decision, saying that Denmark 'was not invited because there was so little use of examinations in Danish schools, due to the examination free *folkehøgskoler*' (Piene, 1961, p. 273).

No After Effects?

In Norwegian educational sources reference to the examination investigations or to the Norwegian Carnegie Committee are extremely rare. Among the few exceptions is an overview article on educational research in Norway from the early 1960s by Professor Johs. Sandven, the successor to Helga Eng as chair of the Institute for Educational Research at the University of Oslo. Sandven mentions the project very briefly, giving no credits for more specific results, with the following paragraph:

> Another attempt at organizing educational research in the 1930's was the establishment of the Norwegian Carnegie Committee to investigate the examination system. The committee was formed in 1937 with Professor Sem Saeland, and after his death, headmaster Joh. Hertzberg, as chairman. Various investigations were undertaken, and the results of several were published in the form of articles and reports. The Carnegie committee did not, however, report to any great extent until after World War II, when an investigation by Olav Sundet on examinations and school work was published. The object of Sundet's research was the important question of the influence of the matriculation examination, at the end of the secondary school, on the day-to-day work in schools, and valuable insights were advanced in this book. (Sandven, 1963, p. 9)

A book on marking and examination policies by Professor Anders Lysne is the only relatively recent research work that has made use of the investigations and findings from the NCC reports. In looking at the limited signs of contributions from the project, however, a fact worth noting is that Kay Piene from 1950 was appointed head of the teacher training unit for secondary school teachers affiliated to the University of Oslo. When he retired in the late 1960s Olav Sundet took over the same position. In this way an outcome of the project was to qualify some of the key scholars engaged in teacher training for general secondary education in Norway for a quarter of a century.

An Early Initiative Concerning Examination Policies

In *Karakterer og kompetanse* (Marking and competence), giving a broad analysis of marking and competence policies in modern educational history in Norway, Professor Anders Lysne (1999) shed light on of some of the negative coincidences that affected the NCC project severely. In 1938 the Minister of Education, Nils Hjelmtveit, appointed a ministerial investigation on examination policies, Eksamensordningskomiteen. This ad hoc committee had as its mandate to go through all aspects of local assessment as well as the external mandatory examinations, and propose reforms. Two of the members of the Norwegian Carnegie Committee, Anton Alexander and Einar Høigård, took part in the work. Alexander would chair the work and Høigård was appointed secretary. The initiative, including the central positions of Alexander and Høigård, would give obvious possibilities to make practical educational use of the competence and findings from the national project, and the NCC milieu might well have been among the pressure groups in the establishment of the ad hoc committee. However, Alexander died after about a year, and Høigaard died during the war. In November 1943, then one of the top leaders of the civil resistance of the teaching profession against the Nazi regime, he was arrested in an attempt to flee to Sweden. Imprisoned, Høigård took his own life so as not to risk betraying resistance activities under torture.

After the war the committee was re-established with Karsten Heli as its new chairman. Heli had, with support from the educational research fund of the capital area under the leadership of Bernhof Ribsskog, made a report on repeaters and other students falling behind in relation to the normal programme of general secondary schooling. Not least through these investigations he had a particular concern for the burdens of the examination programme and the impact it could have for large segments of the secondary school student population. It is in this perspective, perhaps, not surprising that the recommendations from the reorganized committee from 1946 to a large extent would follow a Danish model. In Denmark the pressure from the strong examination-free *folkehøgskoler* sector had led to a compromise where secondary school students could choose between an examination-based programme and a programme without examinations and grading. After some years of further hearings and considerations, however, the recommendations from the committee to follow the Danish approach were set aside.

A Pioneering Project in Educational Research on Secondary Schooling

> The grants from the Carnegie Foundation and Carnegie Corporation have enabled us to start the first scientific educational research concerning the secondary education in Norway.
> (Monroe, 1939, p. 269)

This statement from Einar Høigård at the Dinard conference is a reminder of a different area where it is possible to look for after effects of the IEI project in Norway. Any broader educational research in connection with secondary schooling was not taken up until the mass education reforms of lower and upper secondary schools started from the 1970s.

Support for educational research expanded rapidly in Norway from the 1950s, not least through the establishment of research councils in the decade after the war. This support was, however, mainly channelled into the Institute of Educational Research at the University of Oslo, where the faculty almost unanimously was recruited from the primary school circuit – *folkeskolen*. The segmentation of the teaching profession and teacher education that was visible around the Norwegian Carnegie Committee in the 1930s was furthered for at least three decades, but with the basic school area as dominant.

The Examination-Related Issues Covered in the Norwegian IEI Material

Looking back on the Norwegian part of the IEI project, it is interesting to try to map the main examination-related issues that are expressed through the collection of texts from the decades before the transition to mass education became inevitable. This could be a major analysis on its own, but on the basis of our readings it is, as a start, possible to focus on some characteristic themes and topics.

During the Second World War about 300 Nordic educational researchers and educationalists contributed to a new pedagogic encyclopaedia, *Pedagogisk-Psykologisk Uppslagsbok*, issued in Sweden from 1943. Included in the first volume is an article on 'Examensundersökninger' – examination inquiries – by Laurin Zilliacus. After a general presentation of the IEI Zilliacus summarized research in relation to validity of examination results and the influences of examinations on pedagogy and school work. He then went on to deliberate on a third research area – examinations as a social factor – and drew a map of the discussions in the Carnegie conferences centred on two extreme positions, one conservative restrictive, and the other liberal expansion oriented.

The conservative argument focused on the selection of an intellectual elite while the radical argument focused on individualization and differentiation:

> The conservative position, that at the Carnegie conferences was emphasized by the French delegates, is the one that the function for the examination system is to select an intellectual elite and to guarantee that the focus in the teaching of the school is to educate one. (Zilliacus, 1943, p. 433)[4]

In the Norwegian project and its national surroundings the focus on fair selection and equality for the talented is represented not least by the meritocratic focus on the control of the validity of marking and comparison of the marking of local teachers and results of the systematic peer assessment of the national examinations. A main concern in the investigations of Piene as well as of many other radicals attacking the meritocratic power apparatus has been – and is – to secure a just meritocracy.

A visible elite-oriented approach related to this position can be found in the presentation by Høigård at the 1938 conference, where he referred to the topic of democracy being threatened by massification in the form of over-education starting at secondary schools:

> The great problem today is that democracy allows so many pupils to pass a secondary school. There you have the reason for the International Examinations Inquiry, and I find it very typical that democracy is represented at this Conference. It is today more necessary than it was twenty years ago to select carefully which of the many pupils shall have the opportunity to enter the universities and the high schools, and later to occupy the offices of the State and other leading posts in the country. (Monroe, 1939, p. 285)

This European fear of mass education, articulated among others by Høigård, has different modes, and can from the same years also be found in Karl Mannheim's fear of the differently rigid standardized mass education programme of the German Reich. Still it is interesting to note that the fear of massification finds no parallels in the American experiences of mass secondary education from the inter-war period. From the Carnegie conferences also this difference is denoted by Lauren Zilliacus:

> A radically opposite position has been presented by the American delegates who accepted as a basic principle that furthered schooling beyond the elementary stage should be given all that are interested. Examinations are seen then not as a means to judge or recognize, but as a means to be aware of the competences and abilities of the candidate. (Zilliacus, 1943, p. 434)[5]

In relation to the American approach, one of the interesting statements can be found in the report of Dr W. Learned in the ninth session at the 1938 conference. Learned worked at the Cooperative Test Service and reported on behalf of the leader of the institution, Dr Wood. In his report Dr Learned also commented on American perspectives on the initial and the contemporary approaches to the function of testing:

> The basic ideal underlying the Cooperative Test Service ... was described in the earlier days by various phrases which had, as a common element, the adjective 'democratic'. This adjective has since been largely abandoned because of the many false

> connotations which grew up around it ... In recent years we have used the words 'individualized education' as a convenient and partial designation of the ideal which has prompted our efforts. (Monroe, 1939, p. 293; Lemann, 1999)

In Piene's investigations, the concern for the validity of marking and the national examinations is intertwined with a concern for collegiate teacher-based assessment as necessary institutional quality control of educational fields of knowledge. A number of examples and quality functions of peer deliberations and negotiations over educational knowledge and the mutual learning included within a field or subject are illuminated in his book (1961). His documentation that the Norwegian professional marking system of the inter-war period in general had acceptable validity did not support proposals to introduce expert test-based systems on a broad scale as a substitute for well-developed professional systems. In the Norwegian context use of testing as a functional alternative or supplement to professional assessment and examination was a contested position already in the 1930s, and not least from the late 1950s.

Two quotes from debates on a growing use of intelligence tests in primary schools give some impression of the arguments of the testing sceptics. The first is taken from a parliamentary debate initiated by Per Borten, then a leading member of parliament from the Centre party who from 1965 to1971 was Prime Minister:

> We are all fascinated by numbers – by simplification. The danger in this is that this IQ will follow the child as an undisputed measure of its abilities. ... One must have the right to ask: what has this IQ from first grade to do side by side with results from a leaving exam from the seventh grade' ' (St.forh. 1959, 17. juni, s. 2263)[6]

The questions in the individual initiative from Borten were taken into further consideration in other parliamentary debates in the following years. This led to a statement of principle from the educational committee of the Parliament supporting the established examination and marking practices against any rapid turn to testing or other alternatives.

> The Committee will purely on a basis of principle express that whatever negative aspects the inherited system of examination have, it represents with its national principles a feeling of safety against contingencies that is more thorough than in any other system tried out in this country. One should be very careful in removing such a system until one has, by systematic and comprehensive development work found alternatives that surely work better. (Innst. S. 219, 1960-61: 364)[7]

The work and conclusions by Piene (1961) would to some extent give support to those not prepared to give away the core of the system, the national examinations. However, the limited references to his works give no reason to suppose that the inquiries of the IEI had any broader political impact during the 1960s.

A main concern when examinations and the search for alternatives were set on the agenda of the New Education Fellowship in the years before 1930 was that 'Existing examination systems seriously interfere with educational progress in many countries', and not least that 'Experience indicates that a rigid, mechanistic type of external examining and supervision interferes seriously with good teaching' (*Towards a New Education*, 1930, p. 267). In the context of the Norwegian IEI project the questioning of limits of examinations is to some extent represented in the investigation by Sundet on the impact of examinations on pedagogy and the students' experiences of schooling, as well as in the proposal from the examination policy investigation to introduce meritocracy by choice.

It is interesting in relation to the original initiatives of the New Education Fellowship that the scepticism and distrust toward examinations taken up by Johan Hertzberg in 1935, as well as a large sector of examination-free secondary education, both characteristic features of a common Nordic populist and popular Enlightenment heritage, never would be a matter for more direct investigations, neither in the Norwegian nor in the international setting. These positions can perhaps best be seen as expressions of a Scandinavian educational populism (Lauglo, 1998; Jarning, 1998) that was out of tune with elitist European educational traditions as well as with American approaches to mass education. An indication of the marginal attention towards such positions within the IEI is the fact that in the two printed reports from the 1935 and 1938 conferences there is no documentation of questions or comments raised to the presentations by the participants from the Norwegian project. It is not surprising that unfamiliar and possibly more popular and egalitarian orientations to schooling and assessment did not affect the agenda of the international investigations. It is still worth noting that the deliberations within the framework of the IEI also included some marginal voices.

Notes

[1] When the Nordic countries were invited into the IEI from the mid 1930s there was a deliberate decision to exclude Denmark, due to the strong examination-free school sectors.

[2] The *Artium* in Norway (and Denmark) from 1809 and the *Studenteksamen* in Sweden (and Finland) from 1824, and the functional equivalents in Germany and France, the *Abitur* and the *Baccalauréat*, all belong to a pattern of key national educational institutions from liberal modernity (Müller et al, 1986).

[3] 'Alt I alt er mitt inntrykk det at både forhånds- og eksamenskarakterer må kunne anerkjennes som mer eller mindre riktige uttrykk for elevenes

prestasjoner. Det er en tydelig positiv korrelasjon mellom dem som vil skyldes at de begge måler faglig dyktighet i ett og samme fag.' (Piene, 1961, p. 281)

[4] 'Den konservativa ståndpunkten, vilken vid Carnegie-konferenserna särskilt framhävts av de franska delegaterna, är den att examensväsendet är till för at utvälja en intellektuell elit och för at garantera, att skolans undervisning går ut på att utbilda en dylik' (Zilliacus, 1943, p. 433)

[5] 'En radikalt motsatt uppfattning har framförts av amerikanerna, vilka accepterat som grundprincip att fortsatt utbildning utöver elementärstadiet bör ges åt alla därtil hugade. Examina betraktas därför inte främst som ett medel att fälla eller godkänna uten som ett medel att komma underfund med den examinerades läggning og förutsättningar' (Zilliacus, 1943, p. 434)

[6] 'Vi er alle svake for tall – for å forenkle. Faren ligger I at denne IQ kommer til å hefte ved barnet som et udiskutabelt mål for hva det duger til. ... En må med rette kunne spørre: hva IQ fra første klasse har å gjøre ved siden av en elevs besvarelser ved avgangseksamen i sjuende klasse' (St.forh. 1959, 17. juni, s. 2263).

[7] 'Komiteen vil rent prinsipielt få uttale at hvor mange skyggesider det nedarvede eksamenssystem enn har, så gir det med sin sensur etter landsgyldige retningslinjer en følelse av trygghet mot vilkårlighet og tilfeldighet som vel er større enn noe annet system vi har prøvd her hjemme. En skal være meget varsom med å skille seg med et slikt system før en ved systematiske og omfattende forsøk har funnet frem til noe som en er sikker på er bedre' (Innst. S. 219, 1960-61: 364).

References

Aas, Gro Hanne (2006) *Likhet uten solidaritet. Idehistoriske studier av karakter i utdanning og meritokrati* [Equality without solidarity? Investigations on the intellectual history of marking and meritocracy]. Gothenburg: Institutionen för idehistoria och vetenskapsteori, University of Gothenburg.

Boyd, William (Ed.) (1930) *Towards a New Education*, 54-55. London & New York: Alfred A. Knopf.

Collett, John Peter (1999) *Historien om Universitetet i Oslo* [The history of the University of Oslo]. Oslo: Oslo University Press.

Dahl, Arne O. (1978) *Skoleinspektør Bernhof Ribsskog – en byggmester i norsk skole.* Master's thesis, Institute of Education, University of Oslo.

Jarning, Harald (1998) The Populist Argument: cultural populism and the development of educational theory in Norway, in: Peter Drewek & Christopher Lüth (Eds) *Paedagogica historica, History of Educational Sciences.* Ghent: C.S.H.P.

Jarning, Harald (2003) The Folk High School and General Education, *Skolen 2002-2003* [The national yearbook of history of education in Norway]. Notodden.

Lauglo, Jon (1998) Populism and Education in Norway, in: A. Tjeldvoll (Ed.) *Education and the Scandinavian Welfare State in the Year 2000.* New York: Garland.

Lemann, Nicholas (1999) *The Big Test. The Secret History of the American Meritocracy*. New York: Farrar, Straus & Giroux.

Lysne, Anders (1999) *Karakterer og kompetanse. Stridstema i norsk skolehistorie*. [Character and competence]. Oslo: AVA Forlag.

Monroe, Paul (Ed.) (1936) *Conference on Examintions II*. New York: Colombia University.

Monroe, Paul (Ed.) (1939) *Conference on Examintions III*. New York: Colombia University.

Müller, Detlev, Ringer, Fritz & Simon, Brian (Eds) (1986) *The Rise of the Modern Educational* System. Cambridge: Cambridge University Press.

Østlyngen, Emil & Høigård, Einar (1941) *Pedagogisk psykologi* [Psychology of education]. Oslo: Norsk korrespondanseskole.

Piene, Kay (1953) *Karakterfordelingsnormer, in Festskrift til B. Ribsskog*. [Differentiation of marking]. Oslo: Gyldendal.

Piene, Kai (1961) *Eksamenskarakterer og forhåndskarakterer* [Examination marks and pre-set marks]. Oslo: Cappelen.

Sandven, Johs. (1963) *Educational Research in Norway in the Twentieth Century*. Washington, DC: US Department of Health, Education, and Welfare.

Sundet, Olav (1947) *Eksamen og skolearbeid. Tilskot til granskingane av dei verknadene som avgangsprøvene i den høgre skolen har på det daglege skolearbeidet* [Examinations and school work]. Oslo: Cappelen.

Thuen, Harald & Vaage, Sveinung (2004) *Pedagogiske profiler. Norsk utdanningstenkning fra Holberg til Hernes* [Profiles in Norwegian education]. Oslo: Abstrakt Forlag.

Zilliacus, Lauren (1943) Examensundersøkningar [Examination inquiries], in *Psykologisk Pedagogisk Uppslagsbok* [Psychological Educational Encyclopaedia], 430-435. Stockholm: Natur och Kultur.

Articles from the Active Project Period

Høigård, Einar (1940) Artiumskarakter som konkurransekarakter, *Den høgre Skolen*, 234-243.

Høigård, Einar (1941) Standpunktkarakterer i skriftlige fag ved middelskoleeksamen 1940, sammenholdt med utfallet av tidligere års eksamensprøver, *Den høgre Skolen*, 37-42.

Høigård, Einar (1946-47) Filologer med lektoreksamen, *Norsk pedagogisk årbok*, 23-49.

Piene, Kay (1941) Skriftlig eksamen i matematikk iden høgre skolen, *Den høgre Skolen*, 194-203 and 221-233.

Piene, Kay (1945) Forhåndskarakterer – eksamenskarakterer, *Den høgre Skolen*, 2, 36-42.

Piene, Kay (1945) Topprestasjoner i matematikk ved examen artium – og siden, *Norsk pedagogisk tidsskrift*, 8, 225-233.

Sundet, Olav (1945) Eksamen, *Norsk Pedagogisk Tidsskrift*, 2, 25-30.

Other Publications

Hertzberg, J. (1935) Elevenes innstilling til sitt skolearbeid, *Den høiere Skole*, 19-31.

Høigård, Einar (1942) *Oslo katedralskoles historie*. Oslo: Grøndahl.

Høigård, Einar (1944) *Pedagogisk statistikk i grunntrekk* . Oslo.

Høigård, Einar & Ruge, Herman (1946) *Den norske skoles historie*. Oslo.

Østlyngen, Emil & Høigård, Einar (1941) *Pedagogisk psykologi*. Oslo: Norsk korrespondanseskole.

Piene, Kay (1940) Standpunktkarakterer og eksamenskarakterer ved skriftlig middelskoleeksamen (mimeo). Oslo.

Piene, Kay (1951) *Liberalisme og planøkonomi i norsk skole. Vor Ungdom*. Copenhagen.

Piene, Kay (1953) *Karakterfordelingsnormer, in Festskrift til B. Ribsskog*. Oslo: Gyldendal.

Publications in the Project Area from Other Researchers

Bakke, Karl (1942-43) *Måling av dyktighet i stillelesning. Norsk pedagogisk årbok 1942-43*.

Heli, Karsten (1938) De som kommer til kort, *Norsk Pedagogisk Tidsskrift*, 2-3, 76-88.

Heli, Karsten (1941) *Elever som kommer til kort i den høgre skolen*. Oslo.

Krogset, Lars (1937) Samsvaret mellom folkeskolens og middelskolens eksamenskarakterer, *Den høiere Skole*, 564-566.

Østlyngen, Emil (1939) *Skolen sett fra elevenes standpunkt. Undersøkinger blant folkeskolebarn i Oslo*. Oslo.

Østlyngen, Emil (1942) *Samsvaret mellom skoleytelse og livsytelse*, 49-59. Oslo: Norsk Pedagogisk Tidsskrift.

Østlyngen, Emil (1944) *i regning i de nordiske land* Oslo: Norsk Pedagogisk Tidsskrift.

Østlyngen, Emil (1945) *Standpunktmåling i morsmål og orienteringsfag*. Norsk Pedagogisk Årbok.

Ribsskog, Bernhof (1937) *Lærerprøven. Karakterer og karaktergiving*. Oslo.

Ribsskog, Bernhof (1938) *Karakterer og karaktergiving*. Oslo.

Ribsskog, Bernhof (1942) Melding om den skriftlige avgangsprøven ved Oslo folkeskole 1941, in *Årsmelding om Oslo folkeskole 1940-1941*. Oslo.

Ribsskog, Bernhof (1948) *Gjensittere i folkeskolen*. Oslo.

Sandven, Johs. Sosial innstilling i skoleklassen. Norsk skoleblad 1950, nr 52 og 1951, nr. 1.

Notes on Contributors

Gro Hanne Aas is a senior advisor in the Norwegian Agency for Quality Assurance in Education (NOKUT). She has formerly worked at universities in Norway and Sweden and in the Norwegian Research Council. She holds a PhD in the History of Ideas and Science and has published mainly on the topics of the history of education, and on research and knowledge politics.

David Bartholomew is Professor Emeritus of Statistics at the London School of Economics, United Kingdom. He is a Fellow of the British Academy, a Member of the International Statistical Institute, a Fellow of the Institute of Mathematical Statistics and has served as Honorary Secretary, Treasurer and President of the Royal Statistical Society. He has acted as a consultant on a wide range of statistical matters to many governmental and other organisations.

Ian Deary is Professor of Differential Psychology at the University of Edinburgh, United Kingdom. Since 1997 he has been working with his team on follow-up studies of the Scottish Mental Surveys of 1932 and 1947. He is a Fellow of the British Academy, the Royal Society of Edinburgh, and the Royal College of Physicians of Edinburgh. He is a past President of the International Society for the Study of Individual Differences.

Rita Hofstetter is Professor of History of Education in the Educational Sciences Section of the University of Geneva, Switzerland. She works on the history of education and specialises in the study of the nineteenth and twentieth centuries. Her current research deals with nationalisation of schools, reforms of teacher education and the emergence of educational sciences as a disciplinary field.

Harald Jarning is associate professor at the Department of Education and International Studies at Oslo University College, Norway. His main research interests are the history of basic schooling, the history of higher education, and pedagogy and didactics. He has been editor of the yearbook for educational history in Norway, *Skolen*, and has published mainly on Norwegian history of education and educational research and research policy.

Annukka Jauhiainen is a lecturer in the Department of Education at the University of Turku, Finland.

Martin Lawn is a Professorial Research Fellow at the Centre for Educational Sociology at the University of Edinburgh, United Kingdom. He is the Editor of the *European Educational Research Journal* and ex-Secretary General of the European Educational Research Association. He is a Fellow of the Academy of Social Sciences and has published widely on European educational policy and on the sociology and history of teachers and teaching.

Christian Lundahl is a Postdoctoral Fellow in the Department of Education, Uppsala University, Sweden. He is a member of the research group, Studies in Educational Policy and Educational Philosophy, led by Professor Ulf P. Lundgren. He recently received a four-year grant from the Swedish Research Council to continue his work on assessment in education. Lundahl is also a Director of Education at the National Agency for Education.

Bernard Schneuwly is Professor for Didactics of Language and Dean of the Faculty of Psychology and Educational Sciences at the University of Geneva, Switzerland. Currently, he is working on contents taught in the French mother tongue education classroom, the relationship between teaching, learning and development and the history of educational sciences.

Minna Vuorio-Lehti is a Special Researcher in the Department of Education, University of Turku, Finland.

Florian Waldow is a lecturer and research associate (*Wissenschaftlicher Mitarbeiter*) at Humboldt-University, Berlin, Germany, and a researcher at Uppsala University, Sweden.

Marc Zarrouati is an Assistant Professor at the University of Toulouse, France in both Philosophy of Science (Epistemology) and History of Science. He has a PhD in Theoretical Physics and he was awarded the 'Agrégation' in Mathematics. He also holds a degree in Moral and Political Philosophy. He teaches courses in Philosophy of Education and Educational Sciences at the Teachers' College of the University of Toulouse, where he is currently doing postgraduate work with prospective teachers. He also lectures at the National College of Agronomics (Ecole Nationale de Formation Agronomique). His research interests are in the area of the epistemology and history of educational sciences.